William King's Mortality Books

Volume 1
1795-1832

Transcribed by
Jane Donovan and
Carlton Fletcher

HERITAGE BOOKS
2008

HERITAGE BOOKS
AN IMPRINT OF HERITAGE BOOKS, INC.

Books, CDs, and more—Worldwide

For our listing of thousands of titles see our website at
www.HeritageBooks.com

Published 2008 by
HERITAGE BOOKS, INC.
Publishing Division
100 Railroad Ave. #104
Westminster, Maryland 21157

Copyright © 2001 Jane Donovan and Carlton Fletcher

Other books by the author:

*Records of Dumbarton United Methodist Church:
Volume 1, Baptisms and Marriages 1813-1991*
Jane Donovan

William King's Mortality Books: Volume 2, 1833-1863
Jane Donovan and Carlton Fletcher

All rights reserved. No part of this book may be reproduced or transmitted in any form or by any means, electronic or mechanical, including photocopying, recording or by any information storage and retrieval system without written permission from the author, except for the inclusion of brief quotations in a review.

International Standard Book Number: 978-0-7884-1853-2

Dedication

To the memory of William King, IV

Contents

William King and his *Mortality Books* v

Chronological listing 1

Alphabetical listing 119

William King and his *Mortality Books*

William King was born in County Armagh, Ireland on September 29, 1771, the eldest child of Francis King and his wife, Isabella McCullough King. After the birth of a second child, Esther, in 1773, the family migrated to the U.S., locating in 1775 on a farmstead in Perry County, Pennsylvania, where four more daughters were born, one whose name is not known (1776-1784), Jane (b. 1777), Margaret (b. 1779), and Elizabeth (1781-1858). Francis King died in 1784 of wounds received while serving in the American Revolution.

After his father's death, William was apprenticed to John Shaw of Annapolis, Maryland to learn cabinet-making. According to antiques experts, Shaw's was considered Annapolis's best shop. The English-trained Shaw produced a stream of very creative, diverse artisans. King could scarcely have chosen a better teacher. After completing his apprenticeship in 1792, King remained in Shaw's hire, during which time he became involved in an altercation that resulted in serious injury to an African-American man, which led King to return to Pennsylvania.

King followed his uncle, also named William King, to Georgetown, D.C. in June 1795, and opened a cabinet shop on what is now 31st Street NW below the Chesapeake and Ohio Canal, continuing in business there for nearly sixty years. Uncle William was known as "William Senior" and the cabinet-maker William as "William Junior" to avoid confusion among the fellow citizens of the town. In 1798, he married Mary Fowler "on the bank of the Severn River opposite Annapolis" in a service performed by the Reverend Benton Riggin, a Methodist preacher. William and Mary had seven children (Francis, William, Daniel, Margaret, Isabella, Helen, and Mary; only Francis and Daniel survived to adulthood) before her untimely death at the age of thirty-six, in November 1814. Seven months later William married a second time, to Christina Gozler Fowler, the widow of Mary Fowler King's brother Daniel. This second marriage produced another seven children (William, Mary, Malvina, Henry, James, Thomas Sim, Catherine, John, and Alexander McCaine; Malvina and Alexander died in childhood and Henry died on John C. Frémont's 1849 expedition to California).

As his furniture and coffin business grew and prospered, King trained a number of apprentices, who helped him produce an annual revenue of about $7,000, more than double that of the most successful of his three local competitors. After the White House was destroyed by British invaders in August 1814, King was selected to replace some of the lost furnishings, including four sofas and twenty-four chairs, one of which remains in the White House collection. A shrewd businessman, King also accumulated some Georgetown real estate.

He also experienced a religious conversion and joined the Methodist Church. His experiences in Methodism suggest that King's politics may have been Jacksonian Democrat, as he played a significant role in the Methodist Protestant schism of the late 1820s. The Methodist Protestants left the Methodist denomination over issues of church polity, insisting that lay members of the church should have an equal voice with ordained clergy in church affairs; the movement was strongly connected to the "rise of the common man" of Jacksonian politics. King was among the thirty-seven founding members of the Congress Street Methodist Protestant Church. The building now houses a Christian Science congregation–and the magnificent original 1830 woodwork that a modern observer can only suspect may have been produced by William King.

After King's death in 1854, his son, William Junior, continued the furniture business. The *Mortality Books*' second volume concludes on April 9, 1863 with the 8,503rd coffin produced by this illustrious shop.

William King's *Mortality Books* shed an unprecedented light on aspects of Georgetown and District of Columbia history. Never before available to the public, these ledgers of King's coffin sales provide an unexpected look into the social history of eighteenth and nineteenth century Georgetown, as well as raw data for mortality and demographic studies. Coffin production was a profitable portion of King's prosperous and highly-regarded furniture-making business, as was common for cabinetry artisans of his day. He buried people from all segments of society, from a sitting Vice President of the United States (Elbridge Gerry) to nameless paupers from the Poor House, from the child of President John Quincy Adams to the children of slaves.

Readers of this work should be aware of a number of difficulties when considering King's records. Despite an earnest effort, the presence of errors in this transcription is highly likely. Aside from the inevitable mistakes in reading the original manuscript, instances of confusion, such as between the race of William King's client and the race of the deceased, are possible. If in doubt, the reader should consult the original, now in the collections of the Historical Society of Washington, D.C.

As a rule, surnames correspond to the person who paid for King's services, not to the person being buried. In most cases, the name of the deceased does not appear at all; neither do the words "free" or "slave." "Samuel Anderson's colored man" may be taken to mean that a white man is paying for the burial of his slave, and "Henry Butler (colored man)'s child" may be taken to mean that a free black man has brought his child to be buried, but those determinations are left for the reader to make. King did not always indicate the race of his African-American customers. Joseph Cartwright and Murray Barker, for example, well known free blacks in Georgetown, are not indicated in King's records as "colored." Given names, nicknames, and sobriquets (such as "Old Frank") without surnames are sometimes – but not always – accompanied by a designation of race. The death, for instance, of "Hercules's child" (with no mention of race) is followed, a few years later, by the death of "Hercules (Clagett's colored man)," i.e., his slave.

Each entry is followed by a letter: M, W, or S. M indicates purchase of a mahogany coffin; W indicates walnut, and S stained. A few customers purchased cherry coffins, which are noted.

On a personal note, we wish to express our deep appreciation to Patricia King for permitting us to transcribe the *Mortality Books*.

—*Jane Donovan and Carlton Fletcher*
Washington, D. C.
February 2001

BEALL Lloyd for ------ 8/10/1795 S
LEAR Mr's child 2/21/1796 M
LEAR Mrs 2/21/1796 M
FINNIGAN Mr "about this time" following 2/21/1796 M
TURNER Samuel's child 3/28/1796 M
RICHMOND Mr 4/8/1796 M
TOPPAN Mrs 4/15/1796 S
FORREST I paid for unknown 5/25/1796 S
MARRAY Miss 6/17/1796 W
MORRIS Mr's child 6/27/1796 W
CLAGETT Walter's brother 6/29/1796 M
DAWES Mr charged for unknown 7/6/1796 S
KIRK Mr paid for unknown 7/11/1796 S
KING William Senior's nurse's child 7/11/1796 S
BAILY Jessee's child 7/26/1796 W
BEATTY Major Thomas's child 8/15/1796 M
GOLDIN Miss 8/15/1796 M
BEALL Lloyd's child 8/27/1796 S
SMITH Doctor 8/28/1796 W
CLARK Thomas 8/30/1796 M
Unknown 9/1/1796 S
KING William Senior's child 9/27/1796 M
HENDERSON Mr 11/16/1796 S
CLAGETT James's child 12/9/1796 M
McINTIRE Alexander 9/24/1797 M
LOWNDES Charles's child 10/21/1797 M
MULLIGEN Mr 1/6/1798 S
WORTHINGTON Dr's wife 1/21/1798 M
MATLE Mr 1/26/1798 S
BALCH Stephen B's child 2/7/1798 W
BEATTY Charles A's child 3/1/1798 M
DEAKINS William 3/5/1798 M
COOK James 4/17/1798 M
ENO Edward for ----- 5/12/1798 W
HEDGES Nicholas for wife 6/13/1798 M
PRINGLE John's uncle 6/28/1798 W
OBER Benjamin's child 6/28/1798 W
STONE John for ----- 7/31/1798 M
DAVIS Thomas's child 9/1/1798 S
MARBURY Mr 10/5/1798 M
DANIEL Francis's wife 10/17/1798 W
PAGE Mr 10/26/1798; W

DAVIS Thomas for unknown 12/10/1798 S
FRENCH Mr 12/16/1798 M
HOLMEAD George of Anthony 1/28/1799 W
KROUSE Mr 4/5/1799 W
DALTON Tristram's wife 4/19/1799 M
MOORE John for unknown 4/21/1799 S
BEALL George for unknown 5/3/1799 M
BURNES David 5/9/1799 M
DUNCANSON William M's wife 8/3/1799 M
MONRO Jonathan's child 8/24/1799 S
MONRO Jonathan's wife 8/30/1799 W
WHITE James's child 9/2/1799 S
BEALL Lloyd's child 9/19/1799 S
HENOP Mrs for ----- 9/20/1799 W
MELLIGEN Mr 9/30/1799 W
BROWN Charles's child 10/11/1799 S
DINMORE Mr's child 10/16/1799 W
ADDISON John 10/17/1799 W
DULY Mr 10/19/1799 S
ATKINSON Miss 12/9/1799 W
ATKINSON Mrs for ----- 12/25/1799 S
MORGAN William's child 12/30/1799 W
SCOTT Miss Margarett 1/16/1800 M
ADDY Mr 1/21/1800 W
LONG James's wife 3/4/1800 W
MONROE Jonathan's colored child 3/6/1800 S
STOOPS William's wife 3/10/1800 W
ENGLISH David for ----- 3/30/1800 M
ENGLISH David for a child 3/30/1800 S
ROBERTSON William 4/9/1800 W
GANTT Henry for ----- 4/25/1800 M
KEEPHER Henry for ----- 6/14/1800 S
PLATOR Thomas's child 6/28/1800 W
WADE Mrs for ----- 8/2/1800 S
KNOWLES Joseph E's wife 8/11/1800 M
KENNEDY Matthew's child 8/22/1800 W
DAVIS Thomas for ----- 8/23/1800 W
McLAUGHLIN Charles's colored person, 8/28/1800 S
CRAWFORD Nathaniel's child 8/30/1800 M
PETER Thomas's child 9/1/1800 M
KING Adam's child 9/10/1800 W
RAGON Daniel's child 9/16/1800 W

REINTZLE George 9/29/1800 W
KING George's child 11/2/1800 W
KNOWLES Mr's child 11/5/1800 W
Unknown 11/7/1800 S
DINMORE Richard's child 11/29/1800 S
MITCHELL John's child 12/16/1800 W
SCOTT Gustavus 12/29/1800 M
CLAGETT Walter 1/14/1801 M
JONES James 1/14/1801 M
MASON Stephen T's child 1/26/1801 S
HARRISON Richard's colored woman 2/21/1801 S
BOWIE Alexander's wife 3/30/1801 M
FENTHAM Mrs for ----- 4/11/1801 W
O'FARRELL P 5/11/1801 S
KING Nicholas's child 6/27/1801 S
MASON John T's child 7/22/1801 M
BEALL William D's colored person 7/30/1801 S
HEDGE Mr 8/5/1801 S
BROWN Mr's child 8/10/1801 W
BROWN Mr's child 8/12/1801 W
BARNES Mr's child 8/17/1801 M
CONNOR Mrs for ----- 8/18/1801 S
McLAUGLIN Charles's colored person 8/18/1801 S
OWENS Isaac's child 8/30/1801 W
COZENS Doctor's child 9/2/1801 W
HILTON Mr's child 9/9/1801 W
THRELKELD John for mother 9/10/1801 M
DOUGHTY Mr's child 9/15/1801 M
DINMORE Mr's colored person 9/20/1801 S
DINMORE Mr's colored child 9/20/1801 S
KNOWLES Mrs for ----- 9/22/1801 W
RENSHAW Mrs for ----- 10/8/1801 W
YOUSH Mr's child 10/21/1801 W
WHITE James 10/25/1801 S
HEATH Mr 11/6/1801 W
MASON John T's child 11/7/1801 M
KENNEDY James's child 11/11/1801 W
MACKALL Leonard's child 11/23/1801 W
BAIN Quintin for ----- 11/28/1801 W
BEALL Aquilla's negro girl 11/28/1801 S
HAGNER Peter for ----- 12/21/1801 M
HAGNER Peter's child 12/21/1801 S

COOK Charles 12/24/1801 S
BAIN Quintin's child 1/30/1802 W
NOURSE Mr's child 1/30/1802 W
STODDART Benjamin for ----- 2/13/1802 M
RENNER Mrs Helen 2/23/1802 M
JONES Edward for ----- 3/3/1802 M
GREEN & ENGLISH for colored person 3/4/1802 S
JONES Edward for ----- 3/11/1802 M
MORGAN William's boy 3/11/1802 W
MARBURY William's child 3/13/1802 M
ENGLISH Joseph's child 3/19/1802 S
BEALL Thomas for ----- 3/25/1802 W
BIRTH James's child 3/25/1802 W
STANLY Mr for ----- 3/29/1802 S
BALTZER John's child 4/1/1802 M
WILSON Zadock's wife 4/7/1802 W
WHITE Benjamin 4/7/1802 W
HEWES Mrs's child 4/8/1802 S
MELVIN James's negro boy 4/10/1802 S
Child, name unknown 4/23/1802 S
OWENS Mr 4/30/1802 S
PATTERSON Mr's child 5/4/1802 M
FITZHUGH Mr for ----- 5/18/1802 M
BEALL Mrs 6/12/1802 W
MASON John T's child 6/23/1802 M
MORSELL James S for ----- 6/24/1802 M
ADAM Thomas's chld 7/5/1802 S
GARY Everard's child 7/14/1802 M
BASTEN Charles's child 7/18/1802 W
LIVERS Mr's child 8/2/1802 W
GARDNER Mr's child 8/2/1802 W
BASTEN Charles's boy 8/24/1802 W
HENDERSON Richard 8/30/1802 M
PRICE Mr's child 9/6/1802 M
LINGAN James M for Miss P 9/10/1802 M
TANNEY Francis L 9/20/1802 S
WILLIAMS Samuel 9/22/1802 S
HALLAT Mr 9/24/1802 S
DICK Thomas (Bladensburg) for ----- 9/28/1802 M
JOHNSON Mrs for ----- 10/1/1802 W
Negro child 10/2/1802 S
DEMPSY Mr's child (Alexandria) 10/3/1802 M

McLAUGHLIN Charles for ----- 10/5/1802 M
HENOP Mrs for ----- 10/5/1802 W
SHEPPARD Walter for ----- 10/18/1802 S
BRODHAG Charles F for ----- 10/19/1802 M
HOLMEAD John for ----- 11/1/1802 M
RAGON Daniel's child 11/2/1802 W
ODEN Benjamin's child 11/9/1802 M
WILLIAMS Mr (stage driver) for ----- 11/13/1802 S
KEEPHER Henry's child 11/18/1802 M
DORSEY William H for ----- 11/23/1802 M
HERSEY Benjamin's wife 12/29/1802 M
HARRISON Richard's child 1/15/1803 M
TENNY Isaac for ----- 1/22/1803 M
ODEN Benjamin for ----- 2/6/1803 M
JOHN Leonard H's child 2/9/1803 M
MORE John for ----- 4/1/1803 S
PETER David's child 4/17/1803 M
MOORE John's child 5/10/1803 W
BOWIE Allen 5/22/1803 M
SPEAKE Captain's child 6/7/1803 M
FOWLER Thomas's child 7/17/1803 S
SCOTT John's child 7/19/1803 M
McCUTCHEON James's child 7/21/1803 W
RIND William A's child 7/24/1803 M
COATES James's child 7/29/1803 W
BARWISE Mr's stageman 7/30/1803 S
MITCHELL Mr's child 8/5/1803 S
SLATOR Thomas for ----- 8/7/1803 S
AUBERT Henry for ----- 8/9/1803 W
GRIFFIN Mrs 8/7/1803 S
ABBOT Mr's child 8/25/1803 W
BUTLER Robert for ----- 8/28/1803 S
BROOKS Joseph's child 8/28/1803 W
EVANS Evan for ----- 9/5/1803 W
HARRISON James 9/5/1803 W
KEEPHER Henry's child 9/5/1803 S
CARTER Jacob's child 9/7/1803 S
GARDNER John's child 9/7/1803 W
SIMMONDS William's child 9/13/1803 M
LOWRIE William 9/18/1803 W
HELLEN Walter's child 9/20/1803 M
TRUNNEL Horatio's child 9/23/1803 S

FINAGAN Benjamin's child 9/25/1803 W
CURRAN John for ----- 9/30/1803 M
PETER John's colored child 10/1/1803 S
TOPHOUSE Samuel's child 10/6/1803 W
HARRISON Richard's Fredrick 10/9/1803 S
PATTERSON Edgar's child 10/14/1803 M
ROWS Mr 10/14/1803 W
McCUTCHEON James's child 10/15/1803 W
SEMMES Joseph's wife 10/29/1803 M
ROWLES Joseph E's child 10/29/1803 M
CRUIKSHANK John 11/2/1803 M
CRUIKSHANK Mrs's child 11/7/1803 W
KROUSE John's wife 11/11/1803 M
SPEAKE Mrs's child 11/18/1803 S
PLATER Thomas for a boy 11/22/1803 M
BRUFF Thomas's child 11/29/1803 M
DELAHAY Benjamin's child 12/4/1803 S
HYDE Thomas's colored child 12/24/1803 S
PYE Mrs for ----- 12/31/1803 M
KING William 7/21/1803 M
SPEAK Mrs's Negro child 1/3/1804 S
TOWNSEND Henry for ----- 1/25/1804 S
BECK Richard's child 1/31/1804 M
PETER John's negro woman 2/9/1804 S
KING Adam's child 2/11/1804 S
BANKS John's child 2/19/1804 M
MOORE James's child 2/22/1804 W
NEVITT Thomas's child 3/3/1804 S
FOXALL Henry's ----- 3/7/1804 S
HEISTER General 3/7/1804 M
JOHNS Leonard H's child 3/9/1804 M
LEEK Mr 3/13/1804 S
DUNCASTER Miss Sally's colored child 3/16/1804 S
NIGHT James's wife 3/16/1804 S
REINTZLE Valentine's wife 3/19/1804 M
WILLIAMS Captain's negro boy 3/22/1804 S
BIRTH Mr's child 3/24/1804 W
PEARCE Isaac for ----- 5/1/1804 W
NORRIS Isaac's wife 5/3/1804 W
HARDIN Edward for ----- 5/25/1804 M
MARCH John 6/3/1804 M
MACKEY Alexander's child 6/16/1804 W

KING William's colored child 6/16/1804 S
ISBORN Mrs's child 6/20/1804 W
DeKRAFFT Charles 7/25/1804 W
RANKIN Mr's child 7/25/1804 M
LANHAM Elisha 7/25/1804 S
JONCHEREZ A L's child 8/7/1804 W
DEWES Mr 8/9/1804 M
BROWNING Joseph's child 8/25/1804 W
LAIRD John's child 8/26/1804 M
LAIRD John's wife 8/31/1804 M
ORME Nathaniel 9/12/1804 W
DEGIMS Mr 9/13/1804 W
BEATTY Charles 9/17/1804 M
DUFFY Brian's child 9/17/1804 S
DEVELIN Daniel 9/19/1804 W
LAIRD John for ----- 9/28/1804 M
MITCHELL Doctor 9/30/1804 M
FISHER Mr's child 10/1/1804 S
FRANCIS Mr 10/1/1804 S
CHANDLER Walter S's child 10/4/1804 M
LOVEJOY John's child 10/7/1804 W
PARROTT Richard's child 10/8/1804 M
SHAW & BIRTH for ----- 10/12/1804 S
GALLASPY Mr 10/17/1804 W
ELIASON Mr's child 10/17/1804 W
BARWISE Mr's child 10/17/1804 S
PETER John 10/21/1804 M
BOYD Abraham for ----- 10/27/1804 W
DEAKINS Francis 10/29/1804 M
BARWISE Mr for ----- 10/30/1804 S
SMITH John K's colored child 11/3/1804 S
PARROTT Mr (hatter) 11/19/1804 S
HENOP Mrs's child 11/19/1804 S
TURNER Thomas's child 12/3/1804 M
THAW Joseph's wife 1/3/1805 M
PARROTT Richard's colored person 1/6/1805 S
SMITH John K for ----- 1/7/1805 M
LEE Thomas S's wife 1/24/1805 M
LANG John for ----- 1/24/1805 W
KROUSE John for ----- 1/25/1805 W
KING Adam's child 1/31/1805 S
LAIRD John's child 1/12/1805 M

THOMPSON James for ----- 3/7/1805 M
DINES Jessee 3/8/1805 W
TUCKER Mr 3/11/1805 W
HAWKINS Mrs 3/20/1805 W
SEMMES Joseph's George's wife 4/12/1805 S
BRICE Miss 4/12/1805 M
WHITMORE Benjamin for ----- 4/17/1805 S
DIXON William for ----- 4/27/1805 S
THOMSON John 5/11/1805 S
HODGSON Joseph 5/21/1805 M
DEAKINS Mrs 5/31/1805 M
BROOK Miss Mary's negro girl 6/1/1805 S
HUGHES Miss (at J Laird's) 6/4/1805 M
ANDERSON Mrs 6/18/1805 W
THOMPSON James's child 6/21/1805 M
FORREST Uriah 7/7/1805 M
PRATT John W's child 7/17/1805 M
COX John's Frank 7/27/1805 S
McMURRAY Mr's cartman's child 7/27/1805 S
Old George (gravedigger) 8/10/1805 S
GOSZLER Henry's child 8/10/1805 W
EATHY Hesekiah for ----- 8/16/1805 W
LUFFBOROUGH Nathan's child 8/16/1805 M
LUFFBOROUGH Nathan's child 8/27/1805 M
SAYERS Mr's child 8/31/1805 M
BEALL Mrs Brook's colored child 9/1/1805 S
KROUSE John's Lewis 9/1/1805 S
TALMIE Mr 9/13/1805 W
BAUM Mr's child 9/17/1805 W
WAYMAN Charles 9/27/1805 M
PECK Joseph's wife 9/28/1805 M
CRUST Henry 10/3/1805 M
BANKS John's child 10/4/1805 M
SIMMS Joseph M's child 10/5/1805 W
LAIRD John's housekeeper 10/5/1805 W
HENDERSON Mr 10/6/1805 M
LAINE Mr 10/9/1805 M
MELVIN James's child 10/12/1805 M
KING Nicholas's child 10/14/1805 M
DOUGHTY William's colored child 10/25/1805 S
CRAIG George's mother 10/30/1805 W
STEEL Matthew for a girl 11/1/1805 W

WHITMORE Benjamin's child 11/9/1805 S
DUNLAP John 11/12/1805 M
DUNLOP James's child 11/14/1805 M
PRITCHARD Benjamin's child 11/20/1805 W
MERRY Anthony's Peter 12/3/1805 W
WILLIAMS Elisha O 12/15/1805 M
WALKER James for ----- 12/17/1805 W
LACY Benjamin 12/18/1805 W
MARBURY William's colored woman 12/19/1805 S
STEPTOE Henrietta's child 12/20/1805 S
SMITH Major 12/27/1805 W
MAGRUDER George's wife 1/6/1806 M
DIGGS Mr 1/14/1806 W
REINTZLE John's wife 1/16/1806 M
WOODSIDE John's negro girl 2/1/1806 S
REES Major 2/28/1806 W
NELSON Mr 3/1/1806 S
HENOP Mrs's colored child 3/6/1806 S
FRENCH Mrs 3/12/1806 M
NORRIS Isaac's child 3/16/1806 W
KING George's colored child 4/1/1806 S
SCOTT Margaret for ----- 4/5/1806 M
BEALL Thomas B's John 4/22/1806 S
DUNCASTLE Sarah's colored child 4/24/1806 S
QUADE Walter for ----- 4/27/1806 S
MELVIN James's child 4/28/1806 M
OAKLY John 5/6/1806 M
CRAWFORD William's John 5/9/1806 S
BEALL William D's mother 5/10/1806 W
REINTZLE Anthony 5/21/1806 W
SIMPSON James 5/25/1806 S
DUNCASTLE Sarah's negro woman 6/2/1806 S
RUMNEY John's child 6/17/1806 W
ADAMS John Q's child 6/23/1806 M
MASON John's colored person 6/27/1806 S
GREEN Mrs for ----- 6/30/1806 W
HOLMEAD Anthony for ----- 7/5/1806 W
LIPSCOMB John's child 7/5/1806 W
OWING Mrs 7/11/1806 W
BOYD George's child 7/11/1806 M
STEPHENS James for ----- 7/16/1806 M
QUADE Walter for ----- 7/21/1806 S

HERRITSON Elizabeth for ----- 7/25/1806 S
ADAMS Thomas's child 7/26/1806 W
ANDREWS Mr's child 7/28/1806 W
WEEMS John's child 7/28/1806 M
BAIN Quentin for ----- 8/2/1806 S
WATSON Thomas's child 8/13/1806 S
HALLIDAY Mr's child 8/22/1806 S
KING Marget 8/27/1806 M
WRIGHT Thomas C's child 9/1/1806 W
THOMPSON James's child 9/4/1806 M
BECK Rezin's negro man 9/24/1806 S
WILSON John's child 9/27/1806 M
BLANCHARD William's child 9/29/1806 M
HUGHES Miss for ----- 10/4/1806 M
BROWN Joel's child 10/4/1806 M
LAMBRIGHT George's child 10/4/1806 S
RAGON Daniel's child 10/10/1806 W
LELAND Mr's boy 10/11/1806 S
CLAGETT Mrs's Charles 10/11/1806 S
LOVE Charles's child 10/14/1806 S
FRESH Mr's child 10/15/1806 S
DAVIDSON James for ----- 10/17/1806 M
PRICE Samuel for ----- 10/18/1806 S
MORGAN William for ----- 10/20/1806 S
CRAMPTON Richard for ----- 10/27/1806 M
HEDGES Nicholas's child 10/28/1806 W
HEDGES Nicholas's child 11/3/1806 W
BEALL Upton for a lad 11/8/1806 M
TURNBUL Mrs's child 11/12/1806 S
PETER Robert 11/16/1806 M
THECKER Mr's child 11/20/1806 S
IRWIN William 11/20/1806 M
HILLARY Nicholas for ----- 11/23/1806 W
CONLEY John's child 12/3/1806 S
NAYLOR John H 12/4/1806 S
DIGGS Mrs 12/7/1806 W
ROCK Mr 12/7/1806 S
STORY Mr 12/8/1806 S
DIXON Mr for ----- 12/9/1806 S
HELLEN Walter's child 12/20/1806 M
GANNON James for ----- 12/20/1806 S
NORRIS Isaac for ----- 12/21/1806 W

MAGRUDER Samuel B for ----- 12/26/1806 S
BECK Rezin's negro boy 1/3/1807 S
GALRIGHT William's child 1/15/1807 S
MOUNTZ John for ----- 1/24/1807 S
OFFORD Mr for ----- 1/28/1807 W
BURNS Mrs 1/29/1807 M
REINTZLE Daniel for a lad 1/31/1807 W
COLE Nelly 2/2/1807 S
BROWNING Joseph's child 2/12/1807 W
KURTZ Thomas for Dulen 2/17/1807 S
CORROTHERS G 2/17/1807 S
BEVERLY Robert's child 2/24/1807 M
COLLINS 3/5/1807 S
CURRAN John 3/5/1807 M
LOWRIE Cesar 3/8/1807 W
DUNLOP Henry for ----- 3/17/1807 M
LOWE Walter 3/18/1807 M
COX John's child 3/18/1807 M
MACKALL Benjamin's child 3/19/1807 W
CLOUD Abner's child 3/23/1807 M
BECK Rezin for ----- 3/24/1807 W
MAGRUDER Patrick for ----- 4/4/1807 M
LUFFBOROUGH Nathan's colored child 4/4/1807 S
MELVIN James's child 4/4/1807 M
SHOEMAKER Charles 4/5/1807 S
FAGAN Mr's mother-in-law 4/6/1807 S
GUINNE David for -----4/21/1807 W
MAGRUDER Ninian's black boy 5/5/1807 W
LOVE Charles for ----- 5/14/1807 M
LOVEJOY Samuel 5/23/1807 S
JOHNSON Isaac for ----- 5/25/1807 S
ENGLISH John 6/4/1807 S
LUFFBOROUGH Nathan for ----- 7/2/1807 M
LAMBRIGHT George's child 7/11/1807 S
SWAN Major's child 7/17/1807 M
BALL Richard 7/19/1807 S
STEPTOE Caroline's child 7/31/1807 S
McCUTCHEON Thomas for ----- 8/12/1807 S
MARCH Mrs 8/13/1807 M
WOODSIDES Mr for ----- 8/28/1807 S
CHESLEY Mr's child 9/5/1807 W
COX John's child 9/8/1807 M

COX Mrs John 9/12/1807 M
BAIRD Andrew 9/12/1807 W
RHODES George's child 9/21/1807 W
JORDAN Mary's child 9/21/1807 S
NEVITT Thomas 9/27/1807 S
KEEPHER Henry's child 9/29/1807 M
PETER Thomas's child 10/3/1807 M
ANDERSON Samuel's colored man 10/14/1807 S
CARTER Jacob's child 10/14/1807 S
HINES Daniel 10/16/1807 W
BEALL George 10/17/1807 M
PETER Alexander 10/26/1807 M
HYDE Thomas's child 10/26/1807 W
BECK Richard's colored child 10/28/1807 S
WISE Mr (Alexandria) 11/3/1807 W
MURDOCK Addison's colored women 11/9/1807 S
SLATOR Mr 11/11/1807 S
BOYD Washington for ----- 11/15/1807 W
KEY Francis's Harry 12/9/1807 S
WILSON John for ----- 12/12/1807 S
McPHERSON H & J for ----- 12/13/1807 W
PRITCHARD Benjamin's child 12/20/1807 W
WILLIAMS Jeremiah's child 1/2/1808 M
LELAND John's child 1/11/1808 W
BALTZER John's child 1/21/1808 M
WATERS William's wife 1/26/1808 W
MURDOCK Addison 1/31/1808 M
DAVIDSON James's child 2/9/1808 M
WAIN Mr for ----- 2/13/1808 W
KERR Alexander for child 2/17/1808 M
BEALL Joseph S for ----- 2/17/1808 S
SIMMONS William's child 2/17/1808 M
MAGRATH Jane's child 2/21/1808 S
HARRISON Richard's child 2/29/1808 M
PRICE Samuel's child 3/5/1808 S
KEEPHER Henry 3/14/1808 W
SPEAK Mrs's negro child 3/14/1808 S
FOXALL Henry for ----- 3/17/1808 S
FOXALL Henry for ----- 3/25/1808 S
PARSONS William's child 4/1/1808 S
ORME Archibald for ----- 4/12/1808 W
JOHNSON Isaac's colored woman 4/14/1808 S

GOSZLER Henry's child 4/15/1808 W
MOORE Nathan for ----- 4/19/1808 S
KING James C's child 6/1/1808 W
HYDE Thomas's child 6/24/1808 W
SMITH Edward L's child 6/24/1808 M
MITCHELL John 7/4/1808 W
McINTIRE Samuel for ----- 7/15/1808 M
DePLUX Eugene 7/20/1808 M
PETER David's chld 7/22/1808 M
HILLARY L's child 7/28/1808 S
HARRISON Richard for ----- 7/31/1808 M
RIND William A's child 8/3/1808 M
PATTERSON Edgar's colored child 8/4/1808 W
FERGUSON Mr 8/3/1808 S
TAYLOR Mr's child 8/13/1808 S
MOYERS Samuel's child 8/13/1808 S
MICHINS Mrs's child 8/16/1808 S
BAIRD Mrs's child 8/19/1808 S
RODGERS Thomas's child 8/21/1808 M
McMURRAY William's child 8/23/1808 M
LOVE Charles for ----- 8/25/1808 M
BEALL Thomas B's colored child 8/30/1808 S
ELIASON John's child 8/30/1808 M
TAVANCE John's child 9/3/1808 W
ELIASON John's child 9/3/1808 W
BRADLEY Mrs 9/15/1808 M
ROSS Andrew for wife 9/17/1808 M
DORSEY's Billy's child 9/19/1808 S
BALTZER John 9/26/1808 M
WILLSON Sarah for Miss Dashiell 10/1/1808 M
POLKINHORN Henry's child 10/2/1808 S
McCUTCHEON John for Mrs McCoshine 10/8/1808 W
CORCORAN Mr 10/9/1808 W
KURTZ Thomas for ----- 10/11/1808 M
KELLY Mr 10/14/1808 S
GOSZLER John's child 10/20/1808 W
SAYERS Mr's child 10/21/1808 M
GRAHAM Mr's child 10/21/1808 S
GRAHAM William's child 10/28/1808 S
TURNER Thomas's child 10/29/1808 M
EDWARDS Henry's child 11/6/1808 W
HEATH Mr's child 11/9/1808 S

RETEN Jacob's child 11/9/1808
RIGDEN T for Mr Mitchell 11/9/1808 S
WEEMS Doctor John 11/11/1808 M
SIMMON William's wife 11/20/1808 M
BRONOUGH John W's child 12/7/1808 M
HERSEY Benjamin for Brown 12/11/1808 M
HARRISON Richard's child 12/12/1808 M
SMITH William's daughter 12/16/1808 W
GAINES Richard for ----- 12/17/1808 M
HOYT E J's child 12/17/1808 S
COX John's colored child 12/22/1808 S
MACOMB Mrs's child 1/5/1809 W
SIMPSON John's child 1/6/1809 W
SAYERS John 1/8/1809 M
SHELTON Captain 1/9/1809 M
JAY Absolom 1/15/1809 W
KING George's child 1/18/1809 S
DUNCASTLE Miss S's colored man 1/24/1809 S
FOXALL Henry for son [John] 1/27/1809 M
DAWES Isaac's child 1/30/1809 W
BURNETT Charles A's child 2/1/1809 M
WASHINGTON George's child 2/2/1809 M
DEAKINS Mrs 2/17/1809 M
LANE Mr 2/24/1809 S
SMITH J K for G McCandless 2/26/1809 S
LEATHY 3/21/1809 S
HULL Jacob's child 3/27/1809 W
DUNCASTLE Miss S's colored man 4/8/1809 S
SIMMONS William's child 4/12/1809 M
WHITE Mr's child 4/16/1809 W
ARNOLD Mr's child 4/17/1809 S
SIMMONS William's child 4/19/1809 M
SUTER Alexander's colored woman 4/15/1809 S
THOMSON John for ----- 4/27/1809 M
DUNCASTLE Miss S's negro boy 4/27/1809 S
PETER Thomas's child 4/29/1809 M
PARROTT Richard's black man 5/1/1809 S
CAUSINE Mr's negro woman 5/10/1809 S
LIVERS Mrs J 5/13/1809 M
Unknown 5/14/1809 S
BUSSARD Daniel's Sarah 5/16/1809 S
SMITH William 5/22/1809 W

CLARK William for ----- 5/29/1809 W
BURNET C A's boy 6/4/1809 S
SEMMES's George's child 6/4/1809 S
BAKER D W's son 6/5/1809 S
THOMAS Henry's wife 6/21/1809 S
SLYE Thomas G's child 6/21/1809 W
SMITH Edward L for ----- 6/26/1809 M
DUNCASTLE Miss S's negro child 6/28/1809 S
KEY Philip B's negro man 7/2/1809 S
PARROTT Richard's negro child 7/7/1809 S
FRENCH George for ----- 7/9/1809 M
GRAHAM Mr's child 7/19/1809 S
LIVERS Anthony's child 7/21/1809 W
WILLIAMS Mr's child 7/22/1809 S
ROWLES Joseph E's child 7/23/1809 M
WHITEWOOD Mrs Elizabeth 7/29/1809 M
COUNTEE Dory's girl 7/29/1809 S
FRESH Mr's child 7/30/1809 S
Colored child 8/5/1809 S
TURNER Samuel for Mr Grimes 8/5/1809 M
LONG Samuel 8/17/1809 S
HEWSTEN Charles's child 8/22/1809 W
LOWE Mr's child 8/22/1809 S
TAVANCE John for ----- 8/24/1809 M
BAKER Doctor's negro man 8/26/1809 S
CRAWFORD William's child 9/3/1809 M
ADAMS William 9/5/1809 W
BERRY Mr 9/7/1809 S
LUFFBOROUGH Nathan's child 9/10/1809 M
TRAVERS Nicholas's apprentice Walter 9/11/1809 S
PECK Joseph 9/15/1809 M
McCUTCHEON James for ----- 9/17/1809 S
SMITH Walter for ----- 9/17/1809 M
GRIMES Michael's child 9/20/1809 W
DUNCASTLE Miss S's negro child 9/21/1809 S
BREWER Joseph's child 9/24/1809 M
DUNCASTLE Miss S's negro child 9/25/1809 S
LODDER Joshua's mother-in-law 9/29/1809 S
TRAVERS Nicholas for ----- 10/1/1809 M
KENGLA Lewis's child 10/3/1809 W
WATERS Mr's child 10/3/1809 W
McCUTCHEON Thomas for a girl 10/6/1809 W

PETER Robert Junior 11/11/1809 M
THOMAS John 3rd black child 11/11/1809 S
McCLANN Robert for ----- 11/14/1809 W
BEVERLY Robert's negro child 11/23/1809 S
LYONS Mrs 11/25/1809 S
McCASLER James 11/26/1809 S
GREEN Mrs 11/26/1809 W
SWANN Caleb 11/30/1809 M
CARBERRY Mrs Henry 12/7/1809 W
MARQUAN Mr's son 12/10/1809 S
SPALDING Mr for ----- 12/16/1809 M
HUGHES Miss's negro girl 12/17/1809 S
MOUNTZ John for ----- 12/18/1809 M
A CHILD 12/20/1809 S
BANKS John 1/2/1810 M
BECK Richard's child 1/5/1810 M
PRITCHARD Mrs Benjamin 1/28/1810 W
COATS Doctor 2/8/1810 M
HARSHMAN Mr's daughter 2/9/1810 S
CONLY John's child 2/9/1810 S
HOOVER Mr 2/15/1810 W
QUADE Walter's father 3/1/1810 S
CLARE Benjamin 3/4/1810 M
DOUGHTY Mrs (William's mother) 3/7/1810 M
WILLIAMS Thomas 3/12/1810 M
SPEAKE Mrs 3/20/1810 M
BANKS Mrs's child 3/25/1810 S
PETER John's sister 3/30/1810 M
BECK Richard 4/3/1810 M
HEWIT Thomas 4/13/1810 W
HERSY John C for ----- 4/20/1810 W
ELIASON John's child 4/21/1810 W
McCUTCHEON James 5/8/1810 S
SHORTER Abram's brother 5/18/1810 S
SUTER Alexander's brother Robert 5/20/1810 M
GRIMES Michael's child 5/26/1810 W
DANOON Mr for ----- 6/2/1810 S
BURNETT C A's child 6/3/1810 M
BALTZER George's child 6/6/1810 M
THOMSON George 6/23/1810 M
CROMWELL Jessee's child 6/25/1810 W
Dennis ------'s black boy 7/8/1810 S

BUSHBY William 7/8/1810 W
DAVIS Thomas 7/12/1810 W
SUTER Alexander's negro child 7/19/1810 S
HERSY John C's child 7/21/1810 S
DAVIDSON Samuel 8/1/1810 M
BAKER Mr's child 8/2/1810 S
MORTON William's negro child 8/6/1810 S
GIBBON Mrs 8/9/1810 M
MONROE Thomas's child 8/13/1810 M
HINES John's mother-in-law 8/16/1810 S
McCUTCHEON Thomas's child 8/17/1810 W
DAVIS Mr's son 8/23/1810 S
PETER John's child 8/27/1810 M
TURNER Thomas's negro child 8/29/1810 S
JOHNS Mr's negro woman's child 9/1/1810 W
WITING Colonel 9/4/1810 M
RODGERS Major 9/5/1810 M
BECK Joseph's negro woman 9/9/1810 S
MAYER Henry's child 9/9/1810 S
SMALLWOOD Mr 9/10/1810 S
WALTON James's (colored man) child 9/11/1810 S
DUVALL Gabriel's negro child 9/14/1810 S
HARBAUGH Mr 9/18/1810 S
STEELE Mr 9/21/1810 W
WINFRED Mrs 9/22/1810 S
DUNCASTLE Miss S's negro woman 9/22/1810 S
DULEY Mr for ----- 9/25/1810 W
BURRY Nancy 9/29/1810 S
CAMPBEL Mr's child 9/29/1810 S
WASHINGTON William A 10/4/1810 M
JENKINS Robert 10/7/1810 W
RITTENHOUSE John B's negro woman 10/11/1810 S
CONLEY Patrick 10/14/1810 W
COVER Daniel for ----- 10/20/1810 W
BEALL Ninian's child 10/22/1810 W
RITTENHOUSE John B's child 10/23/1810 M
TUEL Richard's father 10/27/1810 W
ADAMS John for ----- 10/30/1810 W
HARDY William's child 11/1/1810 S
THOMSON Mrs's mother 11/6/1810 W
BAILEY Jessee for ----- 11/14/1810 W
DELAPLANE Joseph for ----- 11/14/1810 M

OWENS Isaac's child 11/19/1810 W
POLK Charles P for ----- 11/25/1810 M
BUSSARD Philip's child 12/5/1810 M
ABBOTT John's child 12/7/1810 M
CRAWFORD William's negro child 12/14/1810 S
COOPER Richard 12/16/1810 S
REINTZLE Daniel's child 12/20/1810 M
JONES Richard's mother 12/25/1810 S
HELLEN Walter for ----- 1/1/1811 M
BARRY James 1/8/1811 S
CHEW Cassy 1/11/1811 W
MORRIS Randal for wife 1/14/1811 W
McKENNY Thomas L's child 1/27/1811 M
GOSZLER George's child 2/5/1811 W
FRENCH George for ----- 2/9/1811 M
MOUNTZ Jacob for ----- 2/15/1811 M
OWENS Isaac's Sam 2/18/1811 S
REINTZLE John 3/13/1811 M
GIBBONS Thomas's child 4/4/1811 W
RENNER John's negro man 4/8/1811 S
MORGAN Evan's child 4/15/1811 S
LANG John's child 4/19/1811 M
RIGDEN William's child 4/23/1811 S
DASHIELL Thomas for ----- 4/23/1811 M
MINOR Mrs 5/1/1811 W
TURNER Thomas's child 5/7/1811 M
FRESH William's child 5/15/1811 S
Patience (Negress) 5/18/1811 S
TURNER Thomas for ----- 5/21/1811 M
OWENS Isaac's child 6/10/1811 W
WOOD Doctor for ----- 6/13/1811 M
THECKER Mrs 6/16/1811 W
BRUSH Mr's child 6/22/1811 M
GAITHER Colonel 6/23/1811 M
BIRCHAN Mrs 6/28/1811 W
SIMPSON Mrs's daughter 7/1/1811 S
CLAGETT Mrs' negro woman 7/2/1811 S
SMOOT Charles 7/2/1811 S
DUFIEFF Mr's child 7/15/1811 W
SIPS Mr's child 7/20/1811 S
PETER John's brother 7/22/1811 M
MORRIS Randal's child 7/24/1811 W

McCLEARY Captain 7/25/1811 M
McMURRAY William for ----- 7/27/1811 M
WHITE Joseph for a girl 7/31/1811 W
CHILDS Henry's child 8/4/1811 M
CARTER Jacob's child 8/6/1811 S
MAYER Henry's child 8/10/1811 S
LAMBRIGHT George 8/15/1811 W
WALKER Elijah 8/17/1811 M
HARBAUGH Leonard for ----- 8/19/1811 S
MORRIS's child 8/19/1811 W
BOSTON Mrs for ----- 8/24/1811 S
HARTLOVE Mr's child 8/31/1811 S
SIMMONS William for a girl 9/3/1811 M
ROWLES Joseph E 9/10/1811 M
MARBURY William's negro woman 9/10/1811 S
DASHIELL Miss S for a girl 9/14/1811 S
DAVIS Charles's mother 9/14/1811 W
GIBBONS Mr's child 9/17/1811 W
LAW Mrs 9/17/1811 S
GROSS Mrs 9/25/1811 S
CAMPBLE Miss for a chld 9/26/1811 S
PEARCE Mr's child 9/27/1811 W
STEWART Doctor for ----- 9/30/1811 M
BOUSCH John C for ----- 9/30/1811 M
CASEY Robert 9/30/1811 M
JOHNSON Mrs 10/1/1811 M
WILSON John's child 10/1/1811 M
WELCH Mrs 10/2/1811 S
GRAHAM William's child 10/10/1811 W
STEWART William's child 10/15/1811 M
StCLAIR John 10/15/1811 M
HILLARD John 10/16/1811 W
McPHERSON Henry's mother 10/17/1811 W
BOHRER Abraham for ----- 10/18/1811 W
HEATH Nathaniel for mother 10/24/1811 W
DAVIDSON James's child 10/26/1811 M
HEATH Nathaniel's child 10/28/1811 M
HEATH Nathaniel's child 10/30/1811 M
ASTON Elizabeth's child 10/31/1811 S
LINGAN Nicholas 11/3/1811M
SMITH Mrs M's daughter 11/3/1811 W
POWELL Mary 11/5/1811 S

ROBERTSON Thomas's brother 11/6/1811 M
WELSH Mr 11/13/1811 S
RAGON Bazil's child 11/14/1811 S
PARROTT Richard's negro woman 11/15/1811 S
RUSSEL John 11/16/1811 S
HUNTER Mr's child 11/18/1811 S
KING George's child 11/20/1811 S
UPPERMAN Henry's child 11/26/1811 W
SMITH Captain's child 11/26/1811 S
KEEN Thomas's child 12/2/1811 S
LANE Robert's mother 12/16/1811 W
MORRIS George's sister-in-law 12/18/1811 W
ORMOT Valentine 12/18/1811 S
SMOOT Samuel's child 12/20/1811 S
DUNCASTLE Miss S's colored man 12/21/1811 S
THOMSON Mr for a boy 12/24/1811 M
BRADFORD William for ----- 12/24/1811 S
SHORTER Abraham's mother 12/26/1811 S
GRAY Mr's child 12/30/1811 S
CRAWFORD William's colored child 12/31/1811 S
GLOYD Mrs's mother 12/31/1811 S
GRAY Mr's child 1/4/1812 S
BOWER Thomas's son 1/5/1812 M
DOUGLAS Mrs 1/6/1812 S
RICHARDSON Mrs 1/7/1812 W
WILLIAMS Jeremiah's black woman 1/9/1812 S
WILLIAMS Jeremiah's black child 1/9/1812 S
KEY F S 's black child 1/15/1812 S
FOSTER Mr 1/15/1812 S
MYERS John's child 1/16/1812 W
Negro Hatfield 1/19/1812 S
BECK Joseph 1/18/1812 W
SMITH Clement's child 1/19/1812 M
COLE Negro Stephen 1/23/1812 S
OLIVE William 1/23/1812 S
OWEN Colonel 1/30/1812 M
RITTENHOUSE Thomas's black girl 2/2/1812 S
COOK Mr's black child 2/2/1812 S
FOWLER Daniel 2/3/1812 W
PETER Mrs Elinor 2/7/1812 M
SPRIGG Mrs 2/7/1812 M
CHILDS Henry 2/9/1812 M

WASHINGTON George's child 2/12/1812 M
NEVIT Joseph's daughter 2/21/1812 M
Negro Macy's child 2/21/1812 S
WOODWARD Mr's child 2/29/1812 S
QUADE Mrs 3/3/1812 S
RIGDEN Thomas's child 3/4/1812 W
Mama Betty 3/10/1812 S
BAKER Doctor William 3/22/1812 W
HEDGES Nicholas's child 3/22/1812 W
JACKSON Mrs 3/23/1812 W
BOON Arnold's child 3/26/1812 W
JACKSON John 4/8/1812 W
JONES Susanna 4/11/1812 M
LUCKET Mrs 4/12/1812 W
BAKER Mr's child 4/17/1812 W
DEAKINS Leonard's child 4/18/1812 W
BLUER John 5/2/1812 S
RISZNER Mrs 5/3/1812 W
KURTZ Daniel's black woman 5/3/1812 S
CATON Mr's child 5/6/1812 W
GEARVIS Mrs 5/7/1812 W
CARLTON Joseph 5/12/1812 M
READEN Henry 5/12/1812 S
A Woman drowned near the Falls Bridge 5/12/1812 S
HARBAUGH Leonard 5/14/1812 S
BOWIE Mrs 5/16/1812 M
KING Nicholas 5/22/1812 M
CRAWFORD William's Bazil 5/22/1812 S
DUCKET Miss Mary 5/25/1812 M
BRANNUM Mrs 5/26/1812 S
COAL Jeremiah's mother 6/8/1812 S
Man that came down the river 6/8/1812 S
A black child (Watt Spokes) 6/8/1812 S
PURDY Mr 6/9/1812 S
WINEBURGER Jacob's child 6/14/1812 W
RUSHER Richard's child 6/19/1812 M
CAMBLE Mashake's child 6/25/1812 S
GIBBON Thomas's child 6/25/1812 W
ENGLISH David's son Thomas 6/26/1812 W
KNOTS Daniel's black woman 6/26/1812 S
MAGRUDER Alexander 6/27/1812 W
SUTER Mrs 7/4/1812 M

CRAWFORD William's black boy 7/5/1812 S
REDEN Henry 7/5/1812 S
RITTER Peter's child 7/6/1812 M
LANDIS Abraham's child 7/9/1812 W
BURNS Mrs' child 7/9/1812 S
GREENFIELD Mrs 7/10/1812 W
CALDER William's child 7/16/1812 M
STEELE Mrs's child 7/20/1812 S
MINN James 7/22/1812 S
RICHARDSON Thomas's child 7/23/1812 W
WEST John's child 7/23/1812 M
EVANS Clarissa's child 7/23/1812 W
RITTER Jacob's child 7/25/1812 W
JONES Richard's child 7/31/1812 S
COOLIDGE Samuel 7/31/1812 M
WISE Mrs 7/31/1812 S
KELLENBERGER child 8/6/1812 S
RAGON Basil's child 8/7/1812 S
Chaves, a black man 8/7/1812 S
BRUFF Thomas's child 8/10/1812 M
COLLINS child 8/10/1812 S
FORREST Henry's child 8/11/1812 M
Nancy a black woman's child 8/13/1812 S
BROWN Clary a black woman's child 8/13/1812 S
DAVIS Edward's child 8/15/1812 W
BOWIE Mrs 8/16/1812 M
BUTLER Charles's child 8/16/1812 W
MYERS John's child 8/16/1812 W
RITTER Peter's child 8/19/1812 M
WILLS Mr's child 8/23/1812 S
CHESTER Mr's child 8/23/1812 S
STEMPLE Mr's child 8/23/1812 W
DOUGHTY William's child 8/28/1812 M
DEVERS James's child 8/30/1812 W
HARTLOVE Mr's child 8/29/1812 S
LEE William's child 8/31/1812 M
WARD Elizabeth's child 9/1/1812 S
LAY Richard's child 9/4/1812 W
GRASON William's child 9/5/1812 M
CARTOR Jacob's child 9/5/1812 W
GIBSON Mr's child 9/7/1812 W
WHITE Mrs 9/9/1812 M

SHERLEY Mr 9/10/1812 S
JONES Mr's child 9/10/1812 S
MORTON William's black child 9/10/1812 S
BANISTER Richard's child 9/14/1812 W
BROWN Joel's child 9/15/1812 M
A black man that died at J. Brown's 9/15/1812 S
TAILOR Captain's child 9/16/1812 S
MILLER Mr's child 9/17/1812 W
COLE Hanah's child 9/17/1812 S
YOUNG Mr 9/18/1812 M
WALLAND Mr's child 9/20/1812 S
THOMSON John C's child 9/20/1812 W
RATCLIF Mrs 9/21/1812 W
SMITH Mrs's child 9/22/1812 M
SHEAPARD Mr's child 9/27/1812 W
SUTER Alexander's black child 9/27/1812 S
GANNON James's child 9/29/1812 W
MARCHEL Mr 10/2/1812 W
READEN Mrs 10/5/1812 S
Thomas's child (a black man) 10/5/1812 S
CLARK Mrs's child 10/8/1812 S
CROWN S T's child 10/9/1812 S
RIDGLEY William G's child 10/20/1812 S
GLEN Mrs's child 10/28/1812 S
MOUNTZ John 10/31/1812 W
RICHARDSON Thomas 11/13/1812 W
LANNUN Rebecka 11/13/1812 S
KING Mary 11/14/1812 M
Cyrus's wife 11/24/1812 S
NICHOLLS William S's black child 11/26/1812 S
KEEPHER Mrs's daughter 11/27/1812 W
CRAGE Robert 12/1/1812 M
PETER David 12/2/1812 M
A black child 12/2/1812 S
CROWN Samuel T 12/23/1812 S
BEATTY Kitty 12/23/1812 M
BOWIE Washington's child 12/31/1812 S
A black woman that died at Langs 12/31/1812 S
MARCHEL Mr [12/1812] S
HAGAN Charles 1/3/1813 S
SEMMES Mary 1/12/1813 M
PARROTT Richard's black boy 1/13/1813 S

BURGES Mrs 2/8/1813 M
BOWMAN Babtist 2/13/1813 S
WOOD Mr 2/19/1813 W
LEE Nancy's black man William 2/21/1813 S
NEWTON Mrs's child 2/21/1813 S
BUSSARD Daniel 3/3/1813 M
BARNES Mathew 3/9/1813 S
TUTTLE Mrs 3/10/1813 S
Minty 3/10/1813 S
THOMSON John 3/12/1813 S
MASON Thomas 3/12/1813 M
WIPPLE Oliver 3/16/1813 M
CRUTTENDEN Mr's child 3/17/1813 W
WILSON John's child 3/31/1813 S
WAGNER Jacob's black child 4/6/1813 S
DUNCASTEL Sally 4/9/1813 M
CLAGGETT Mrs's black woman 4/12/1813 S
STULL Captain's child 4/15/1813 M
WHITE Mr's child 4/16/1813 S
Safa child 4/20/1813 S
STEWART William's child 5/1/1813 M
UPPERMAN George's child 5/8/1813 W
CRAWFORD William's black boy 5/10/1813 S
STONE Edward's child 5/14/1813 W
WILLIAMS John a black man 5/15/1813 S
PECK M A's black girl 5/16/1813 S
ROBERTSON Mr's child 5/20/1813 S
LAY Richard's child 5/24/1813 W
WHANN David 5/24/1813 M
MORSELL Mrs 5/31/1813 M
HARRIS James a black man 6/1/1813 S
CHESTER Samuel's child 6/3/1813 S
McDONNAL L a black man for his mother 6/5/1813 S
PORTER's child 6/10/1813 S
WILLIAMS James (a black man)'s child 6/12/1813 S
LYON Mr's child 6/18/1813 M
GIBSON Mr's child 6/28/1813 S
PARSONS William's child 6/28/1813 M
WALES Mrs's child 6/27/1813 M
FOXALL Henry's black child 6/27/1813 S
TAILOR Benjamin's child 7/1/1813 S
BARBER Barna's daughter 7/5/1813 S

FRIZE Mr's child 7/7/1813 S
George a black man's child 7/7/1813 S
HALLENBECK Mrs 7/6/1813 M
KING Joseph's child 7/14/1813 M
TIFFIN Edward's child 7/16/1813 M
VINSON John 7/17/1813 S
COMBS Mrs 7/27/1813 S
NEWTON Miss 7/28/1813 S
NORMAN Betsey 7/31/1813 S
ADAMS Isaac's child 8/8/1813 S
EDMONSON Mrs 8/10/1813 S
JOHNS Dennis's child 8/19/1813 M
Charlot's child a black man 8/20/1813 W
PETER Mrs 8/21/1813 M
NEWTON Walter's child 8/25/1813 W
PEARCE Mrs's child 8/25/1813 W
McMURRY Joseph 9/1/1813 M
ADAMS Mrs 9/3/1813 W
STORM James's child 9/4/1813 M
WILSON Isaac's child 9/4/1813 M
A Negro Woman 9/6/1813 S
GODDARD John B's child 9/6/1813 W
KING Margrat's son 9/6/1813 M
HILLARY Nicholas's child 9/14/1813 W
TOLSTON Sarah's child colored 9/14/1813 S
ASTAN Peggy's child 9/17/1813 S
BECK Mrs 9/20/1813 M
HARTLOVE's child 9/20/1813 s
FOX Sally 9/24/1813 W
MORRIS Mr's child 9/24/1813 W
CAMPBLE Mrs 9/25/1813 M
RUSSELL Mrs 9/25/1813 W
WEAVER Mr's child 9/27/1813 S
RITTER Jacob 10/1/1813 W
ROBERTSON Thomas's son 10/2/1813 W
HOTT Mr's child 10/3/1813 W
WILSON John's child 10/4/1813 M
KING Mr (Labann)'s child 10/4/1813 S
LUTZ John's child 10/5/1813 W
CRAWFORD William's black child 10/5/1813 S
FITZHUGH Samuel's child 10/7/1813 M
RICHMOND Mr's child 10/7/1813 S

RICHMOND Mrs 10/7/1813 S
BUSSARD Philip's child 10/10/1813 M
THOMSON Mr 10/10/1813 M
POLKINHORN Henry 10/15/1813 W
Negro Dolly 10/18/1813 S
HANSON A C's child 10/23/1813 M
PETER George's black man 10/24/1813 S
SLATOR William 10/24/1813 S
MAFFITT Samuel 10/26/1813 M
THORP Thomas's child 10/27/1813 S
SIP Mr's child 11/2/1813 S
HIGHT Mrs 11/2/1813 S
LEO Mr's black boy 11/3/1813 S
NEVIT James 11/3/1813 S
HANSON A C's child 11/4/1813 M
CLINE David's child 11/5/1813 W
CAMPBLE Mashack's child 11/5/1813 S
ALFIND Mr's daughter 11/5/1813 S
HART John's child 11/8/1813 W
RUNNELS Margrat 11/15/1813 S
KURTS Daniel's black woman 11/15/1813 S
BOON Mrs 11/17/1813 W
MURDOCK John's child 11/20/1813 S
BALTZER George 11/23/1813 W
PARSONS William's child 11/23/1813 M
THUMBERT William's boy 11/23/1813 S
CLEGGET Mrs 11/24/1813 W
KENT Mrs 11/24/1813 M
RINGGOLD Mrs 11/29/1813 M
MIM Peter 12/3/1813 M
McKENNEY William's black girl 12/2/1813 S
FREEMAN Mrs's black man 12/2/1813 S
DUFFY Brian 12/7/1813 W
NICHOLLS William S's child 12/11/1813 M
PARSON William's father 12/11/1813 W
FOX Mary 12/13/1813 W
HALLY Harriot's daughter 12/14/1813 S
McDANIEL John's child 12/16/1813 W
STODDERT Benjamin 12/19/1813 M
KING Old Mr 12/22/1813 S
WEEMS Mrs's black girl 12/27/1813 S
BOWIE Washington's child 12/28/1813 S

BRUMWELL Mrs 1/2/1814 W
BOWIE Mrs of Bladensburg 1/4/1814 W
MARBURY Miss E 1/7/1814 M
MARBURY William's black woman 1/7/1814 S
MITCHELL Mrs 1/12/1814 M
DAVIS Mrs 1/16/1814 S
FENWICK Mrs's ralation 1/22/1814 S
WILLIAMS Mrs 1/23/1814 W
WIRT John's child 1/23/1814 M
BRAY William 1/24/1814 S
WALTERS T's black child 1/25/1814 S
ADAMS Thomas's black woman 2/1/1814 S
KENNEDY Mr's child 2/5/1814 S
PARSONS James 2/6/1814 W
SHELBY Mrs 2/9/1814 S
PETER Mrs Ann 2/9/1814 M
THOMSON Mrs 2/11/1814 S
BUTLER Lucy's son 2/15/1814 S
HAGERTY John's child 2/16/1814 W
SONN Doctor 2/17/1814 S
FENWICK Mrs 2/20/1814 S
YOUNG Charles 2/23/1814 M
KNIGHT Mr's child 2/23/1814 S
SIMMONS Miss 2/28/1814 M
COOLIDGE Miss Peggy 3/4/1814 M
SIMMES Paul a colored man 3/4/1814 W
WILLIAMS Mr 3/6/1814 M
WHANN William's black boy 3/10/1814 S
MYERS Mr 3/12/1814 W
HOPKINS Edward 3/13/1814 M
JACKMAN William 3/20/1814 S
MORGAN Mr 3/20/1814 S
SMITH Mrs 3/23/1814 M
LIVINGSTON Mrs 3/23/1814 M
BUTLER Trecy a colored 3/28/1814 S
BOWN John C's child 3/30/1814 W
PETER George's child 3/31/1814 M
JOHNCHEREZ A L's child 3/31/1814 W
WHANN William's black child 3/31/1814 S
HURTLE Joseph's child 4/5/1814 M
RODES Mrs's child 4/11/1814 S
LAIN Robert 4/13/1814 S

Levi's father in law a colored man 4/14/1814 S
McKENNEY William's black girl 4/15/1814 S
RODS Mrs 4/20/1814 S
HICKASON Mr's black man 4/21/1814 S
PARIS Mrs 4/23/1814 W
HICKASON Mr's black woman 4/24/1814 S
WELCH Methew 4/28/1814 W
FORD James (a black man)'s child 5/1/1814 S
SIMSON Kitty 5/1/1814 S
FORD Mrs 5/3/1814 W
JONES Lawrence 5/4/1814 W
CONNER Mrs 5/8/1814 S
CANDIS's son in law 5/13/1814 S
FORD Mr's black woman 5/16/1814 S
WILSON Mrs's child 5/18/1814 S
LANDSDEL Mr's child 5/23/1814 S
PETER George's child 5/28/1814 M
LANDSDEL Mr's child 6/4/1814 S
RITTENHOUSE John B 6/5/1814 M
PRITCHARD Benjamin's child 6/10/1814 W
GODY Mrs 6/21/1814 W
ADDISON Mr E 6/23/1814 M
GROVES Mrs 6/24/1814 W
KILRICE Mrs 7/1/1814 W
GRASON Mrs 7/4/1814 S
WHITE Charles C's child 7/5/1814 W
BAKER John's son 7/9/1814 M
KING Little Mary 7/10/1814 M
SMITH Clement's child 7/14/1814 M
MAGRUDER Miss Rachal 7/14/1814 M
PLATOR Mrs 7/14/1814 M
SMITH Mr's child 7/14/1814 W
CLARK Saterlee's child 8/1/1814 M
LAMBERT Morris's child 8/3/1814 W
MARCH Hanah's child 8/6/1814 S
TURNER Betsey's child 8/9/1814 S
WINDOM Charles's child 8/10/1814 W
DUVALL William 8/11/1814 W
MAGRUDER Dr's black man 8/15/1814 S
DAVIS Penney 8/18/1814 W
DANT Henry 8/25/1814 S
MACCUBBIN Richard 8/30/1814 M

CALDER William's child 9/2/1814 M
TOLIVER James for 2 soldiers 9/2/1814 S (2 coffins, both S)
POWERS Mrs 9/2/1814 S
PEAVE Qualia 9/6/1814 S
RUFFINS Robert 9/6/1814 S
RAMSEY Andrew's child 9/10/1814 M
YEATS Lieutenant 9/10/1814 S
TUBBERVIL Richard 9/15/1814 M
TOLIVER James for a soldier 9/18/1814 S
Levi's child 9/9/20/1814 S
PATTERSON Dr's child 9/21/1814 M
SHERLOCK John's child 9/21/1814 S
KINSAL Mrs's daughter 9/23/1814 W
MARBURY William's child 9/25/1814 S
CHESTER Samuel's son 9/27/1814 S
ANDERSON Mr at Whites 9/28/1814 S
NEWTON Walter's brother 9/29/1814 S
GROSS Jacob 9/29/1814 S
DYER Aaron 10/5/1814 W
LAIRD John's black child 10/6/1814 S
ROBERTSON Joseph 10/6/1814 S
McCLAIN Duncan's child 10/11/1814 S
MANUAL 10/12/1814 S
OLIGLE Harris's child 10/15/1814 W
MOYERS Samuel's child 10/17/1814 W
KING Little Hellen 10/18/1814 M
FRENCH Mr 10/22/1814 S
SWAN Mr's child 10/26/1814 S
HART John's child 10/28/1814 W
BOLTON Isaac 10/30/1814 W
WILSON Thomas 10/30/1814 W
WHALIN Mary 10/31/1814 S
KINSEL Mr 11/11/1814 S
GEORGE Enoch's child 11/6/1814 W
ROBERTSON H B's child 11/8/1814 S
ASTON Peggey's child 11/9/1814 S
ARNOLD Mr 11/14/1814 W
LANN Mr 11/15/1814 W
DARCEY William's black boy 11/17/1814 S
REINTZEL Maria 11/18/1814 W
SKIDMORE Samuel 11/21/1814 S
LAINE John 11/22/1814 S

GERRY Elbridge 11/24/1814 M
BALL Aquala 12/1/1814 W
ROWLUND George 12/10/1814 S
BALL Mr 12/14/1814 W
WHALEN Nicholas's child 12/16/1814 S
MANCHIET Mrs 12/17/1814 W
Black man at Landes 12/18/1814 S
HEISE John C's child 12/18/1814 W
HOLTZMAN Jacob 12/23/1814 M
SHAW James 12/27/1814 W
BRENT Richard 12/31/1814 M
STEPHENS Miss 12/31/1814 W
ROUNDS Zekel's child 12/31/1814 S
CATON Mr's child 12/31/1814 W
WOODLAND Jane's husband 12/31/1814 S
NEVIT Mr 1/4/1815 S
LOUNDS Mrs 1/5/1815 W
COOK Beck 1/5/1815 S
KING Mr 1/7/1815 S
BACENS Mrs 1/8/1815 S
WEST Mr 1/8/1815 S
FENNECEY James 1/10/1815 S
HARDEN Mrs 1/12/1815 S
KING Mr 1/12/1815 S
DUVALL Mrs's child 1/12/1815 S
GARY Everard 1/13/1815 M
JACKSON Mrs 1/13/1815 W
GOSZLER John's child 1/15/1815 W
PERRY Mr 1/15/1815 W
JOHNSON John 1/15/1815 S
Andrew 1/16/1815 S
BACENS Mr's child 1/16/1815 S
WILSON John A (George) 1/18/1815 S
PAIN William 1/18/1815 W
BAKER ~~Zachariah~~ Mrs 1/19/1815 M
EASTON Mr 1/19/1815 S
FELIOUS Jacob's black woman 1/19/1815 S
KING Miss 1/21/1815 S
HARDEN Thomas 1/21/1815 S
BACEN Mrs's child 1/21/1815 S
MASON John's Tom 1/26/1815 S
PENDRED Mrs 1/28/1815 W

CHILDS Cassey 1/29/1815 S
WHALEN Mrs 1/29/1815 S
HAGON Mrs 1/31/1815 S
LYLES Jacob 1/31/1815 S
MAGRUDER Mrs 1/31/1815 M
SEMMES Cravan 1/31/1815 W
MILLER Mr's child 2/1/1815 W
GRIFFIN Mr's child 2/1/1815 S
GOLDSBOROUGH John 2/2/1815 W
McCUTCHEN Thomas 2/3/1815 W
LYLES Mrs 2/4/1815 S
OTT Mrs 2/4/1815 M
GUSTINE Robert J's child 2/4/1815 M
ROCH Mrs 2/4/1815 S
GIBBON Mrs 2/4/1815 W
MIM Polly 2/8/1815 W
HOBLER William C 2/9/1815 W
COLE Beckey 2/9/1815 S
SMITH Thomas's son 2/10/1815 S
GRAHAM Mr's black man 2/10/1815 S
AIR John 2/12/1815 S
WINDBURY Mrs 2/12/1815 W
STONE Mrs 2/12/1815 M
GOSZLER Anthony 2/12/1815 W
DAVIS Samuel (woman) 2/13/1815 S
PLATOR Thomas (black man) 2/15/1815 S
Statia a black woman 2/15/1815 S
GILDCREST Mr a soldier 2/16/1815 S
PAUL Mrs 2/16/1815 S
GILDY John 2/16/1815 W
WARRING Mrs's boy 2/16/1815 S
PHILIPS Mr 2/17/1815 S
ISAACS Mr 2/18/1815 W
MAHORNY Mr 2/18/1815 W
BROWN Mr 2/18/1815 S
EASTERDAY Mrs 2/18/1815 S
MITCHELL John's black man 2/20/1815 S
DAVIS John 2/20/1815 S
HADON John 2/21/1815 S
WILSON Mr 2/21/1815 W
BANSELL William 2/23/1815 W
LOVEJOY Elizabeth 2/24/1815 W

SALMON Mrs 2/24/1815 S
BROOKS Mr's black man 2/24/1815 S
McCUTCHEON John 2/26/1815 W
WEEDEN Mrs's son 2/27/1815 S
BEATTY Thomas 2/28/1815 M
Thomas's child (a colored man) 2/28/1815 S
HAGERTY John's child 3/1/1815 S
RUTH Henry 3/6/1815 W
ROBERTSON Mrs 3/8/1815 W
KROUSE John's Harry 3/9/1815 S
DALENA Matthew 3/9/1815 W
STEWART David 3/9/1815 M
RINGGOLD Tench's colored man 3/9/1815 S
BUTLER William a colored man 3/9/1815 S
DONNELSON Mr 3/11/1815 S
REED Mr 3/13/1815 W
WILSON Richard 3/13/1815 M
SIMMONS Mrs 3/14/1815 W
RIDGWAY Mr 3/14/1815 S
ALLEN Mr 3/14/1815 S
CLEGET Mrs 3/18/1815 S
BROWN Parson's wife colored woman 3/18/1815 S
NORRIS Benjamin 3/18/1815 W
DEVENAY Patrick 3/19/1815 W
EDWARDS John 3/23/1815 S
HOLLINGHEAD John 3/23/1815 M
RIDGWAY James 3/24/1815 S
COBET Mrs 3/27/1815 W
JOHNS Mrs 3/28/1815 M
RIDGWAY Mrs 3/30/1815 S
NEEDAM William A 4/1/1815 W
GUSTINE Samuel 4/3/1815 M
JONES Mrs 4/4/1815 S
MACKEY Mrs 4/5/1815 M
KNIGHT Mr's child 4/5/1815 S
BAKER William's child 4/6/1815 M
KING Mary 4/6/1815 M
PRITCHARD Mr 4/8/1815 W
ROBERTSON Thomas' colored boy 4/13/1815 S
PRICE Thomas 4/14/1815 W
BEATY John 4/15/1815 M
BERRY Mrs 4/15/1815 M

SHREVES Mr 4/18/1815 W
Colored man at C. Shorter's 4/19/1815 S
CRAIG George 4/19/1815 W
LOUNDS Francis 4/23/1815 M
WEST Mrs 4/24/1815 M
SCREVENER Mr 4/25/1815 S
TUCKER Benjamin 4/26/1815 S
LOWERY John's coloured woman 4/27/1815 S
LOUFBOROUGH Nathan's black woman 5/2/1815 S
KING Enoch's mother 5/2/1815 S
HICKASON John 5/5/1815 W
SPRIGG Orsburn 5/8/1815 m
WILLIAMS Benjamin's mother 5/8/1815 S
WIRT John's child 5/16/1815 M
BURCH James's mother 5/16/1815 W
HALL Richard 5/19/1815 M
A Captain of G W P Custis's vessell 5/20/1815 S
YOUNG Martha 5/25/1815 M
A Black child 5/25/1815 S
SMITH Clement's black child 5/30/1815 S
GLOYD Mrs's son 6/5/1815 W
NEALL H 6/7/1815 S
MULLIGAN Mrs 6/15/1815 M
BERRY Mr's child 6/19/1815 W
STILLING Mrs 6/20/1815 S
SHAW John 6/22/1815 W
MAGRUDER Miss Patty 6/27/1815 W
SHARP Mrs 6/30/1815 W
FRENCH George's 2 children 7/5/1815 M
FORREST Mrs 7/6/1815 M
HOLTZMAN Mrs 7/9/1815 W
FOXALL Henry's black child 7/23/1815 S
DAWSON Mr's child 7/25/1815 S
KEY Philip B 7/29/1815 M
GODDART John B's child 7/31/1815 W
FLETCHER James's child 7/31/1815 S
MALONY James's wife 7/31/1815 W
VARDEN Mrs 8/3/1815 S
FEILD William's girl 8/4/1815 S
ANDREWS Mrs's child 8/4/1815 W
CLARK Daniel 8/4/1815 M
LEE Miss Nancy's black child 8/5/1815 S

WILLIAMS William's child 8/5/1815 W
TANNAR Mr 8/8/1815 W
RENALDS John's child 8/8/1815 M
DAVIS Mrs's daughter 8/9/1815 S
BARN Nancy's child 8/10/1815 S
POOL Nancy's child 8/13/1815 S
A Child that Nancy Pool nursed 8/14/1815 S
HODGES Benjamin's daughter 8/14/1815 M
MAGRUDER Mrs's daughter 8/14/1815 W
A Black child at Mr Langs 8/16/1815 S
SHREVE Mr's child 8/18/1815 S
MORRELL John's child 8/18/1815 W
MELVIN Mrs 8/20/1815 M
RIDGWAY Mr's child 8/21/1815 S
A Black woman at Duports 8/21/1815 S
BROWN Lucy's child 8/30/1815 S
MADERA Mrs's child 8/30/1815 S
Philip's child 8/31/1815 S
HENDERSON John's child 8/31/1815 W
THOMSON Charles 9/2/1815 S
SMITH Mrs 9/2/1815 M
WILLIAMS Mrs 9/3/1815 W
FREDERICK's child 9/3/1815 S
FREEMAN Mrs's black child 9/4/1815 S
SIM Mrs 9/4/1815 M
BROWN Mr's child 9/5/1815 W
RIDGWAY Leven's child 9/7/1815 S
JOHNS Leonard H's child 9/8/1815 M
BUTLER Charles's child 9/10/1815 W
BOWIE Washington's child 9/11/1815 S
MARQUAL Mrs's child 9/11/1815 S
ROBERTSON Mrs 9/13/1815 S
HALL Eliza's child 9/13/1815 S
WASHINGTON George's child 9/17/1815 M
McDANIEL George's child 9/17/1815 W
GOADWIN Mrs's child 9/17/1815 S
DUCKET Bazil 9/18/1815 M
GRASON Sally's son 9/21/1815 S
KING James's child 9/23/1815 S
HOWKE Joseph's child 9/23/1815 W
KEEPHER Mrs 9/24/1815 S
HOLLAND Mr's child 9/25/1815 S

THOMSON Mr's child 9/25/1815 S
CRANNEL Jesse's child 9/25/1815 M
LINGAN Mrs's black child 10/1/1815 S
BRYAN T 10/2/1815 S
THOMSON John C's child 10/5/1815 W
COVER Richard's child 10/7/1815 M
BROOK Miss Latty 10/12/1815 M
CHRIEN Mrs 10/16/1815 W
WATKINS Mrs 10/17/1815 M
CHEW Mrs 10/17/1815 W
CROW John's child 10/27/1815 W
CUPPERSMITH Henry 10/28/1815 W
TRUNNEL Horatio's child 10/29/1815 S
CARR John 10/30/1815 S
HOLLY's mother in law 10/30/1815 S
HELLEN Walter 10/31/1815 M
SLATOR Davis 10/31/1815 M
CLEMENTS Joseph 11/4/1815 S
TAYLOR Mr's child 11/4/1815 S
HILLARY Lewis's wife 11/9/1815 W
PACKHAM Caleb's child 11/10/1815 W
CHILY Mrs 11/12/1815 S
CLEGET Mrs' black man 11/15/1815 S
DAVIS Mrs 11/18/1815 M
MORDOCK Mrs 11/19/1815 W
KEY F S's black child 11/19/1815 S
CRAIGE Charles 11/20/1815 W
NICHOLSON Mr's father 11/20/1815 S
PRICE Mr 11/22/1815 W
EWELL Thomas's child 11/25/1815 M
JONES Thomas's son 11/27/1815 S
NEALL Charles 11/29/1815 W
BEALL Ninian's black girl 12/8/1815 S
CALDER William's child 12/10/1815 M
FRENCH Charles 12/12/1815 M
GOSZLER George's child 12/16/1815 W
DELLENGER Fredreck 12/17/1815 W
CRAWFORD William's 2 children 12/21/1815 M
NEWTON Clement's black woman 12/23/1815 S
ENGLISH David's colored girl 12/23/1815 S
WHITE Charles C's child 12/24/1815 M
McCASHIN Catharine 12/25/1815

MORRISON John 12/31/1815 W
KIRKWOOD Peter 1/2/1816 S
ROBY Leonard 1/4/1816 S
HIGDON Mr's child 1/4/1816
FOX Ceph 1/6/1816 W
FOX Bartelton 1/6/1816 W
DAVIS James 1/7/1816 W
REMINGTON Mr's daughter 1/9/1816 S
CLEMENTS Benjamin 1/10/1816 W
CARTER James's child 1/11/1816 W
CLARK Baily 1/11/1816 M
CAIN Catharine 1/11/1816 S
RITTER Peter's brother 1/15/1816 W
CREEGER Mrs 1/16/1816 W
CONEGE Mrs 1/25/1816 W
CRAVEN William's child 1/25/1816 S
ROBERTSON Mrs 1/26/1816 W
BOND Mrs 1/30/1816 S
RIDGWAY Leven 1/30/1816 S
WIRT Philip's child 2/1/1816 M
HILLARY Miss 2/5/1816 S
BUTLER Robert 2/8/1816 S
CLEMENTS Mrs 2/10/1816 S
FOXALL Mrs 2/10/1816 M
GEORGE Mrs 2/10/1816 W
MORSELL J S's colored child 2/16/1816 S
SPRIGG Samuel's child 2/16/1816 M
STRECH Mrs 2/20/1816 M
GODDART Mrs 2/26/1816 W
WILLIAMS John S's child 3/3/1816 S
HERRON John 3/3/1816
RITTER Mrs 3/3/1816 W
CRARN E 3/7/1816 S
RETCLIF Joseph's child 3/11/1816 W
POOL Lewis's child 3/13/1816 W
TURNER Thomas 3/16/1816 M
CAMBLE Mrs 3/17/1816 W
MAFFIT Thomas 3/17/1816 M
BROOK James B's woman 3/17/1816 S
DANT Mr's child 3/21/1816 W
HOLMAN Mr's black man 3/21/1816 S
OWENS Elizabeth 3/25/1816 W

NALLY Mr 4/1/1816 S
RETCLEF Joseph's black woman 4/1/1816 S
MULLIGAN James 4/1/1816 M
MAGRUDER Patrick's child 4/6/1816 M
McCARTY Thomas 4/7/1816 M
DUVALL Mrs 4/10/1816 M
STANFORD Richard 4/10/1816 M
RIYE Mrs' child 4/14/1816 S
RIDGLEY William G's child 4/15/1816 M
WILLY Jarvander 4/16/1816 W
COLCLAZER Thomas's child 4/20/1816 S
MACKEY Alexander 4/22/1816 M
PICKRELL John's child 4/22/1816 W
GUSTINE Ann 4/24/1816 M
BROW Adam 4/25/1816 S
KENNEDY Miss 4/26/1816 W
REED Jane 5/1/1816 W
MILLIGAN Joseph's child 5/5/1816 M
RAGAN John 5/5/1816 W
BOWER Eversfield 5/8/1816 M
MORRIS George's child 5/9/1816 W
DICK Jimmy 5/10/1816 S
GELASPY Mr 5/10/1816 W
RENTZEL Andrew 5/12/1816 W
OGDON Mrs 5/15/1816 M
MORRIS Garret's wife 5/15/1816 S
KING Isabela 5/10/1816 M
BROWN William's child 5/24/1816 S
MILLS Mr 5/25/1816 S
ROBERT a colored man 5/25/1816 S
PITT George 5/25/1816 M
SOMMER Nathan's mother 5/28/1816 S
RIDGLEY William G's child 5/28/1816 M
JONES Mr's child 5/30/1816 W
BLAGROVE William's child 6/10/1816 S
NEWTON John 6/12/1816 W
GRAY Mr's child 6/15/1816 S
BROWN Milly 6/15/1816 S
BUTLER Frank 6/16/1816 S
SPARROW John 6/25/1816 S
DUNCAN John 6/27/1816 S
ROSS Charlotty's child 6/29/1816 S

PATTERSON Edgar's child 7/2/1816 M
MACKEY William's child 7/2/1816 W
ECKELHART Mr's child 7/2/1816 S
BEAN William's child 7/2/1816 W
ROSS Charlotty 7/3/1816 S
WILSON Mrs 7/5/1816 W
CISELL Mrs 7/6/1816 W
DIGGS William's child 7/8/1816 M
MAGRUDER Mrs D 7/11/1816 M
RIND Wm A's child 7/14/1816 S
DUVALL Miss 7/14/1816 W
HAWKINS William's child 7/15/1816 S
COOK Thomas's black girl 7/18/1816 S
WIPOR Ruben's child 7/18/1816 W
HAUP Mr's child 7/20/1816 S
TATEHAM Colonel's boy 7/21/1816 S
LANDIS Abraham's child 7/23/1816 W
FITZGERALD Mr 7/26/1816 M
HALLENBECK William's child 7/27/1816 W
PUTMAN Mr's child 7/27/1816 W
DABNEY Mary 7/27/1816 S
CRAWFORD William's black woman 7/28/1816 S
A MAN that was drowned 7/29/1816 S
JOHNSON E 7/31/1816 S
CLEGET Bishop 8/3/1816 M
GIBSON John's child 8/4/1816 W
LAY Richard's child 8/5/1816 M
CLEGET Jane's black woman 8/7/1816 S
CARMAN Mrs 8/9/1816 S
BARNES Lucy's child 8/13/1816 S
BROOK Charles's child 8/17/1816 S
BEVAN Jerom's child 8/17/1816 W
WELLS Richard's child 8/20/1816 M
OBER Robert's child 8/20/1816 M
JONES John's son 8/27/1816 W
PARKS John's child 8/27/1816 S
George's wife 8/30/1816 S
HART John's child 8/30/1816 W
MORE Mrs's child 8/30/1816 S
FAGAN Mr's child 8/31/1816 S
CISEL Mr's child 9/3/1816 S
GROSS Thomas's child 9/3/1816 S

ONEAL John's child 9/3/1816 S
BOWYER Mrs's child 9/3/1816 S
NEWTON Walter's child 9/6/1816 W
CLEMENTS Mr 9/6/1816 S
EDWARDS Mr's child 9/6/1816 S
WILLIAMS William's child 9/8/1816 W
BEVAN Jerom's child 9/9/1816 W
BECK Truman's black girl 9/11/1816 S
WISE Mr's child 9/13/1816 S
KING Ambrose's child 9/18/1816 S
WILLIAMS Eli's colored woman 9/19/1816 S
NICHOLLS William S's child 9/19/1816 M
BARBARA's child (a colored woman) 9/20/1816 S
MACKALL B F's child 9/24/1816 M
BROWN Mr (stagedriver)'s child 9/25/1816 W
OBRIAN Joseph 9/26/1816 S
GRANT William (a colored man)'s child 9/27/1816 W
WILLIAMS Mrs 9/28/1816 M
HEBORAN John colored man 9/28/1816 S
BURDECK Henry's child 10/2/1816 W
Man that died at Mr Chrten 10/2/1816 W
SIMMES Ignatious' child 10/5/1816 M
GODDART John B's child 10/5/1816 W
HINES John 10/8/1816 W
BOSWELL Mrs 10/9/1816 W
Mary (a colored woman)'s mother 10/9/1816 S
JOHNSON (a colored woman)'s child 10/11/1816 S
LEAR Tobis 10/14/1816 M
RENTZEL Valentine's black man 10/15/1816 S
SHORTER Ned's child 10/17/1816 S
COOPER Mrs 10/19/1816 S
ROADS William 10/24/1816 S
COLINS Joseph S' child 10/24/1816 M
DITTY John 10/26/1816 W
SPOWROW Mr's child 10/28/1816 S
OVERTON John's child 10/28/1816 S
WILLIAMS Mrs 10/31/1816 M
MORGAN Mordoca 11/7/1816 W
ANDERSON Andrew 11/9/1816 W
FOX Parmealy 11/9/1816 W
MARTIN Miss's child 11/20/1816 S
A WOMAN that died at Graces 11/21/1816 S

GODDART Mr's child 11/23/1816 W
CRUIKSHANK John 11/25/1816 M
CLARK J D's child 11/25/1816 M
SILPS Thomas's child a colored man 11/25/1816 S
BARKER Thomas a colored man's wife 11/28/1816 S
CRAWFORD William 11/28/1816 M
HAGERTY John's child 11/30/1816 W
HEBORAN Peter's child 11/30/1816 S
THRELKELD John's Grace 11/30/1816 S
McKELDEN Andrew 12/5/1816 W
CAMBLE John 12/9/1816 M
FLONES Charles 12/9/1816 W
MITCHELL Judson's brother 12/19/1816 W
THOMSON Nancy 12/23/1816 S
BELT Joseph S 12/23/1816 M
FORD Mr 1/1/1817 S
CARSON Mr's child 1/1/1817 S
ROBERTS Mrs 1/8/1817 M
GIBSON Mr 1/9/1817 S
TURNER Sara 1/12/1817 S
WARTON James's son 1/12/1817 S
SQUAW William 1/16/1817 S
ROBERTS Mr's child 1/17/1817 M
WILEY Mary 1/21/1817 W
KING Ignatius's child 1/23/1817 S
OWENS Singleton 1/29/1817 w
GUSTINE Green 1/30/1817 M
EDMUNSON Desham's child 1/31/1817 S
JONES Thomas's child 1/31/1817 S
HOLLY John 2/8/1817 S
BUTLER Nancy 2/14/1817 S
YATES Mrs 2/16/1817 W
ANDERSON Mr 2/16/1817 W
BENTON Mrs 2/20/1817 S
QUEEN Mrs 2/21/1817 W
COLE George's child 2/21/1817 S
ATEASON Mrs 2/27/1817 S
KEELER John 2/27/1817 S
WEASNER Mr 2/27/1817 S
RUSSELL Basil 3/6/1817 S
DAWS Edward's child 3/8/1817 M
BROWN Nelly's sister 3/10/1817 S

WILSON William 3/12/1817 M
YATS Mrs's daughter 3/12/1817 S
BUTLER's child 3/12/1817 S
TENNEY Isaac 3/15/1817 M
HILSMER Mrs 3/24/1817 W
CARTON Louisa 3/24/1817 S
NEWTON Clement's son 3/25/1817 W
CRAWFORD Mrs's black child 3/27/1817 S
Old Davy's wife 3/31/1817 S
SPARROW Mr's child 4/2/1817 S
BRISCO George 4/2/1817 M
WIRT John's child 4/7/1817 M
STILES Mrs's mother 4/8/1817 S
McKELDIN Mrs's child 4/13/1817 W
BRODWEL James's child 4/16/1817 W
SWAN Mr's child 4/17/1817 S
GERNES Henry's child 4/17/1817 S
WALKER Mr's child 4/18/1817 M
RIGGS Mrs 4/18/1817 M
REED Mrs's child 4/20/1817 S
ONEAL John's child 4/21/1817 S
HALL Henry Low 5/10/1817 M
OFFUT Bazil 5/12/1817 W
BRADY Caleb's son 5/12/1817 S
SHAAFF Arthur 5/17/1817 M
TURNER Samuel's child 5/21/1817 M
HAGAN Miss 5/22/1817 S
HOOVER Peter's child 5/22/1817 S
RUSH Samuel 5/24/1817 S
A MAN that was drowned 5/28/1817 S
CROW John's child 6/6/1817 W
BROOK James B's boy 6/8/1817 S
RUSSELL F A's child 6/9/1817 M
JONES John 6/9/1817 S
FEILDS William 6/18/1817 W
NEAL Leonard 6/19/1817 M
BURGER Richard's child 6/30/1817 M
MARKWOOD Mrs 7/2/1817 M
NORRIS Mr's child 7/2/1817 S
WINGARD Abraham's son 7/3/1817 M
Ana colored woman child 7/9/1817 S
RENNER Daniel's child 7/17/1817 M

FREEMAN Mrs's black woman 7/18/1817 S
BERRY Mrs 7/21/1817 W
BEDDOW James' black man 7/21/1817 S
MITCHELL John's black child 7/29/1817 S
DEAN Mr's child 7/29/1817 S
ELIASON John's child 7/30/1817 S
GREVER Robert's child 7/21/1817 W
HILLARY Lewis's wife 8/2/1817 W
JONES Richard's child 8/3/1817 S
ATWOOD John's child 8/4/1817 W
McKENNAY Samuel's child 8/4/1817 S
McDANIEL Mrs's child 8/4/1817 S
ELIOT Linde 8/5/1817 W
DAVIS Mr's child 8/5/1817 S
MIDDLETON Mr's child 8/5/1817 M
ELIASON Mrs 8/6/1817 M
PIFER Henry's child 8/12/1817 M
ANDREWS Mrs's child 8/13/1817 W
REED Mrs 8/13/1817 S
WATERS Thomas's black woman 8/13/1817 S
WATERS Thomas's black child 8/13/1817 S
ANDREWSON Samuel 8/14/1817 S
WHALEN Nicholas's child 8/14/1817 S
BROOK Miss 8/16/1817 W
BRADWELL James's father 8/18/1817 W
CROWN William's child 8/23/1817 S
CARTON Jacob's child 8/26/1817 W
THUMBERT William's child 8/27/1817 M
HILTON Mr's child 8/27/1817 W
CLARK J D's child 8/31/1817 M
BROOK J B's child 8/31/1817 M
HANDY S W's child 9/1/1817 M
HILLEARY Nicholas's child 9/3/1817 W
WEBB Mr 9/3/1817 W
HIGDEN Nelly's child 9/5/1817 S
BACCUS Mr's child 9/6/1817 W
TRAVERS John's black boy 9/8/1817 S
JEWELL Wm's child 9/8/1817 W
SHECKELL R's child 9/13/1817 W
REINTZEL Anthony 9/14/1817 M
LUPTON Mr's child 9/16/1817 S
KING Eliza's black child 9/20/1817 S

FIELDS Mathew 9/21/1817 S
MUD Thomas's child 9/21/1817 M
SMITH John K's black child 9/23/1817 S
RUSSIE Mrs 9/23/1817 W
A Color'd man's child 9/29/1817 S
MILLER Captain 9/30/1817 M
SMITH Mr's child [9/1817] S
LACY Benjamin 10/1/1817 W
THOMPSON Mr's child 10/1/1817 S
A man drown'd at the falls 10/1/1817 S
PEABODY Miss Adeline 10/10/1817 M
COOPER Mary's child 10/12/1817 S
MACKALL Mr's child 10/14/1817 S
SMITH Mr 10/14/1817 W
LANDES Abraham's child 10/27/1817 W
McDANIEL Leonard 11/1/1817 S
POOL Mrs 11/17/1817 W
MILLER Elizabeth 11/23/1817 W
COLCLAZER Thomas's black child 11/27/1817 S
KIRK Thomas 11/28/1817 M
SIFFORD Mrs 11/28/1817 W
HOAGLAND Isaac 11/30/1817 W
McKENNEY William's child 11/25/1817 M
A Child at E Patterson's factory 11/17/1817 S
JOHNCHEREZ A L 12/1/1817 M
GOULDING Mr's child 12/1/1817 W
GIBSON Mrs 12/4/1817 W
WASHINGTON George's child 12/6/1817 M
MAGRUDER Thomas 12/9/1817 M
WEIGHTMAN Mr's child 12/10/1817 W
WARTON James's child 12/15/1817 W
TURNER Mrs 12/15/1817 M
ADAMS Mr 12/22/1817 S
BOYD Mr 12/24/1817 S
OTT John's child 1/3/1818 M
BARNS Nancy 1/7/1818 S
BOWIE Robert 1/12/1818 M
A child in the country 1/12/1818 s
LYONS John's black woman 1/18/1818 W
Aunt Lucy 1/19/1818 W
BLAGROVE H B's child 1/22/1818 S
McPHERSON Mrs 1/22/1818 W

MARBURY Wm's black girl 1/23/1818 S
LOWE Mrs 1/27/1818 M
ARNY Mr's boy 1/31/1818 S
JOHNSON Isaac's son 2/3/1818 W
PEALE Mary 2/4/1818 S
RODGERS Mrs 2/13/1818 M
SMITH Captain Thomas 2/15/1818 S
HUNT Mrs's child 2/15/1818 W
PAINE Wm's sister 2/16/1818 W
Old Kitty 2/16/1818 S
FELSON Alexander's child 2/17/1818 S
WATHEN Mrs 2/19/1818 S
HILLEARY John 2/20/1818 M
NICHOLSON Thos H 2/25/1818 S
WHARTON Mrs 3/1/1818 M
WOOD John 3/10/1818 S
TRUNNEL Horatio's son 3/11/1818 W
John 3/12/1818 S
PARADISE Mr's child 3/13/1818 S
RANDOLPH Mr's man 3/14/1818 S
SWETT Samuel Junr 3/14/1818 M
KNOWLES Mrs 3/10/1818 M
FRYE Daniel's 2 children 3/11/1818 M
A black child at Mrs Villard's 3/19/1818 S
NORRIS Stephen's child 3/20/1818 S
HOLT Lawrence O 3/23/1818 M
LANG William's black boy 3/23/1818 S
TRAIL Mr 3/25/1818 S
HALL Miss 3/25/1818 M
LEVIS Mr's child 3/25/1818 W
WIRT John 3/25/1818 M
MILLER Wm 3/25/1818 W
HARP Aquilla's child 4/1/1818 S
WEISNER Mr 4/6/1818 W
OTT John 4/9/1818 M
WHANN Wm's black woman 4/11/1818 S
CHANDLER W S's black woman 4/17/1818 S
FORD J 4/18/1818 S
A colored child 4/21/1818 S
WILEY John's child 4/22/1818 M
Betty 4/22/1818 S
ANDERSON David 4/23/1818 S

SMITH Wm 4/25/1818 W
GREY Vincent's child 5/1/1818 S
HUNTER Mr's child 5/2/1818 S
BLAGROVE Mr 5/4/1818 W
GANTT T T 5/6/1818 M
PICKRELL B's woman 5/8/1818 S
DIGGS Thomas's woman 5/8/1818 S
HILL Mr 5/13/1818 S
BAKER John's man 5/15/1818 S
CLAXTON John 5/16/1818 S
WILEY Mrs 5/16/1818 W
BURGESS R's black child 5/23/1818 S
TYLER Mr 5/23/1818 M
FRENCH James 5/26/1818 W
ADAMS Mary 5/27/1818 S
BROWN Mr's child 5/29/1818 W
WILSON John A's black child 5/30/1818 S
HEBRON John's black child 5/31/1818 S
Priscilla's child 6/1/1818 S
BARLOW Mrs 6/1/1818 M
ELSY Doctor 6/7/1818 M
Jane 6/15/1818 S
FORREST Henry's child 6/20/1818 M
PICKFORD John B 6/20/1818 W
BELL Elenor 6/21/1818 M
CARTER James's relation 6/23/1818 S
BLAGGE Mr's child 6/24/1818 M
MURDOCK John's child 6/27/1818 S
SMITH Clement's two children 7/3/1818 M
BOONE Mr 7/4/1818 S
A COLORED woman 7/9/1818 S
MORRIS Randall 7/9/1818 S
COXEN Washington's child 7/10/1818 S
RUSSELL F A's child 7/11/1818 M
WALL John 7/13/1818 S
JAMES Benjamin 7/13/1818 S
THOMAS Mr 7/13/1818 S
LYONS John's black child 7/16/1818 S
SIMMONS Mrs 7/16/1818 M
COLLINS John's child 7/16/1818 S
Maria's child 7/18/1818 S
TOWNLY Mrs's child 7/24/1818 M

COLCLAZER Thomas's child 7/24/1818 s
A Black woman 7/24/1818 S
MACKINALL Mr's son 7/24/1818 S
SMITH John K 7/24/1818 M
BARN Ned's child 7/28/1818 S
PRATT Mrs's black child 7/31/1818 S
GIBSON John's child 8/3/1818 S
HERBERT Francis's child 8/3/1818 W
HALL Edward's man 8/7/1818 S
GOOD Wm's black child 8/9/1818 S
GREEN Wm's child 8/11/1818 S
BOAMAN Raphael's child 8/12/1818 S
HILL Mr's child 8/13/1818 W
GREAVES John's child 8/13/1818 S
GRIFFIN T B's child 8/14/1818 W
DUFFY Wm's chld 8/15/1818 S
REED Mr's child 8/15/1818 W
RAY Mr's child 8/16/1818 W
MAGRUDER Hellen 8/17/1818 M
ABBOTT John's black child 8/17/1818 S
GREENWELL Mr's child 8/17/1818 S
HUTCHIN Mr's child 8/18/1818 S
SHIELD Mr's child 8/18/1818 S
SHARP Mrs' child 8/20/1818 S
COLLINS James's child 8/21/1818 S
MELVIN Alexander 8/22/1818 M
LATIMORE Stephen 8/22/1818 M
KURTZ D's child 8/22/1818 W
DIGG Wm's child 8/22/1818 M
GRUMBLE Mr's child 8/22/1818 S
POINTER Ann's child 8/24/1818 S
BIDDASON Daniel's child 8/25/1818 S
BIRTH John 8/26/1818 W
RIFFLE Mr's sister's child 8/27/1818 S
DYKUS Wm's child 8/27/1818 S
CLOXON Mr's child 8/30/1818 S
ROBERTS Wm's black child 8/30/1818 S
McCOY Mr's child 8/30/1818 S
Nancy's child 8/30/1818 S
STONE John B 9/1/1818 S
BUTLER Louisa's child 9/1/1818 S
BARKER Murray's child 9/3/1818 S

COLLINS James's child 9/4/1818 S
PARKER Elonor's black girl 9/6/1818 S
TUCKER Enoch's child 8/6/1818 M
WOOD Ann 9/6/1818 M
ROBERTSON Mrs's child 9/8/1818 S
WATKINS Mrs's black child 9/8/1818 S
GREEN John's child 9/10/1818 M
DAVIS Maria's child 9/10/1818 S
CHANDLER Fanny's child 9/10/1818 S
CLARKE J D's child 9/12/1818 S
RIDGEWAY Mr's child 9/12/1818 S
RIDGELY Wm G's child 9/14/1818 M
KING Melvina 9/14/1818 M
MACKALL Benjamin's child 9/15/1818 M
PAINE Elizabeth's child 9/15/1818 S
LAW Mr 9/15/1818 S
HAWKINS Charles's child 9/15/1818 S
PICKERELL Benjamin's child 9/16/1818 S
LANNUM Norman 9/16/1818 S
MAGRAW Mrs 9/17/1818 W
MOORE Joseph's child 9/17/1818 S
WIRT Philip 9/18/1818 W
LINKIN Mr's child 9/21/1818 S
James 9/21/1818 S
WATERS Mr 9/21/1818 M
CLEMENTSON Geo's child 9/22/1818 S
LOVELESS Mr's child 9/23/1818 S
BRONOUGH John's black woman 9/24/1818 S
SHARP Mrs 9/24/1818 S
BUTLER Mary's sister 9/25/1818 S
BIRTH Mrs 9/27/1818 W
SHAY Mr's child 9/28/1818 S
RIDGEWAY Eden's child 9/30/1818 S
CORCORAN Mr's child 9/30/1818 S
HERSEY J C's child 9/30/1818 W
JAMES Mrs 10/1/1818 S
MORAN Miss 10/1/1818 S
WILEY John's black boy 10/3/1818 S
BENFIELD Mrs 10/6/1818 W
GREENWELL Mr's child 10/9/1818 S
BLANCHARD Doctor's child 10/11/1818 M
EDMONSON Mr's child 10/12/1818 S

GEORGE Thomas 10/16/1818 S
DUVALL Wm 10/16/1818 W
PICKERELL Benjamin's child 10/17/1818 S
FORD John G's black man 10/18/1818 S
MONFORD Wm's child 10/18/1818 S
WATERS Thomas's child 10/18/1818 M
LATHROPE Mr's child 10/19/1818 M
WILSON James's child 10/21/1818 M
HOPE Thos's child 10/22/1818 S
McCHESNEY D's child 10/24/1818 M
WILLIAMS Major 10/26/1818 M
SMITH Clement's black man 11/2/1818 S
SMITH Athony's child 11/3/1818 W
DAVIS Amos's child 11/5/1818 S
ARNAY Joseph's lad 11/5/1818 S
ARMSTRONG Robert 11/5/1818 S
HARPER Dr's woman 11/5/1818 S
SALTER Ann 11/5/1818 S
COATS Miss 11/7/1818 W
SPALDING Mrs 11/7/1818 S
PARKER Mrs 11/9/1818 W
WEBSTER Miss 11/15/1818 W
BROOK James's black girl 11/17/1818 S
COOPER 11/17/1818 S
JONES F P's child 11/18/1818 S
SEMMES James's child 11/18/1818 W
MAGRUDER Samuel B 11/18/1818 W
PARSON William's young man 11/20/1818 S
MACKEY Mrs 11/26/1818 M
FULLALOVE James's child 11/26/1818 W
Charles a colored man's child 12/5/1818 S
BROWN James a colored man 12/5/1818 S
HUGHES Jacob 12/7/1818 W
KEARNES Miss 12/7/1818 W
MORE John's child 12/7/1818 S
WEBSTER E 12/8/1818 W
BEALL Mrs's colored woman 12/8/1818 S
MACKENALL Mr 12/8/1818 S
COOK Mr 12/12/1818 M
McTEVRAN Henry's black man 12/15/1818 S
WIMEN Mrs's child 12/19/1818 S
MOXLEY Mr's child 12/19/1818 S

BROOKS Mrs 12/19/1818 S
RATCLIFFE Mr a colored man's child 12/21/1818 S
RUSSELL Mr 12/22/1818 S
ROBERTSON John's child 12/22/1818 W
NICHOLSON Mr 12/22/1818 S
HILL Richard (a colored man)'s child 12/22/1818 S
NUGENT Eli's child 12/28/1818 S
OBER Gustavus 1/3/1819 m
WOOLLARD Samuel's child 1/11/1819 S
SMITH Clement's child 1/11/1819 M
CARLISLE Christopher 1/20/1819 M
FORREST Mrs's grand child 1/20/1819 M
A Black child 1/26/1819 S
SIMPSON Captain 1/27/1819 S
JACKSON John 1/30/1819 M
WISE Helen 2/3/1819 S
OFFITT Mrs 2/7/1819 W
MASON Armstead T 2/8/1819 M
JENISELL John 2/10/1819 S
HILTON Mrs 2/22/1819 S
LANEY Charles 3/2/1819 S
GREENTREE Mrs 3/10/1819 M
GRAHAM Mary 3/11/1819 S
TRAVERS George 3/11/1819 M
JANISELL Mrs's child 3/14/1819 S
JONES Richard's sister 3/14/1819 S
SMITH J K's colored child 3/17/1819 S
WILEY John 3/21/1819 M
SHANKS Wm 3/22/1819 S
COPANG Mr 3/24/1819 S
LEWIS Mrs 3/28/1819 M
PAULEY Mrs 4/1/1819 W
CREAGER Mrs 4/3/1819 S
FRENCH Mrs's black woman 4/4/1819 S
A Negro 4/9/1819 S
HARPER N 4/9/1819 S
WINGARD A's child 4/9/1819 M
CLARK Thomas 4/15/1819 M
Letitia's child 4/15/1819 S
JONES Mr 4/24/1819 S
ALLEN William's wife 4/24/1819 S
ROBERTSON Mrs 4/24/1819 W

MUNRO Robt 4/30/1819 M
BARRETT Mrs 5/1/1819 W
HARRISON G's woman 5/1/1819 S
SHAAFF J 5/1/1819 M
FOX Mrs 5/3/1819 W
MAGRUDER Wm O 5/5/1819 W
MUDD T J's child 5/8/1819 S
DIXON Mrs 5/14/1819 W
BROWN Wm 5/18/1819 S
PUMFREY Lloyd's woman 5/18/1819 S
COOPER Mrs 5/25/1819 S
DYERS Mrs 5/27/1819 S
A Black man 6/2/1819 S
GLENN Mrs 6/2/1819 S
KNOT Mr's son 6/6/1819 S
SMITH Mrs 6/9/1819 S
PILES Mrs 6/10/1819 W
A Black child 6/13/1819 S
ROBERTSON Wm 6/13/1819 S
EDMUNDSON Miss 6/17/1819 W
McMANNERS Mrs's child 6/18/1819 S
JEWET Nathaniel's child 6/19/1819 W
JACKSON Samuel's child 6/19/1819 S
CLAGETT Jane's Sally 6/19/1819 S
BACOCK Mr's son 6/22/1819 S
COLLINS's child 6/24/1819 S
JARVIS Mrs 6/27/1819 S
TAYLOE Charlotte's mother 6/27/1819 S
BAKER Zackriah's child 7/3/1819 W
LANDES Mrs Abr's child 7/5/1819 W
De LONGUERVILLE Mr 7/6/1819 M
GREEN Sally 7/7/1819 S
LINKENS Mr's child 7/10/1819 S
RICHARD 7/12/1819 S
WALKER Elizabeth 7/16/1819 W
CHORTERS John 6/16/1819 S
MASON Elizabeth 7/18/1819 M
ROWE James 7/19/1819 S
BARKER Andrew's father 7/23/1819 S
BAKER John's child 7/26/1819 M
MAGRUDER Mrs S B 7/26/1819 W
DIXON Thomas's child 7/28/1819 W

GREY Wm's wife 7/28/1819 W
BUNNEL Mr's child 7/29/1819 W
GIBSON John's child 7/29/1819 S
BLAGGE John's black child 7/29/1819 S
HARP Miss's child 7/31/1819 S
MAYFIELD Henry's child 8/1/1819 W
BARNS Ned 8/1/1819 S
WILSON Levi 8/2/1819 W
FRYE Nath's child 8/2/1819 M
QUEEN Austin 8/4/1819 S
WHITNEY Mr's 2 children 8/5/1819 S
WHITE Robert's child 8/7/1819 W
WHITE C C 's child 8/10/1819 W
GRAY Hugh's child 8/10/1819 S
MASSEY Thomas's child 8/11/1819 S
FORREST Henry's woman 8/11/1819 S
BOWIE Mrs 8/14/1819 M
GITTINGS Miss 8/14/1819 W
SEMMES Mrs 8/15/1819 W
HUNTER Mr 8/15/1819 S
THOMAS Miss 8/18/1819 W
WILSON James R 8/18/1819 M
MISCY Mr's child 8/19/1819 M
McKENNY William's child 8/20/1819 M
SMITH Mr's child 8/21/1819 W
MAGRAW Benjamin's child 8/21/1819 W
NEWTON Walter's child 8/20/1819 W
NICHOLSON Mr's son 8/24/1819 W
McKENNY William's child 8/24/1819 M
KING Zachariah's child 8/26/1819 S
CLAGGET Jane's woman 8/26/1819 S
MOYERS Samuel's child 8/26/1819 W
STONE Edward's child 8/26/1819 W
COLLINGWOOD Samuel's child 8/27/1819 W
GOLDSBOROUGH Charles W's man 8/29/1819 S
SEMMY R T's child 8/29/1819 W
RENNER Daniel's child 8/30/1819 M
MUDD Thomas J's child 8/30/1819 S
BRADFORD Wm's wife's sister 8/31/1819 S
HINES John's child 9/1/1819 W
TURNER Mary 9/1/1819 M
DIXON James's child 9/2/1819 W

BRYAN Mr's child 9/2/1819 S
ANDREWS Mrs's child 9/2/1819 W
BIAS Cooke's wife 9/2/1819 S
MATHEWS Mr's child 9/3/1819 S
ABBOT John's child 9/4/1819 M
WILLIAMS William 9/6/1819 M
JONES Mr's child 9/7/1819 S
SMALLWOOD Horatio's child 9/7/1819 W
COVER George's child 9/7/1819 M
LEVETT Samuel 9/9/1819 M
NICHOLSON Mr's child 9/9/1819 S
LYONS John's brother-in-law's child 9/13/1819 W
GREENWELL Mr's child 9/13/1819 S
MACKALL B F's child 9/13/1819 M
CARTER Mrs 9/17/1819 W
JONES R's sister's child 9/18/1819 S
JONES R's sister's child 9/20/1819 S
SMITH Mr's child 9/20/1819 M
BLAGGE John's child 9/22/1819 M
FITZHUGH Janet 9/23/1819 M
HARRISON Gustavus's child 9/23/1819 M
FULLALOVE Mr's child 9/25/1819 S
KEY Mr's black woman 9/24/1819 S
MAGRUDER Mrs 9/27/1819 W
RITCHIE Abner 9/27/1819 M
SMITH Mrs 9/28/1819 W
DALANY Mrs 9/28/1819 S
ONEAL Mrs 10/1/1819 W
CHISLEY Zadoc's child 10/6/1819 M
GILES John's child 10/6/1819 W
BEALL Thomas of George 10/6/1819 M
GRIFFIN T B's brother 10/6/1819 W
PRESSEY Mrs 10/7/1819 S
KING Miss 10/7/1819 M
CRITTENDEN Joel's child 10/7/1819 M
GITTING Mrs 10/8/1819 W
STARNES Mrs's child 10/8/1819 W
HUFF Mr 10/8/1819 S
ASHTON Mr's child 10/9/1819 W
BIGGS Thomas 10/9/1819 S
BRADY Caleb's child 10/9/1819 S
BROOK Joseph's child 10/12/1819 W

NEVIT William's child 10/12/1819 W
ELLIS Mrs's child 10/15/1819 S
RATCLIFF Joseph's child 10/17/1819 M
CHANDLER Walter S's son 10/19/1819 M
NICHOLSON Mrs 10/23/1819 S
BLANCHARD William's child 10/30/1819 M
SIM Thomas's black man 10/30/1819 S
DAVIS George's child 11/3/1819 W
LOWE Miss 11/5/1819 M
ROSS Mrs 11/8/1819 M
KIRBY Robert's child 11/16/1819 W
GODDART Mrs 11/18/1819 M
CLEGGET Mrs 11/21/1819 M
ELVIN Mr's child 11/23/1819 S
WISE Mr 11/27/1819 W
STEWART Mrs's child 11/30/1819 S
OFFIT Mrs 12/3/1819 W
SIM Thomas's black girl 12/4/1819 S
BOWMAN Mr 12/6/1819 W
RITTENHOUSE Mrs's black child 12/6/1819 S
GRAHAM John's child 12/17/1819 M
HOLT Mrs 12/20/1819 M
GODDERT James's child 12/22/1819 M
THOMAS Mrs 12/23/1819 S
WATERS T G's child 12/25/1819 M
SHLEY John D 12/28/1819 W
PAIN Mr 12/30/1819 S
MONFORD William's child 12/30/1819 S
HUFF Mrs's child 12/30/1819 S
HARP Mr's child 1/2/1820 S
HILLS Mrs 1/3/1820 W
BEAL Samuel 1/7/1820 W
WINGARD Abraham 1/11/1820 M
HAWKINS Walter 1/11/1820 S
BURNET Mrs 1/16/1820 S
BAKER John's mother 1/17/1820 M
CHANDLER W S's black man 1/24/1820 S
STEWART Hugh 1/26/1820 M
LANG John 1/27/1820 M
CRAGIN Mr's child 1/28/1820 S
CALDER James's black woman 1/30/1820 S
LATHROP John 1/30/1820 W

HAWKINS Charles's child 1/30/1820 S
A MAN that died at Mr Dyer's 2/2/1820 S
HILL R's child 2/3/1820 S
Old Cissay 2/4/1820 S
Old McDaniel 2/8/1820 S
READ child 2/9/1820 W
WELCH Miss 2/12/1820 S
RAGAN Bazil's son 2/12/1820 W
RENSHAR Mr 2/12/1820 W
HAWKINS Walter's child 2/21/1820 S
BOOTH Mr 2/22/1820 S
MITCHEL J 2/22/1820 S
WATTERS T's black man 3/6/1820 S
CROSS Mrs 3/11/1820 M
HOLT Mrs 3/15/1820 M
GILHAM B 3/20/1820 S
TRAVERS Mrs 3/21/1820 W
Old Tom 3/21/1820 S
BEDDO William 3/28/1820 S
HOLTZMAN George's child 3/31/1820 M
LAYLAND Mr 3/31/1820 W
HENDERSON Sarah's black man 4/7/1820 S
JONES Solomon's child 4/12/1820 S
McCOY Mr's child 4/12/1820 S
BOSWELL Mrs 4/13/1820 W
HOPKINS Mrs 4/19/1820 W
NEAL John's wife 4/19/1820 S
BURNET Charles A's black woman 4/29/1820 S
James 4/29/1820 S
AVARD Samson 5/3/1820 S
KURTZ Mrs 5/6/1820 M
TAYLO John's child 5/6/1820 S
ROSS Lamkin 5/8/1820 S
HULL Jacob 5/12/1820 W
WHANN Mrs 5/12/1820 M
MARBURY Leonard's child 5/17/1820 M
MORDOCK John's child 5/21/1820 W
Negro Joseph 5/23/1820 S
LANG Mrs 5/23/1820 S
ELLIS Mrs 5/26/1820 W
DUCKET Miss 5/30/1820 M
MELLEY Bazil 6/5/1820 S

JONES Mrs 6/5/1820 W
HOLT John's child 6/7/1820 M
CHARRY Mr 6/8/1820 S
WASHINGTON George's son 6/11/1820 M
CLARK George's son 6/11/1820 M
LIVERS Mr's child 6/11/1820 W
HAGERTY John 6/13/1820 W
PIFER Mr 6/13/1820 S
PIFER Mr's child 6/13/1820 S
RIND William's child 6/15/1820 W
MORDOCK John 6/19/1820 W
KING Ignatious's child 6/19/1820 S
REEDER Thomas's child 6/21/1820 M
ALLIN William's brother 6/21/1820 S
JACKSON Samuel's child 6/22/1820 S
O'BRIAN William 6/25/1820 M
JONES C L's child 6/27/1820 S
MACKALL B's black woman 6/27/1820 S
HAWKINS Walter's child 6/27/1820 S
KNIGHT Mr's child 6/27/1820 S
NICHOLS Mr 7/1/1820 S
GREEN James 7/1/1820 M
WHELAN Mrs 7/2/1820 S
HAGARTY Mrs's child 7/2/1820 W
WASHINGTON Mrs 7/2/1820 M
A Child that died at L Hill's 7/3/1820 M
WELLS Richard's child 7/5/1820 M
BARKLEY John's child 7/7/1820 M
SCHULTZ Henry 7/7/1820 M
MORGAN Mr 7/9/1820 S
ARNOLD Mr 7/12/1820 S
WILSON Grace's child 7/14/1820 M
TRAVERS John's black child 7/15/1820 S
WHITE Charles C's child 7/16/1820 W
STEWART William's child 7/20/1820 M
RICH Mr 7/22/1820 W
TRUNNEL Henry's child 7/24/1820 W
CARLAN William 7/26/1820 W
LAUB Jacob 7/27/1820 M
Cyrus 7/27/1820 S
VALLARD R H L's child 7/27/1820 W
THERLY Mr 7/31/1820 S

George's child 7/31/1820 W
ROBERTSON John's child 7/31/1820 W
SCOTT Alexander's Sam 8/3/1820 M
BANISTER Richard's child 8/4/1820 S
JACKSON Samuel's child 8/5/1820 S
NICHOLLS Mrs's child 8/6/1820 S
JONES F P's child 8/6/1820 S
DUN Samuel's child 8/9/1820 W
HALL Brice's child 8/10/1820 S
MAYER Adam's child 8/12/1820 W
AVARD Mrs's child 8/12/1820 S
SHAAFF Mrs's son 8/12/1820 M
NEWTON Walter's child 8/13/1820 W
MAY Mrs 8/13/1820 S
CLARK Samuel's black child 8/16/1820 S
EATHY George's child 8/17/1820 W
BAKER Z's child 8/18/1820 W
McCAULY William's child 8/18/1820 S
DUGLASS Mr's child 8/18/1820 S
STEEL Mr's child 8/18/1820 W
HEBNER Frederick's child 8/19/1820 W
TOLBERT Mr (of Alexandria)'s son 8/25/1820 S
Miles a black man's child 8/26/1820 S
WADE Mr's child 8/27/1820 W
THOMAS Jennet's child 8/28/1820 S
McDANIEL E 8/29/1820 W
MARBURY Lucy's child 8/30/1820 S
A CHILD that died at Gunn 8/31/1820 S
HUTTON Dafny's child 8/31/1820 S
KURTZ Daniel's black woman 9/4/1820 S
BOHRER Jacob's son 9/4/1820 W
PETER Mr's child 9/4/1820 M
ORM T's child 9/6/1820 W
JACKSON Jasper 9/6/1820 M
PALMER John's child 9/8/1820 M
KRAUSE John 9/9/1820 M
BRENNER Mr's child 9/9/1820 W
A STRANGER 9/9/1820 S
WILLIAMS Daniel 9/12/1820 S
BOWMAN Nat's child 9/14/1820 S
BOHRER Abraham's child 9/15/1820 W
BERRY Mr 9/15/1820 S

NICHOLLS Mrs 9/15/1820 S
WILLIAM Jeremiah's black child 9/16/1820 S
CORCORAN Thomas's black woman 9/17/1820 S
MILLER James's child 9/18/1820 W
McCOY John's child 9/20/1820 S
ABBOT John's child 9/21/1820 M
WATERS John's child 9/22/1820 W
Hercules's child 9/22/1820 S
SEMMES Raphel's child 9/23/1820 M
DASHEALON Miss 9/23/1820 S
SCOTT Thomas 9/24/1820 W
GANTT Live 9/24/1820 S
Milly's child 9/25/1820 S
KELLY John's child 9/27/1820 S
RENNER Daniel's child 9/27/1820 S
PEARCE Mrs's child 9/28/1820 M
CALAHAN Mr's child 9/28/1820 S
SKINNER Mr's child 10/1/1820 W
DUNLOP George 10/1/1820 M
BEALL T B 10/1/1820 M
WARD Ulysses's nephew 10/2/1820 W
HAGERTY Mrs's child 10/2/1820 W
OFFITT T B 10/2/1820 W
ADAMS Henry's child 10/6/1820 S
WISE Charles 10/7/1820 W
LANNUM Elisha's child 10/7/1820 W
CORCORAN Mrs 10/9/1820 W
SWAN J 10/9/1820 S
DAY Mr's child 10/10/1820 S
CHISHAM John 10/10/1820 S
CONNTEE Richard 10/11/1820 M
WEEMS Elisha's black woman 10/11/1820 S
SCOTT Alexander's son 10/11/1820 M
BEALL Rinsey 10/11/1820 W
MILLER George 10/15/1820 W
STEEL Mrs 10/15/1820 S
DAY Mrs 10/17/1820 S
JOHNSON Henry 10/22/1820 S
STEEL Mr's child 10/22/1820 W
CRAVEN William's child 10/24/1820 S
JACKSON Joseph's child 10/26/1820 W
DAY child 10/26/1820 S

HUTCHENS Mrs 10/26/1820 W
DAY Mrs 10/26/1820 S
WETZEL F 10/31/1820 W
DUNLOP James Junr's child 11/2/1820 M
WROTH Mrs 11/2/1820 S
CUSTIS Mr's man 11/3/1820 S
WOOD E's daughter 11/4/1820 S
LAMAR R 11/6/1820 M
DELANY Mrs 11/11/1820 S
CAMPBELL Com. 11/13/1820 M
LOWE Miss 11/15/1820 M
ROBERTSON William 11/16/1820 S
TIVINE Mrs 11/17/1820 S
TRUNNEL Mr's mother-in-law 11/19/1820 W
O'BRIEN Mrs 11/19/1820 W
REINTZEL D's black woman 11/20/1820 S
ROSS William's child 11/20/1820 S
BUTLER Mary 11/27/1820 S
PETER Columbia 12/4/1820 M
THUNBLERT William's child 12/8/1820 M
WOOLLARD Samuel 12/13/1820 S
POOL Mrs 12/18/1820 S
BEALL Mrs's girl 12/18/1820 S
JONES Dennis's black child 12/21/1820 S
ALFRED D 12/21/1820 S
MOXLEY Mr's child 12/24/1820 S
WEEDEN William 12/27/1820 S
BOHRER Barbary 1/3/1821 W
LIVERS Ignatious 1/8/1821 W
A ---- Over the river got by Mr Lawrence 1/16/1821 S
Grace (colored woman) 1/20/1821 S
BARN Ann's child 1/26/1821 S
BLAGE Benjamin 2/1/1821 S
CALDER William's daughter 2/5/1821 M
MUMFORD William (colored man) 2/6/1821 S
PYFER Henry's child 2/9/1821 M
BAKER S 2/11/1821 M
SHIVENER John 2/14/1821 M
STILLS Mr's daughter 2/19/1821 W
REDHEFFER Mr 2/20/1821 M
RATHIN R 3/6/1821 S
REEDER John 3/6/1821 W

BENSON Mrs's child 3/10/1821 S
CARBURY Lewes's child 3/10/1821 W
LEWES child 3/10/1821 S
REED Mrs 3/14/1821 M
LUCY 3/22/1821 S
RABBIT Mr's child 3/24/1821 S
RICHARDS Mrs 3/26/1821 S
SKEGS William 3/26/1821 S
MITCHELL Miss 3/28/1821 W
MORSELL J S's colored child 3/28/1821 S
HALL Elisha 4/1/1821 W
BOOTH Mr's daughter 4/2/1821 S
SHEAPERD L's child 4/11/1821 W
RUTHFORD Mrs 4/12/1821 W
PARSONS Mrs 4/14/1821 M
BRUFF Mrs 4/15/1821 W
MAYFIELD William 4/22/1821 W
ESTLERMAN Mrs 4/23/1821 W
BOHRER Jacob's black woman 4/25/1821 S
ELIASON John Jr 4/30/1821 W
SPALDING Mrs 4/30/1821 W
BROWN Clary's son 4/26/1821 S
Dodd (Colored woman) 4/29/1821 S
THAW Joseph's child 5/4/1821 M
SMOOT Mrs's child 5/5/1821 M
PATTENGER Thomas's colored woman 5/5/1821 S
THAW Joseph's child 5/12/1821 M
SMITH Henry (colored man)'s child 5/12/1821 S
HIGDON Mrs 5/16/1821 S
BOHRER Mrs 5/22/1821 W
A Sailor 5/26/1821 S
PATTENGER Thomas's child 5/27/1821 M
HODNET James 5/28/1821 W
GIBSON Richard's father 5/29/1821 W
MAYFIELD Benjamin's son 5/30/1821 M
FITZHUGH Richard 5/31/1821 W
A Drowned man 6/1/1821 S
ROSS Mr 6/6/1821 M
MORLAND Mrs's child 6/7/1821 S
WEAVER Mr 6/10/1821 S
DAYE A 6/10/1821 W
MORGAN Mr 6/12/1821 S

ELVINS Mr 6/13/1821 S
KING George's child 6/23/1821 M
MUNFORD Sarah (colored woman)'s child 6/23/1821 S
BEALL W B's daughter 7/9/1821 W
KEASOM Mrs 7/10/1821 W
KIRBY R's child 7/10/1821 W
SMITH Mr (colored man) 7/12/1821 S
JOHNS L H (colored man) 7/19/1821 S
SHEAPARD L's child 7/19/1821 W
BAKER John's child 7/20/1821 M
BLAIR Miss 7/24/1821 M
MacDANIEL G's son 7/27/1821 M
HEMFLEY Henry 7/27/1821 W
WATKINS Mr's child 7/27/1821 S
HOLTZMAN John's child 8/1/1821 W
JARBOW William 8/1/1821 W
KNIGHT Mrs 8/3/1821 W
KING William's child 8/3/1821 S
WILHOUN George's colored child 8/3/1821 S
McKENNEY T L's Tom 8/7/1821 S
FORMAN Mrs 8/8/1821 W
FOX E J 8/8/1821 M
BIAS Pally's child (colored man) 8/11/1821 S
ROBERTSON Mr's child at Curtis 8/13/1821 W
FURGASON Mr 8/14/1821 W
BAKER Polly 8/16/1821 S
COBLER James's child 8/18/1821 W
MEEM George's child 8/20/1821 W
RAGON Mary 8/23/1821 W
COLE (colored man)'s son-in-law 8/23/1821 S
MACDANIEL Mrs 8/24/1821 M
THOMSON Mrs 8/25/1821 W
LEE Elinor's child 8/27/1821 W
SPARROW Mr's child 8/28/1821 W
VANESSON Peter's child 8/29/1821 W
SHORTER C (colored man)'s mother 8/30/1821 S
TAILOR Miss at Nelson 8/30/1821 S
CONNERS Robert's child 8/30/1821 S
CALDER William at Kile's 8/31/1821 S
CARRALL Lucy's child 8/31/1821 W
SHEID Miss Ann J 8/31/1821 M
WHITE C C's (colored) child 8/2/1821 S

BARCLEY J D's child 9/1/1821 M
GROSS Jacob 9/1/1821 S
BROOKS Dafnay (colored man)'s child 9/2/1821 S
WREN John 9/3/1821 M
TILLY James 9/4/1821 W cherry
DENNESON John's child 9/5/1821 W
HUTCHENS Mr Castar's child 9/9/1821 S
THOMAS Captain's wife's child 9/11/1821 S
SMITH Josias (colored man)'s child 9/12/1821 S
ENGLISH David Senr's child 9/14/1821 M
WETNEY Mr's child 9/15/1821 W
BIAS Smithy (colored man)'s child 9/16/1821 S
SHAAFF Mrs's colored boy 9/17/1821 S
LEE Miss 9/18/1821 W
MILLER Mrs 9/19/1821 W
CRUET Mr 9/19/1821 W
PETTENGILL Mr's child 9/19/1821 W
ELVINS Mr 9/20/1821 W
PROCTOR Benedict (colored man) 9/21/1821 S
KNABS William's child 9/25/1821 W
PARROTT Richard's colored child 9/26/1821 S
MAGRUDER Mary Ann 9/27/1821 M
CRAIG Lewis 9/28/1821 W
McDANIEL George's child 9/28/1821 M
ROBINSON Mrs 9/29/1821 W
UPPERMAN Jacob 9/29/1821 W
PALMAR Elisha 9/30/1821 W
DECKER James 10/1/1821 S
HUSLER Joseph's child 10/1/1821 W
HART John's child 10/2/1821 W
George's daughter (colored woman) 10/3/1821 S
REYNOLDS Mrs's child 10/3/1821 W
PAINE Jacob's daughter 10/3/1821 W
HILLEARY Lewis (colored man) 10/3/1821 W
FREEMAN Robert 10/4/1821 S
BALL Betsey's child 10/4/1821 S
McCAN Arthur 10/5/1821 S
KNIGHT William 10/6/1821 M
MILLER James's child 10/7/1821 W
TOLMIE Mrs's grandchild 10/9/1821 W
HEARD Mrs 10/9/1821 W
ATWATER William C's child 10/10/1821 M

KING George 10/11/1821 M
BALL Lewis 10/11/1821 S
McCOY Mr's child 10/11/1821 S
MARAND Mr 10/12/1821 S
JARVIS Mrs 10/12/1821 S
NOURSE Michael's child 10/13/1821 W cherry
MAGRUDER Lycurgus's child 10/14/1821 M
POOL Ann 10/14/1821 S
HODGES Thomas C 10/15/1821 M
WHEATLEY Mrs 10/16/1821 W cherry
DOYNE Joseph 10/17/1821 M
PRITCHARD Mrs's child 10/17/1821 S
MAYFIELD Henry's child 10/18/1821 S
MILLER Mrs's daughter 10/19/1821 W
JONES Dennis's child 10/19/1821 M
DAVIS Samuel's brother (colored man) 10/20/1821 S
COLLINGWOOD Samuel 10/21/1821 W
KING William Sr 10/19/1821 M
McKENNEY William's child 10/21/1821 M
HILLEARY Tilman's daughter 10/22/1821 W
SCOTT Mrs 10/23/1821 M
MARBURY William's colored child 10/24/1821 S
KING John 10/24/1821 M
REEDER Mrs's child 10/25/1821 W
SCOTT Mr's child 10/27/1821 S
A Woman at Spalding's 10/27/1821 S
COX Mr's child 10/27/1821 S
McCOMB General's child 10/29/1821 M
MATTINGLY Mrs 10/29/1821 S
COX William 10/30/1821 S
BEALL N's brother-in-law 10/31/1821 S
FALLS Sally (colored woman) 10/31/1821 S
MORGAN Mrs 11/2/1821 W
SOUTHNER Mrs 11/3/1821 W
FIPP William 11/3/1821 S
PETER Elizabeth 11/4/1821 M
TRAVERS John 11/5/1821 M
PRITCHARD Mr's child 11/5/1821 S
Nancy (colored woman)'s father 11/10/1821 S
JENKINS Matthew's daughter 11/12/1821 S
COXEN Mr's child 11/12/1821 S
RIGGS Romulus's child 11/13/1821 M

WILLIAM James's child 11/13/1821 S
CONTEE Mrs 11/14/1821 M
MOUNTS John's child 11/15/1821 M
DAWS Benjamin's child 11/15/1821 W
Kitty (colored woman) 11/15/1821 S
DAVIS Samuel's brother 11/15/1821 S
ARNAY Mrs 11/18/1821 W
RIDGWAY Mrs 11/21/1821 W
THOMSON William (colored)'s child 11/21/1821 S
WHITE Mr 11/22/1821 S
CURRANT Jane (colored woman)'s daughter 11/22/1821 S
MARKWARD William 11/25/1821 W
CANNON Mr 11/25/1821 W
BUTLER Sally (colored woman)'s mother 11/26/1821 S
BROOKS Mrs 11/26/1821 S
MAGRUDER Mr 11/27/1821 W
CHANDLER Walter S's colored woman 11/10/1821 S
GRIM Mrs 12/2/1821 W
WHITE C C's child 12/2/1821 W
CHAPMAN Henry 12/6/1821 M
----- Mrs 12/8/1821 S
SPEAR Mrs's child 12/8/1821 S
CRANFORD Mrs (colored woman) 12/8/1821 S
DEAKINS Mrs 12/11/1821 S
WALLICE Mrs 12/13/1821 W
BROOKS Thomas 12/17/1821 M
STEWART William's child 12/18/1821 M
OVERTON John (colored man)'s child 12/19/1821 S
GOULDING Mr's child 12/26/1821 S
BURMISTAN Mrs 12/26/1821 M
KING Margrat 12/28/1821 M
JONES F P's child 12/31/1821 S
CHUB Nancy (colored woman) 12/31/1821 S
LOWNDES F's Isaac 1/3/1822 S
HARP James's child 1/4/1822 S
HARP James' child 1/6/1822 S
HARP James' child 1/9/1822 S
HUSLER Joseph 1/11/1822 W
ROSS Andrew 1/13/1822 M
POWERS R's child 1/15/1822 S
BROWN John (colored man)'s relation 1/15/1822 S
HAYSWOOD Mr 1/16/1822 S

Thomas (colored man)'s child 1/17/1822 S
LOWNDS Ann 1/18/1822 M
WELLS Mrs 1/19/1822 S
KNOX Mrs 1/19/1822 S
ELDERKIN Mr's child 1/26/1822 W
SWINK W 1/27/1822 W
BROOKS William 1/27/1822 S
WEBB John 2/2/1822 S
LANNIN Elisha 2/2/1822 W
FOWLER Mrs 2/4/1822 W
PETTET Mrs 2/6/1822 W
PLANT Eliza's child (colored woman) 2/9/1822 S
~~SHOEMAKER Mrs 2/9/1822~~
MORE Joseph's wife's sister 2/17/1822 S
GARDNER Mr's child 2/22/1822 S
GRANT William (colored man)'s child 2/23/1822 S
COOK Mrs 2/26/1822 M
MARQUARD Charles's child 3/1/1822 M
NICHOLSON Mr 3/3/1822 S
BROWN Sam 3/5/1822 S
BURNET Charles A's child 3/5/1822 M
BAUTCHER Mr's child 3/10/1822 W
HUGHS J 3/12/1822 W
TYLER Mrs 3/13/1822 W
ROBERTSON Mr (laborer)'s child 3/20/1822 S
DOUGLAS Mr 3/20/1822 M
JONES Mrs 3/20/1822 M
SMITH Ann's child 3/20/1822 S
PETER John (colored man) 4/8/1822 S
SMITH Clement's child 4/8/1822 M
NEEDAM George 4/9/1822 W
GARDNER Thomas 4/14/1822 S
EDMUNSON Edward 4/15/1822 W
WHITE Mr's mother 4/15/1822 S
TURNER James 4/15/1822 S
SMITH Thomas's child 4/15/1822 S
WOODMAN Mr 4/17/1822 S
JONES Miss 4/22/1822 W
RIND Mrs 4/25/1822 W
BEASLY Mrs 4/25/1822 W
RUSH Paty 4/25/1822 S
PATTERSON Edward (colored man) 4/28/1822 S

BUTLER Mary 4/28/1822 S
WILLIAMS Mr's boy 5/4/1822 S
HEDGES Mrs 5/11/1822 M
BUTLER Henry's child 5/11/1822 S
KILGORE Mrs 5/23/1822 M
NEWGENT Eli (colored man)'s child 5/25/1822 S
CARBURY Henry 5/27/1822 M
COLLINS Lillemen 5/28/1822 S
SIMMONS Samsen 6/3/1822 W
HENDERSON John's child 6/6/1822 W
NORMAN John's mother (colored man) 6/6/1822 S
PEARCE William 6/8/1822 S
HERMANCE Ann 6/9/1822 M
FEARSON Joseph's child 6/14/1822 W
BECK Mrs 6/18/1822 W
MORSELL J S's George 6/23/1822 S
THUMBERT William's child 6/24/1822 M
CARTER Jane's mother (colored woman) 6/25/1822 S
MUMBY R's child 6/26/1822 W
WATERS John's child 6/26/1822 W
BUSEY J 6/26/1822 S
CARBURY Lewis's child 7/1/1822 W
WARING Miss Nelly 7/5/1822 M
Candis's son 7/4/1822 S
WOOLHAM Mr 7/7/1822 S
KEY F S' son 7/9/1822 M
MORE John's child 7/11/1822 S
BUTLER L (colored man)'s child 7/16/1822 S
BOWER James's child 7/17/1822 W
MAUGH John 7/17/1822 S
KING Mrs's child 7/18/1822 M
HILTON Perry's child 7/20/1822 S
NEVIT John's child 7/20/1822 S
STRICH Mr 7/22/1822 M
RIND W A Jr's child 7/22/1822 W
NEWGENT Eli's mother-in-law 7/25/1822 S
KING Edward's child 7/25/1822 W
UPPERMAN Mrs 7/25/1822 W
DULEY Barton 8/2/1822 W
LOVE Mrs 8/3/1822 M
ADDISON W D's colored woman 8/4/1822 S
FITZGERALD Mary's child 8/5/1822 M

A Foundling at Havenlar 8/9/1822 S
MAGRUDER Robert P 8/11/1822 M
DAWES Benjamin's child 8/11/1822 W
WHEELER Clement 8/11/1822 M
MARON Mrs 8/21/1822 M
PETTINGILL Mr's child 8/25/1822 W
THOMSON William's colored woman 8/28/1822 S
BUTLER Charles's child 8/28/1822 S
TURNER Thomas's colored woman 9/2/1822 S
QUEEN Anthony (colored man) 9/3/1822 S
HARP Elizabeth's child 9/6/1822 S
GILLIS George's colored child 9/6/1822 S
VANNESIN Peter's child 9/6/1822 M
MORRIS Jeret (colored man)'s relation 9/7/1822 S
KIRBY Robert's colored child 9/9/1822 S
CROW John's child 9/9/1822 W
HARDON Miss 9/13/1822 W
LYONS Mrs 9/16/1822 M
WASHINGTON Lund's child 9/17/1822 M
UPPERMAN Henry's child 9/20/1822 M
McCOMB Mrs 9/20/1822 M
PARKE David 9/21/1822 S
BAIRN John's granddaughter 9/22/1822 M
MOYERS Samuel's grandchild 9/22/1822 W
TAYLOE John's child 9/24/1822 M
WINEBURGER J's relation 9/25/1822 W
NEWTON Lewis 9/30/1822 W
SYMINGTON James's child 10/2/1822 W
BENSON Mrs 10/4/1822 W
ROBY Mr 10/5/1822 W
BROOKS Dafney (colored woman)'s child 10/6/1822 S
MICDONNAL P 10/6/1822 S
TOLMEY James 10/8/1822 W
HODSON Mrs (colored woman) 10/8/1822 S
TUCKER Samuel's child 10/9/1822 S
LIVELY Mr 10/11/1822 W
PYFER Henry's child 10/11/1822 M
FREZIER Thomas 10/12/1822 W
REEDER Mr's child 10/13/1822 W
WATSON James 10/13/1822 M
HOPE Tom's wife 10/14/1822 S
MAHONY George's child 10/15/1822 W

WHITE Mrs 10/18/1822 S
HULL Mrs's mother 10/21/1822 S
BEAN Mrs 10/24/1822 S
HART Mrs 10/24/1822 W
MORGAN William 10/28/1822 W
REAVER Mr's child 10/29/1822 S
SWAN Nancy (colored woman) 10/30/1822 S
BRANNUM Mrs 10/31/1822 S
MORE Joseph's relation (colored woman) 11/2/1822 S
DAWSON Charles 11/2/1822 M
MAFFITT William 11/3/1822 W
MILLIGAN Joseph's child 11/4/1822 W
COLLINS Mrs's child 11/4/1822 S
MOOR Charles's daughter 11/6/1822 S
STEMBLE Henry's colored child 11/6/1822 S
LIVINGSTON C 11/6/1822 W
FRENCH Mrs 11/12/1822 W
ROBERTSON Mrs 11/15/1822 S
SCOTT Allen's colored woman 11/20/1822 S
KNOLES Thomas 11/23/1822 M
KROUZE Mrs 11/24/1822 W
LIPSCOMB W C's child 11/24/1822 W
HALL Sally (colored woman) 11/24/1822 S
LEVIS Mr's child 11/27/1822 W
MORE Vincent 11/27/1822 W
MASSEY Samuel 11/27/1822 W
HARRISON Gustavus's colored woman 11/27/1822 S
MORGAN Mrs 12/8/1822 M
COLLINS Ann's child 12/8/1822 S
FAHEY Mr 12/10/1822
HANSON Mrs 12/10/1822 W
MAKALL Benjamin 12/12/1822 M
KING Mrs 12/13/1822 M
OFFUTT William 12/13/1822 W
CALHOON Mrs (colored woman) 12/13/1822 S
UPPERMAN Mr 12/14/1822 W
RICHARDS Caleb 12/15/1822 W
PATTERSON Edger's colored woman 12/16/1822 S
TAYLOR Daniel 12/16/1822 S
BRADFIELD John's child 12/16/1822 S
POTTS Samuel's child 12/16/1822 M
LANG William's daughter 12/16/1822 W

WILLIAMS Eli 12/30/1822 M
PARROTT R's colored man 12/30/1822 S
CAMPBELL Meshac's mother-in-law 1/1/1823 W
HOPE Tom 1/2/1823 S
YATES John 1/2/1823 M
THOMPSON Benjamin 1/3/1823 S
KEHIM Robert 1/4/1823 S
PARROTT Richard 1/5/1823 M
GOSZLER Mrs 1/9/1823 S
NORRIS Mrs's child 1/12/1823 S
BAKER John's child 1/14/1823 M
CRUET Mr' child 1/15/1823 S
BUTLER Henry (colored man)'s child 1/15/1823 S
MAY Mr's child 1/18/1823 W
POTTS Samuel's colored man 1/19/1823 S
BENSON Mr's child 1/20/1823 S
ADAMS Hannah 1/21/1823 W
WATERS T G's colored child 1/21/1823 S
STEWART Miss Margaret 1/22/1823 M
LIVERY Mrs 1/26/1823 W
PECKHAM William 1/29/1823 W
BOWIE Thomas 1/30/1823 M
PANE William 1/31/1823 W
GAITHER G R's child 2/6/1823 S
SLYE Mrs (Robert's wife) 2/6/1823 M
WILSON Lawrence 2/6/1823 S
FOLIO Mrs's child 2/6/1823 S
SMITH Mrs 2/8/1823 W
PAYNE Mrs 2/8/1823 S
BRONAUGH J W's daughter 2/10/1823 M
COXEN W's child 2/17/1823 S
McDANIEL John's child 2/18/1823 W
ROBERTSON Mr 2/19/1823 W
CLARKE Mrs (Samuel's mother) 2/19/1823 W
HIGDEN Mr 2/20/1823 S
RICHARDS Mrs 2/22/1823 S
MILLER Hezekiah's child 2/27/1823 S
~~LETCHER~~ Care (colored woman)'s mother 3/4/1823 S
A Colored woman at Gideon Davis's 3/4/1823 S
DUNLOP James 3/5/1823 M
MAGRUDER Ninian 3/5/1823 M
PEALE Charly (colored man) 3/7/1823 S

LYONS Miss E 3/7/1823 M
MOYERS Samuel's child 3/15/1823 W
GARRETSON John (colored man)'s child 3/18/1823 S
ANDREWS Miss's child 3/18/1823 S
LEE Caroline 3/24/1823 S
JACKSON Joseph's child 3/26/1823 W
BEDLEY Mrs's child 3/26/1823 S
Theresa (colored woman) 3/28/1823 S
LEE Mr 4/2/1823 W
HARRIS Luke 4/4/1823 W
CARTER James 4/5/1823 S
HOOVER Mrs Peter 4/8/1823 S
CRUIKSHANK Charles's child 4/9/1823 W
BROODWELL James's child 4/15/1823 W
THOMPSON William Jr's child 4/16/1823 M
MITCHEL Hannah's child 4/17/1823 S
KELLY John 4/22/1823 W
SMOOT Samuel's child 4/26/1823 S
BROWN William (colored man) 4/29/1823 S
WELLS Richard's child 5/9/1823 M
MARLBRO John's girl 5/13/1823 S
Sally (colored woman) 5/15/1823 S
HINES Mary Ann 5/16/1823 S
CHESLEY Mrs 5/21/1823 W
FAGAN Mr's child 5/21/1823 S
A Man per Mr Custis 5/21/1823 S
FRASIER John's child 5/31/1823 S
DONALDSON Mrs 6/4/1823 W
CORCORAN Mrs 6/4/1823 M
Clare's mother (colored woman) 6/10/1823 S
HARRISON Gustavus's child 6/10/1823 M
GREEN James (colored man)'s child 6/10/1823 S
ERRINSHAW Mrs 6/18/1823 W
BELT James's child 6/20/1823 M
WILLIAMS John 6/21/1823 S
PECKHAM Mrs's son 6/25/1823 W
STINCHCOMB A S's child 6/27/1823 S
TRAVERS Mr 6/30/1823 W
McILVAINE C's child 7/1/1823 M
ROBERTSON Mrs's colored man 7/3/1823 S
JACKSON Mrs 7/4/1823 W
DUCKET Isaac 7/4/1823 M

DAWES B's colored girl 7/7/1823 S
ATWOOD John's child 7/12/1823 W
TOWSON Colonel N's child 7/15/1823 M
KURTZ David's child 7/19/1823 W
HELEN Mr's colored man 7/19/1823 S
LEE Jane's child 7/23/1823 S
JONES Morris 7/24/1823 S
FENWICK Mrs 7/24/1823 S
BEALL B W 7/25/1823 W
BEALL Mrs B's colored child 7/26/1823 S
EATHY George 7/30/1823 W
DICKSON Mrs 7/31/1823 W
----- Mrs's child 8/3/1823 S
KNOWLES John 8/4/1823 W
DEAN Felix's child 8/4/1823 S
GREATRAKE L's child 8/4/1823 W
NEWTON Walter's child 8/5/1823 W
YOUNG Jacob 8/6/1823 W
QUEEN Mr Richard's child 8/7/1823 W
HUTTON Mrs 8/7/1823 M
BRADY Michael 8/8/1823 W
MAGRUDER George 8/11/1823 M
HARDISTAY Mr's child 8/11/1823 M
MARKRITIER Stephen 8/12/1823 S
HEBNER Frederic's child 8/16/1823 W
MILES William's child 8/21/1823 S
HARP Mrs 8/22/1823 S
GERMAN Valentine's child 8/25/1823 S
PUMPHREY Lloyd's child 8/27/1823 M
MASON George's child 8/28/1823 M
BEALL W B's daughter 8/30/1823 W
STEWART Henry 8/31/1823 W
PERRY Mrs 8/31/1823 W
FRENCH Mrs's man 9/1/1823 S
COOKENDORFER Leonard 9/4/1823 W
LUCAS William's child 9/4/1823 S
SNOWDEN Richard 9/4/1823 M
SIM Thomas for colored woman 9/6/1823 S
SMALLWOOD Mrs's boy 9/7/1823 S
TUCKER Enoch's child 9/7/1823 M
A Boatman 9/7/1823 S
JENKINS Mrs 9/9/1823 S

OGLE Mr's child 9/11/1823 S
HOOVER Peter's child 9/11/1823 S
PETER John's child 9/11/1823 M
SCOTT Mrs 9/12/1823 S
ROUNDS Lettie (colored woman)'s child 9/13/1823 S
JACKSON Richard 9/16/1823 M
McPHERSON John 9/16/1823 M
SKIDMORE Mr's child 9/18/1823 W
PETTINGALE Mr's child 9/20/1823 W
LAMB Mr's child 9/22/1823 W
OULD Robert's child 9/22/1823 W
BEALL Mrs B 9/23/1823 M
PAUL Anthony 9/24/1823 W
TRYON Mrs 9/25/1823 W
GRIFFIN Mr 9/26/1823 S
NORRIS Mrs's child 9/26/1823 S
FECHTIG Lewis R 9/26/1823 M
HAYNES Mrs 9/28/1823 M
HAYNES Mrs's servant 9/28/1823 W
WILLIAMS Mrs 9/29/1823 S
NEWTON Mr 9/29/1823 W
ELLIS Mrs's child 9/30/1823 S
HOPKINSON Francis 9/30/1823 W
ROBERTSON John's child 10/2/1823 S
CRAWFORD Sarah's colored child 10/4/1823 S
BURROWS Mrs 10/5/1823 W
SMITH Abner (colored man)'s child 10/6/1823 W
MARSHAL R H's colored woman 10/6/1823 S
WHEELER Ignatius colored man 10/7/1823 W
RICHARDSON J's child 10/7/1823 S
PETER Sarah 10/8/1823 M
MIMKIN Mrs's daughter 10/12/1823 S
DeMYER John's child 10/13/1823 S
BRADY Mrs in Virginia 10/16/1823 W
THOMPSON Mrs 10/16/1823 S
DAVIS Sarah's child 10/17/1823 S
GEESLER Mr's child 10/19/1823 W
BENNET Mr's child 10/19/1823 W
McCLOSKEY Mr 10/19/1823 S
SMITH John's child 10/19/1823 W
NORRIS Mrs's son 10/21/1823 S
HUTTON James's child 10/21/1823 M

TANEY A J 10/23/1823 M
A Colored woman at T Beck's house 10/24/1823 S
BIAS Cynthia's child 10/25/1823 S
AYRES Mrs's child 10/26/1823 S
BANNISTER Richard's child 10/29/1823 S
BENTZ Adam 10/29/1823 S
RHEY Mr's child 10/30/1823 S
REINTZEL Samuel's child 10/30/1823 W
PERLEY Mr's child 11/2/1823 S
OBER Robert's child 11/2/1823 M
CALHOUN William's child 11/4/1823 S
BRADY Caleb Senr 11/4/1823 W
SHERMAN Peter 11/5/1823 W
HILLEARY Nicholas 11/6/1823 S
RYE Mr's child 11/7/1823 S
HOLT John and Sopha Skagg's child 11/7/1823 W
KUHNS William 11/10/1823 W
MAYFIELD Mrs's child 11/10/1823 S
MUSTIN Thomas's child 11/11/1823 M
MADDOX Mr's child 11/12/1823 M
STEELE Charles's child 11/13/1823 S
HILTON John's child 11/15/1823 W
BROWN James's child 11/16/1823 S
LOVELESS Mrs's child 11/17/1823 S
DAVIS Sarah (colored woman)'s child 11/17/1823 S
SWAIN William 11/19/1823 S
LANHAM Mrs's child 11/20/1823 W
PETTIT William 11/21/1823 W
NEWTON James's child 11/22/1823 W
MUDD Harriet's child 11/22/1823 W
HUTCHINS John's child 11/22/1823 S
THOMPSON William Senr 11/23/1823 M
NEUGENT Eli (colored man)'s child 11/23/1823 S
WARRING Mrs 11/23/1823 M
LAIRD John's colored child 11/23/1823 S
BROOKES Daphne (colored woman)'s child 11/23/1823 S
REDMAN James 11/23/1823 M
OBER Robert's child 11/24/1823 M
LUFBOROUGH Mrs 11/27/1823 M
SPARROW Mr 11/27/1823 S
DAWES Benjamin's child 11/30/1823 W
HAVEY Mr's child 12/6/1823 S

MURPHY 12/6/1823 S
Old Sam 12/6/1823 S
GREUHM Frederic 12/4/1823 M
SMART Mrs's child 12/7/1823 W
STULL John J's child 12/7/1823 M
HOLTZMAN John's child 12/8/1823 W
STEWART Miss 12/8/1823 W
RICE George 12/8/1823 S
MARBURY Luke 12/10/1823 S
HOMANS Benjamin 12/11/1823 M
POWEL Ann (colored woman)'s child 12/17/1823 S
CLARKE Ann Maria 12/17/1823 M
A Colored child at H Addison's 12/17/1823 S
ROBINSON John's child 12/20/1823 W
McKENNY Samuel's child 12/21/1823 M
MORE Jesse's child 12/22/1823 W
ADDISON Henry's child 12/23/1823 M
MORTON William's child 12/23/1823 W
SMITH Clement's colored child 12/30/1823 S
TILLEY Charles's child 12/30/1823 W
POLK David's child 12/31/1823 M
BISHOP Mr's child 1/1/1824 S
KING James's mother (at the foundry) 1/11/1824 S
GREEN Simon 1/14/1824 S
BARTLET Isaac's child W
SMITH Caroline 1/24/1824 M
BUTLER P 1/27/1824 S
BAKER John's child 1/27/1824 M
WHITNEY Jared's child 2/1/1824 W
ROBERTSON Mrs's mother (pauper) 2/2/1824 S
FENWICK Clara (colored woman)'s child 2/2/1824 S
TURNER Samuel 2/3/1824 M
A Pauper at William Turner's 2/4/1824 S
FORREST Henry's colored woman 2/4/1824 S
KEILER Mr 2/5/1824 S
ADDISON Henry's child 2/6/1824 W
PHILISTIN Mrs 2/6/1824 W
GREEN Mrs 2/7/1824 S
FAGAN Daniel's child 2/8/1824 S
DEGGES William's child 2/9/1824 M
LIBBY Joseph's child 2/11/1824 M
ROBERTSON H B's colored child 2/11/1824 S

LIPSCOMB Jesse's child 2/12/1824 W
BUTLER Mary (colored woman)'s child 2/14/1824 S
ROBB John 2/16/1824 W
COGER Mrs (colored woman) 2/18/1824 S
BEALL Basil 2/18/1824 S
CLARKE John D's child 2/18/1824 M
WHEATLEY Mr's child 2/19/1824 W
KING John (the labourer)'s wife 2/21/1824 S
BARNES's Frank 2/21/1824 S
SHAW Catherine 2/22/1824 M
RAGON Daniel 2/23/1824 S
McKEE Mr's child 2/23/1824 S
WILLIAMS James's child 2/23/1824 S
POTTS Samuel's colored child 2/23/1824 S
NICHOLAS (colored man)'s son 2/23/1824 S
FREEMAN Constant 3/1/1824 M
SLYE Robt's child 3/8/1824 M
CLARKE William's child 3/8/1824 W
CUTTING Nathaniel 3/9/1824 W
BAYLEY William 3/9/1824 W
BUSEY Mrs 3/11/1824 W
FORTUNE William's wife's sister 3/11/1824 S
Agnes (colored woman) 3/11/1824 S
HARRY Mrs 3/14/1824 S
ROUNDS Ezekiel 3/20/1824 S
KENDEL Eliza (colored woman)'s child 3/20/1824 S
LAIRD William's child 3/20/1824 M
FLEET Henry (colored man) 3/20/1824 W
WHITE Thomas C 3/24/1824 W
MOREHOUSE Mr 3/24/1824 S
PETER George's child 3/25/1824 M
WILLIAMS Mr's child at the foundry 3/25/1824 W
TUEL Mrs 3/26/1824 S
OFFUTT Rebecca 3/28/1824 W
HERBERT Mrs 4/1/1824 S
OWENS Isaac jr's child 4/1/1824 S
OLPHIN Mrs 4/3/1824 S
BRADLEY Thomas 4/4/1824 M
NOBLE Mrs 4/10/1824 W
THOMAS Jared (colored man)'s child 4/11/1824 S
GIBSON William 4/11/1824 M
DIDENHOOVER Mr 4/13/1824 W

NICHOLLS Mrs 4/15/1824 S
WILLIAMS Mr 4/20/1824 S
WILLIAMS Jeremiah's boy 4/23/1824 S
TURNAR Jane 4/23/1824 S
GREER James's girl 4/26/1824 S
LOVEJOY Zedekiah's child 4/5/1824 W
STEVENSON Betsey (colored woman)'s child 5/4/1824 S
JACOBS John 5/4/1824 S
GRIMES John 5/6/1824 S
McDANIEL T 5/14/1824 S
PETER Mrs George 5/14/1824 M
ENGLISH David Jr's child 5/15/1824 S
RIDGWAY Levin 5/21/1824 S
GREEN James (colored man)'s child 5/24/1824 S
BUTLER Henry's colored woman's child 5/31/1824 S
KIRK Mrs's colored child 6/1/1824 S
MYERS Mrs John 6/2/1824 W
MASTERS Levi 6/6/1824 S
BIRTH James's Ned 6/6/1824 s
SIFFORD Isaac 6/12/1824 S
BLAIR William's child 6/22/1824 W
BAKER Mary 6/24/1824 S
PARKER William's child 6/25/1824 W
POTTS Samuel J's child 6/26/1824 M
A drowned child 6/27/1824 S
TUEL Ross's child 6/27/1824 S
WILSON Thomas 6/28/1824 M
DEAKINS Leonard 6/29/1824 M
WEBSTER Mrs's grandchild 7/4/1824 S
HENDERSON Doctor's man 7/8/1824 S
HAZEL Henry's child 7/9/1824 M
KIRK A M's child 7/9/1824 M
MARBURY William's Maria 7/12/1824 S
BROWN James 7/13/1824 S
A drowned man 7/15/1824 S
ROBINSON John's child 7/24/1824 W
PAGET William's child 7/28/1824 S
JOHNSON Susan (colored woman)'s child 7/28/1824 S
BROWN Hen's child 7/28/1824 S
BOSSWELL Ben's servant's child 7/29/1824 W
SIFFORD Mrs's child 7/29/1824 S
DAVIDSON Lewis G's boy 8/2/1824 S

GETTY Robt's child 8/2/1824 M
GREEN James (colored man)'s child 8/3/1824 S
A Foundling child 8/3/1824 S
LINTHICUM O M's child 8/5/1824 M
LUCAS Bennet's child 8/6/1824 S
BEALL M (colored woman) 8/8/1824 S
SULLIVAN Mrs's child 8/8/1824 S
BENNET Mr's child 8/9/1824 W
BOARMAN Mr's child 8/9/1824 W
SHECKELS Richard's child 8/9/1824 W
CARTER Betsey (colored woman) 8/10/1824 S
BOWIE Washington's daughter 8/11/1824 M
ANDERSON Charlotte (colored woman) 8/13/1824 W
A child at Mrs Shiveley's 8/14/1824 S
WETZEL John 8/16/1824 W
HENDERSON Thos's child 8/18/1824 M
ELLIS Hezekiah's child 8/21/1824 S
BLACK Eliza 8/21/1824 S
DEAVER Mr's child 8/21/1824 W
NORRIS Mrs 8/24/1824 S
SEWALL Lewis's child 8/27/1824 S
~~FECHTIG Lewis R~~ 8/28/1824 M
FOWLER Mr's child 8/31/1824 W
BROWN Henry's child 9/6/1824 S
HERN Elizabeth 9/6/1824 S
SHAAF Mrs's colored child 9/8/1824 S
RIDGEWAY Mr's child 9/8/1824 S
CALDER William 9/10/1824 M
CLARK John's son 9/12/1824 S
HERVEY Mr's child 9/14/1824 S
PLATER Patsey Miss 9/14/1824 M
PLATER Mr's woman 9/14/1824 S
OWENS Isaac Jr 9/17/1824 M
A colored woman at Mr McGill's 9/17/1824 S
BURGESS Richard's child 9/23/1824 M
DAWES Mrs Ben 9/26/1824 W
LANHAM Mrs A 9/28/1824 M
HOSKINS Jeff 9/29/1824 W
COBB James D's nephew 9/29/1824 W
WARD Mrs Eliz 10/1/1824 S
STINCHCOMB A S's child 10/3/1824 S
GRIFFIN Mrs 10/7/1824 W

BROOKE Thomas 10/8/1824 M
SCOTT Sabrett 10/11/1824 W
GANTT Fielder 10/12/1824 M
LEEDE Frederick M 10/13/1824 S
KEARNS Mr 10/15/1824 S
STEELE Mrs 10/25/1824 W
WOOD Mrs Ann 11/1/1824 W
MATTINGLY Mrs 11/2/1824 S
KNOWLES William's child 11/6/1824 W
SUTER A's colored child 11/10/1824 S
McNEAR William's child 11/11/1824 W
EDMONDSON Thomas 11/20/1824 W
WILLIAMS Mrs's child 11/24/1824 S
Old Harry 11/25/1824 S
LAMBERT Maurice 12/6/1824 M
CONNER Robert's child 12/8/1824 S
HOLTZMAN Harriet 12/15/1824 W
WATERS T G's mother 12/20/1824 M
MULLAKIN Mrs 12/20/1824 M
MARLO Thomas (colored man)'s child 12/21/1824 S
COVER John (colored man)'s child 12/21/1824 S
DAVEY Mrs 12/23/1824 W
BALTZER Joseph 12/25/1824 W
MORE John 12/28/1824 S
BARCLAY Mary Ann 12/29/1824 W
STODDART Mr's child 12/29/1824 S
GOSZLER George's child 1/13/1825 W
CRUIKSHANK Charles's child 1/14/1825 M
BAILY James C (waterman) 1/23/1825 W
Negro Celia 1/25/1825 S
BAKER Nancy 1/26/1825 W
RIDGEWAY Mrs 1/27/1825 S
MARZINGO Mrs 1/28/1825 M
Negro Beale 1/29/1825 S
LEESH Mr's child 1/30/1825 W
CONROD Godfry's child 1/31/1825 M
WEISNER Thomas 1/31/1825 S
RADCLIFFE Mrs 2/16/1825 M
KING William 2/17/1825 S
KING William's child 2/17/1825 S
BOWIE John 2/19/1825 M
HERVEY Jane 2/20/1825 M

CLAGGETT William 2/26/1825 M
WHITE Eliza's child 2/28/1825 S
Ned (colored man)'s child 3/2/1825 S
REEVES Mrs 3/3/1825 S
HARRISON Dr. John 3/6/1825 M
DUCKER Moses (colored man) 3/10/1825 S
GRIFFIN T B's child 3/10/1825 W
STOUT Mr 3/22/1825 W
DENNINGTON Mr 3/31/1825 W
LEWIS Marcus 4/1/1825 W
STILES Mr 4/5/1825 W
DUVALL Miss (of P G Co) 4/11/1825 W
GIBSON Samuel 4/16/1825 M
NORRIS James 4/20/1825 S
TRAVERS Nicholas's child 4/22/1825 W
KITTS Priscilla (colored woman)'s granddaughter 4/23/1825 S
CUSTIS Mrs's grandchild 4/25/1825 M
DODGE Francis's colored boy 4/26/1825 S
McKEWEN Mr's child 4/26/1824 W
WASHINGTON Lund's grandchild 4/26/1825 S
WILSON Isaac's child 4/29/1824 M
ERMANDINGER Jno S 4/29/1825 S
HAWKINS Chas (colored man) 4/29/1825 S
COCKELY Mrs Frances 5/1/1825 W
SOUTHERLAND Thos Y 5/8/1825 M
PARSONS William's apprentice (John Reynolds) 5/11/1825 S
KNOX John's child 5/12/1825 S
HANSON (colored man)'s child 5/12/1825 S
HALL Flora (colored woman) 5/16/1825 S
CHANDLER W S 5/19/1825 M
WHITE Robt's child 5/19/1825 W
TAYLOR Mrs's child 5/20/1825 S
DANDRIGE Wm (colored man)'s mother 5/20/1825 S
ROBERTSON Mrs Eliza 5/20/1825 M
GRAYSON Sally 5/21/1825 S
BOND Thomas (seaman) 5/22/1825 S
SMOOT Samuel's child 5/25/1825 S
Hercules (colored man) 6/1/1825 W
HALLER Geo W's child 6/1/1825 M
MORTON William's colored child 6/3/1825
SHECKELL Richd's child 6/8/1825 W
WALKER Elizabeth (colored woman)'s child 6/11/1825 S

Cassey (colored woman) 6/15/1825 S
GUEST Job's child 6/20/1825 M
BARNES Mrs 6/22/1825 W
VILLARD Mrs Sophia 6/22/1825 M
CHEW Miss (Delphi Mills) 6/26/1825 W
ELLIS Joshua's child 6/27/1825 S
CROW John's child 6/28/1825 W
GRIMES Michael's mother 7/2/1825 S
A Colored woman 7/5/1825 S
CLEMENTSON George's colored boy 7/7/1825 S
KIRBY Robt's colored child 7/9/1825 S
RIDGEWAY Mr's child 7/11/1825 S
TANNER Mr 9/11/1825 S
CHEW Robt F's child 7/12/1825 W
HALL Kitty (colored woman) 7/16/1825 S
MATTINGLY Mr 7/16/1825 S
FOWLER Catherine's child 7/18/1825 S
A Negro child at McCandlass's 7/20/1825 S
CLEMENTSON Ed's child 7/22/1825 W
A Negro child at McCandlass's 7/22/1825 S
STROMAN Mr's child 7/23/1825 S
CORCORAN Thomas's colored child 7/23/1825 S
ADDISON Henry's child 7/24/1825 W
DAVIDSON L G's colored man 7/26/1825 S
PETER George's colored woman's child 7/28/1825 S
PETER George's colored woman's child 7/31/1825 S
A child at Josias Smith (colored man)'s 7/20/1825 S
ELLIOTT Mrs's child 8/2/1825 M
COKELY Mrs's child 8/4/1825 W
PRATHER Mr 8/7/1825 S
BELT Mrs (PG Co) 8/7/1825 M
SMITH Thomas (colored man)'s child 8/8/1825 S
Negro Rachel (Hackey) 8/9/1825 S
ADAMS Chas 8/11/1825 S
FREEMAN J D's child 8/11/1825 W
TURNER William's child 8/14/1825 S
SMITH John K's child 8/15/1825 M
COVER Miss 8/16/1825 W
McPERSON J H 8/16/1825 M
DAVIS Sally 8/18/1825 S
BURGESS Richard's child 8/24/1825 S
PELTON Asahel 8/27/1825 S

DECKER Mrs 8/29/1825 S
HOLMES Wm 8/29/1825 M
ANDERSON Philip (colored man)'s child 9/1/1825 S
TIERNAN Mr 9/8/1825 S
MACKEY William 9/10/1825 M
RAWLINGS Samuel 9/13/1825 W
WHALEN Bridget 9/16/1825 S
CLARKE William's child 9/21/1825 W
CHRISTAN Thomas (seaman) 9/25/1825 S
GOOD Wm's colored man 9/29/1825 S
COLLINS Rachel 9/30/1825 S
SCOTT Mrs A (Montgomery County) 10/7/1825 W
HOLTZMAN George W 10/9/1825 M
GUEST Job's child 10/9/1825 M
BROWN Catherine 10/12/1825 S
RODIER Peter's child 10/12/1825 S
LEVIS Ed's child 10/12/1825 S
TUCKER Samuel's child 10/14/1825 W
BURGH Mr's child 10/15/1825 S
FEARSON Wm 10/16/1825 W
TILLEY Charles's child 10/22/1825 W
HALL Brice's child 10/23/1825 W
ASHTON E's child 10/24/1825 S
CORCORAN Thomas's woman 10/28/1825 S
WATERS Mr T G 11/1/1825 M
EASTON Deb's child 11/5/1825 S
FENWICK Francis 11/9/1825 S
A colored woman at James Wharton's 11/11/1825 W
DUNLOP James's child 11/14/1825 M
LAIRD Wm's child 11/17/1825
CHESLEY Thomas (colored man)'s wife 11/24/1825 S
McCULCHEAR Mrs 11/29/1825 W
BALTZER Mrs 11/29/1825 W
BUTLER Sarah (colored woman) 12/1/1825 S
A Foundling child 12/1/1825 S
CONNELLY Thos 12/3/1825 W
CLARK Mr's child 12/3/1825 S
LEEK Mr's child 12/3/1825 S
BOWIE Miss Margaret 12/5/1825 M
HAWKINS James 12/9/1825 M
TURNER Thomas's child 12/10/1825 S
SIMMONS Mrs 12/11/1825 S

HOLTZMAN George's colored girl 12/12/1825 S
COVER George's child 12/14/1825 S
COGSWELL Joseph 12/20/1825 S
BUTLER Henny (colored woman)'s child 12/24/1825 S
MARBURY Adam (colored man)'s wife 12/24/1825 S
WATERS Jno 12/25/1825 W
MAGRUDER Samuel (PG Co) 12/25/1825 W
CARBERRY Lewis's child 12/26/1825 W
BAKER Mary 12/28/1825 S
BROWN Jane's child 12/28/1825 S
HALLER David 12/28/1825 W
LEUCAS Henry 12/29/1825 S
HODGE Robt (colored man)'s wife's daughter 12/30/1825 W
BARBER Barney 12/30/1825 S
KEACH Suckey's husband 1/2/1826 S
KINCADE James's colored child 1/2/1826 S
SHRYBROCK Mr's child 1/12/1826 S
KURTZ Daniel (colored woman) 1/16/1826 S
SPALDING Richard 1/18/1826 S
PYFER Henry's child 1/26/1826 M
TOULSON Nancy (colored woman) 1/28/1826 S
TRAVERS Chas 1/31/1826 S
ADAMS Betsey 1/31/1826 s
CHEW Robt's man 2/1/1826 S
HAWKINS Walter (colored man)'s wife 2/5/1826 S
NEVITT Mrs 2/5/1826 S
CHAPMAN David 2/8/1826 M
CARMICHAEL Mrs 2/9/1826 W
PAYNE Josias 2/9/1826 S
NALLY Mr 2/13/1826 S
BARNES John 2/13/1826 M
NEWTON Walter 2/14/1826 S
DOUGLASS Mrs 2/16/1826 W
DIXON Thomas 2/17/1826 W
WAUGH Mr's child 2/17/1826 W
ROSS Richard seaman 2/18/1826 S
CLEMENTSON Geo Senr 2/19/1826 M
MELVIN Jas 2/20/1826 W
PALMER Ann 2/21/1826 S
A Child 2/23/1826 W
FORREST Henry 2/25/1826 M
SHORTER Clem 2/27/1826 S

BARCLAY Mrs 3/6/1826 W
HYDE James 3/12/1826 W
PAYNE Isaac 3/13/1826 S
PATTEN Mrs 3/15/1826 M
COKELY Lewis (colored man) 3/16/1826 S
QUANDER Sally (colored woman) 3/17/1826 S
WIRT Sarah's daughter 3/20/1826 W
WILLIAMS Brooke's colored woman 3/20/1826 S
MORGAN William's grandchild 3/21/1826 W
LEVINE Daniel 3/24/1826 S
SEWELL Joseph's son 3/25/1826 W
WALKER Mrs 3/28/1826 S
DODGE Francis's Abe 3/28/1826 S
BAKER John W's colored man 3/30/1826 S
GUEST Job's child 4/1/1826 M
A Colored Woman 4/5/1826 S
HEDGE Cassey 4/6/1826 S
BOSWELL Benjamin Senr 4/9/1826 S
VANHORN Mrs 4/10/1826 S
SCHLEY Mrs 4/12/1826 W
BOWIE Washington 4/13/1826 M
CHEW Philip's wife (colored woman) 4/15/1826 S
HAYNES Staley 4/19/1826 W
CLARK Jane 4/20/1826 W
BRUMBLY Mrs 4/22/1826 M
MAYFIELD Benjamin 4/23/1826 W
CONNER Patrick's wife 4/24/1826 W
LEE Alfred's brother 4/26/1826 S
WIMSETT Mrs 4/28/1826 S
KURTZ Thomas 5/1/1826 W
SPARROW Mrs 5/2/1826 S
ASHTON Margaret .5/3/1826 W
ENGLISH Mary 5/3/1826 M
WILSON H G's brother 5/5/1826 W
LEACH Mrs 5/7/1826 S
BRADLEY Mr's child 5/8/1826 S
KIRK Mary 5/8/1826 M
A Colored Man 5/9/1826 S
PARSON William's child 5/9/1826 W
ADAMS Miss's child 5/12/1826 W
WALKER David's child 5/15/1826 M
A Colored Boy 5/27/1826 S

NEALE Leonard 5/28/1826 S
MACKALL Leonard's Dinah 5/30/1826 S
WILLIAMS Joseph's wife 5/2/1826 S
WENTWORTH Matthias 6/1/1826 S
THOMPSON Juliana 6/2/1826 S
CHICK Joseph's wife 6/10/1826 S
PAYNE Thomas's child 6/11/1826 W
RINGGOLD Mary 6/11/1826 M
PURPOX John (colored man) 6/15/1826 S
CLARKE William's child 6/19/1826 S
SIFFORD Mrs's child 6/22/1826 S
FLETCHER James's child 6/23/1826 S
CROW John's child 6/23/1826 W
A Child 6/25/1826 S
Harriet's child (colored) 6/26/1826 S
FROST Louisa (colored woman) 6/26/1826 S
COOKENDORFER Mrs's colored woman 6/28/1826 S
DONALDSON Thomas's wife 6/28/1826 S
THOMPSON Susanah 7/1/1826 S
CRUTTENDEN Joel's child 7/1/1826 M
PALMER John 7/3/1826 W
NACE Mary's child (colored) 7/10/1826 S
SMITH Clement's boy 7/12/1826 S
SMITH Lewis's child 7/21/1826 S
KING Andrew's child (colored) 7/23/1826 S
NICHOLLS I S's colored child 7/25/1826 S
PERLEY Mrs's child 7/26/1826 S
WEIGHTMAN Mr's child 7/28/1826 S
WEIGHTMAN Mr's child 7/31/1826 S
MCDANIEL Mr's child 7/4/1826 S
TOWNLY Charles 8/3/1826 S
KING Henry Senr 8/6/1826 M
DUFIEFF Cherubim 8/7/1826 W
COOKE Thomas 8/9/1826 M
WARD Mr's child 8/9/1826 S
KELLY Mrs 8/10/1826 S
WHITE Richard's child 8/11/1826 W
BRYANT Mr's child 8/12/1826 S
A Colored Man 8/13/1826 S
PARKER George Senr 8/14/1826 W
JACKSON Philip's child (colored) 8/14/1826 S
ROLLING William's daughter 8/15/1826 S

HUGHES Archy 8/15/1826 S
NEVINS's child 8/15/1826 S
KENT Gov.'s wife 8/15/1826 M
RAGON Basil's grandchild 8/16/1826 W
SHAW Mrs 8/17/1826 W
STULL Mrs 8/17/1826 M
AIKINS Mr's wife 8/19/1826 S
THRELKELD Mrs E 8/20/1826 M
BOSWELL Mrs 8/25/1826 S
COOKE John B 8/25/1826 M
WHITE John's child 8/25/1826 W
RIGDEN Mrs 8/26/1826 W
THRELKELD Miss E 8/28/1826 M
ABBOTT John's colored child 8/28/1826 S
PLANT Eliza's child 8/28/1826 S
HARTLOVE John's child 8/30/1826 W
FURGERSON Eleonar's mother (colored woman) 9/6/1826 S
WILLIE John 9/10/1826 S
KNOX John's wife 9/6/1826 S
BOWIE William 9/11/1826 M
WILLIAMS Mrs 9/11/1826 W
MAGILL Mrs 9/12/1826 M
PETERS Harriet (colored woman) 9/12/1826 S
ELLIS Joshua's child 9/14/1826 W
TANNER Paul 9/15/1826 S
STROMAN Mr's child 9/16/1826 S
NICHOLLSON Thomas's son 9/19/1826 W
ABBOTT Mr's colored child 9/20/1826 S
SMITH Lewis's son 9/22/1826 W
McNEAR Daniel's child 9/25/1826 S
DEMENT Richard's wife 9/25/1826 W
MORGAN Aquila's child 9/28/1826 S
CLORIVERE Joseph (priest) 9/30/1826 M
MORE Charles's daughter (colored) 10/1/1826 S
BROOKE Daphne's child (colored) 10/1/1826 S
WHALEN Michael 10/5/1826 S
GIBSON Joseph's child 10/5/1826 M
BAKER Zachariah's child 10/5/1826 W
TURBY John 10/6/1826 S
KING Adam 10/6/1826 W
RATCLIFFE Joseph's child 10/9/1826 M
BECK Mrs Dorcas 10/10/1826 M

HEADERSON Nicholas's wife 10/12/1826 S
JOHNSON Isaac 10/13/1826 S
SIMONDS Nelly's grandchild 10/13/1826 S
THOMPSON Mrs's colored girl (Seth) 10/14/1826 S
MARSH Sally's child 10/17/1826 S
PEABODY Mrs 10/21/1826 W
MORE William (colored man) 10/21/1826 S
DIMENT Richard's mother 10/23/1826 W
MILLER William 10/23/1826 S
SHORTER A (colored man) 10/25/1826 S
LAMBERT Mrs 10/26/1826 M
HENDERSON Polly 10/28/1826 S
KENNEDY Mrs 10/31/1826 M
HENDERSON Doctor's child 10/31/1826 M
BAKER John W's colored man 11/2/1826 S
NORRIS R's sister-in-law 11/3/1826 S
LYON John's nephew 11/4/1826 M
ISWELL William's child 11/7/1826 M
KENT Joseph's son 11/11/1826 M
CORCORAN John 11/15/1826 S
BUTLER Charles's child 11/16/1826 W
WILLSON Z 11/18/1826 W
SHAW L's daughter 11/19/1826 M
BAKER Mrs 11/21/1826 M
TAYLOR Sally 11/22/1826 S
McKENNY Samuel's child 11/22/1826 M
HALL F M 11/24/1826 M
COLLINS Mrs 11/24/1826 S
RIDGEWAY Mrs 11/26/1826 S
NOVEL Jane's child (colored) 11/26/1826 S
CARTWRIGHT Joseph's child 12/1/1826 S
DUNN Samuel's child 12/3/1826 W
YOUNG Adam's wife 12/3/1826 W
MOXLEY's child (colored) 12/5/1826 S
CONNER Robert's child 12/5/1826 S
CLARKSON Mrs 12/8/1826 S
CLEMENTSON George Jr 12/9/1826 W
WHITLOW J B (colored man)'s child 12/13/1826 S
LEACH Mrs 12/14/1826 S
Old Kit's grandchild 12/16/1826 S
BROWN Betty 12/20/1826 S
Susan 12/22/1826 S

PEAKE John's child 12/23/1826 S
POOLEY Mrs 12/24/1826 S
MATTHEWS Henry's child 12/27/1826 S
McPHERSON Henry's colored child 12/31/1826 S
LAIDLER Elenor 1/4/1827 M
EDWARDS Mrs 1/4/1827 W
BUTLER Dinah (colored woman) 1/7/1827 S
HUTCHINSON John S 1/7/1827 M
BRADLEY's child (colored) 1/10/1827 S
CLARKE Mrs 1/10/1827 W
MOXLEY Samuel's child 1/11/1827 S
HOSKINS John 1/13/1827 S
McGILL John 1/17/1827 M
McCANDLESS's man 1/18/1827 S
BELT Sarah 1/22/1827 M
REMICK M D 1/22/1827 S
WARNER Nicholas's daughter (colored) 1/22/1827 S
KERR William 1/23/1827 M
BEATTY John 1/23/1827 M
SHREVE Benjamin of Virginia 1/27/1827 W
PIERS Aquila's wife 1/28/1827 S
WATTS Mary's child (colored) 1/30/1827 S
SMALLWOOD Daniel's wife 1/30/1827 S
SHAW Lemuel's colored child 1/30/1827 S
WATERS John's child 1/13/1827 W
CORCORAN Mrs 2/1/1827 S
STODDART Mr 2/7/1827 W
MIX E's child 2/7/1827 W
BROOKES Mary 2/9/1827 M
BURCH Ann 2/11/1827 W
CLARK Mr 2/14/1827 S
CONNER Mrs 2/16/1827 S
ROBERTSON J P 2/18/1827 W
WILLSON Mrs Isaac 2/19/1827 W
ENGLISH Mrs 2/19/1827 M
McDONALD Mrs (colored) 2/21/1827 S
COLE Ambrose (colored) 2/24/1827 S
PEABODY John 2/26/1827 W
GOSLER Henry Senr 3/4/1827 W
BENSON L M (sailor) 3/7/1827 S
NEWTON Mrs W's child 3/10/1827 S
BAUGHMAN Mrs 3/12/1827 S

LINTHICUM O M's child 3/16/1827 M
MAGRUDER Mrs George B 3/16/1827 M
PAUL Mrs's child 3/24/1827 S
ATTWATER William C's mother-in-law 3/28/1827 W
BROWN John's child 3/28/1827 W
WATERS William (Virginia) 3/29/1827 W
SUTER Richard's grandchild 3/30/1827 S
GRAY Alfred's brother (colored man) William 4/2/1827 S
BEALL Ann 4/10/1827 M
JACKSON Benedict (colored man) 4/11/1827 S
SHERRIFF Mrs of Bladensburg 4/14/1827 W
BELT James's child 4/16/1827 M
PRIOR George (colored man) 4/16/1827 S
JONES Horatio's colored man 4/18/1827 S
LAIRD William's child 4/21/1827 M
A Colored woman at poor house 4/21/1827 S
Hercules (Clagett's colored man) 4/27/1827 S
WOLTZ Mrs 4/30/1827 W
CROWLEY Miss 5/1/1827 S
McDANIELS Mrs's child 5/1/1827 W
GODFREY Mr's mother 5/2/1827 W
COVER Mrs 5/2/1827 M
BEALL Jerry (colored man) 5/4/1827 S
MOXLEY Samuel's father 5/5/1827 W
JOHNSON Peter (colored man) 5/8/1827 S
MURPHY Mrs 5/11/1827 S
BAKER Z's child 5/17/1827 W
GROSS Thomas's child 5/21/1827 S
PAYNE Jacob 5/22/1827 W
MAY John 5/22/1827 W
PARDONSON James 5/24/1827 S
MORAN Mrs 5/25/1827 S
GROSS Thomas's child 5/28/1827 S
SIM Doctor's black boy 6/4/1827 S
BELL Rachel 6/8/1827 S
CLARK Eliza's child (colored) 6/10/1827 S
KINCADE James 6/11/1827 M
MURPHY Martha's child (colored) 6/12/1827 S
COLCLAZER Jacob's child 6/13/1827 S
REINTZEL's Charles 6/17/1827 S
KINCADE Martha 6/18/1827 M
McDANIELS Mr's child 6/19/1827 S

CLARK Eliza (colored woman) 6/26/1827 S
BALCH Mrs 6/28/1827 M
RYE Mr's child 7/3/1827 S
HENDERSON Thomas's child 7/5/1827 M
ROUNDS Martin 7/8/1827 S
ANDERSON William 7/9/1827 S
BEARD Captain's child 7/14/1827 S
BISHOP Mr's child 7/15/1827 S
SCOTT Jessie's colored child 7/21/1827 S
LEVINE William's wife (colored) 7/21/1827 S
BROWN Joel's child 7/26/1827 W
CLEMENTSON John's child 7/27/1827 W
HUTCHINS John's child 7/27/1827 S
FREELOT Mr 8/1/1827 S
WILLSON James C's child 8/1/1827 M
VANESSEN Peter's colored child 8/2/1827 S
RUTRIE William 8/2/1827 W
LELAND John 8/7/1827 W
SYLVESTER Mr's child 8/8/1827 W
MITCHELL Mr 8/10/1827 W
TAYLOR Nellie's grandchild (colored) 8/13/1827 S
PUMPHREY Lloyd's father 8/14/1827 S
PAYN John's father 8/14/1827 S
HAILE Mrs's child 8/16/1827 W
McDANIEL John's child 8/16/1827 W
WILLSON John A's colored child 8/19/1827 S
BOWLINE Joseph's wife 8/20/1827 S
GEESLING Mrs's child 8/20/1827 W
SPARROW Mr's child 8/21/1827 S
JACKSON Susan's child (colored) 8/24/1827 S
BRYANT Mr's wife 8/24/1827 S
SMITH Thomas's child (colored) 8/27/1827 S
WALKER S S's child 8/28/1827 M
GRIMES Leonard 9/1/1827 S
HARRISON Gus.'s child 9/4/1827 M
KING Andrew's wife 9/6/1827 S
LUCKETT Ig. 9/7/1827 S
HOLT Ralph 9/9/1827 W
SEWALL Mrs 9/10/1827 W
BROOKE Betsy (colored woman) 9/12/1827 S
COLE Frank (colored man) 9/13/1827 S
A drowned colored man 9/14/1827 S

MUSE Lindsay's sister (colored woman) 9/14/1827 W
BROWN Mrs Joel 9/16/1827 W
BRENT Elizabeth 9/17/1827 W
EVERET Joseph 9/18/1827 S
MAQUIRE Hugh's wife 9/21/1827 M
RIFFLE Joseph 9/22/1827 S
RATRIE William Senr 9/23/1827 W
WILLSON John 9/25/1827 S
WILLSON Mrs's colored woman 9/26/1827 S
CROW John's child 9/27/1827 W
LAW Horace 9/27/1827 S
KING J H's child 9/29/1827 M
SCOTT Mrs Horatio 10/2/1827 M
KING Ignatius's mother 10/3/1827 S
SWIFT Lieut.'s child 10/3/1827 M
CLEMENT John's child 10/7/1827 W
WHITE Josabed's wife 10/7/1827 W
BOWIE Thomas (PG County) 10/8/1827 M
HOLTZMAN Mrs George's child 10/12/1827 W
NICHOLLS Mrs Sarah 10/14/1827 M
STEELE Samuel's daughter 10/15/1827 W
SHIVELY Mrs 10/16/1827 S
EVERSFIELD Mary (colored woman) 10/17/1827 S
LEVINS Eliza's child (colored) 10/18/1827 S
CHANDLER Mrs's colored woman 10/20/1827 S
FREEMAN Miss Mary 10/23/1827 W
DEAN Felix's child 10/27/1827 S
BUTLER Charles 11/1/1827 S
CLARK Mrs's child 11/3/1827 S
KING Andrew's child 11/5/1827 S
SCOTT James's son (colored man) 11/13/1827 S
HUGHES Richard (colored man) 11/14/1827 S
KING Ignatius's wife at the foundry 11/14/1827 W
LEAR Walter 11/17/1827 S
BOWIE Humphrey 11/19/1827 M
MAUPIN Mrs 11/20/1827 S
CLARK Samuel's girl 11/22/1827 S
HARDIE Robert 11/27/1827 W
HOLSTON James 11/28/1827 S
BEALL Mrs 11/28/1827 S
Sarah 11/29/1827 S
MOXLEY Samuel's child 12/3/1827 W

OTTINGER Charles 12/6/1827 S
LINGAN George 12/9/1827 S
BRADSHAW Mrs 12/10/1827 S
BAKER J W's colored woman 12/10/1827 S
HOOBLER John 12/26/1827 S
SHIELDS Patty 1/3/1828 S
DADE Harry's child 1/3/1828 S
A Man at Tenlytown (Noveres) 1/4/1828 S
TWYFORD Smith's child 1/4/1828
WHITNEY William's father 1/8/1828 W
BRADEY Caleb's child 1/9/1828 S
NICHOLSON James 1/12/1828 W
BUTLER Electius's child (colored) 1/14/1828 S
GLASCO Sally 1/19/1828 S
WATTSON Mr 1/20/1828 M
MOXLEY Samuel's colored man 1/25/1828 S
TURNER Thomas's colored child 1/25/1828 S
SPALDING Enoch 2/2/1828 S
WEISNER Mrs 2/6/1828 S
THOMAS Anthony's father (colored) 2/8/1828 S
BEADLE A's child 2/10/1828 S
RHODES William 2/13/1828 M
ASHTON E's child 2/13/1828 S
PHILIPS Mrs 2/14/1828 S
A drowned colored man 2/19/1828 S
TURNER Thomas's John 2/19/1828 S
COLEMAN Mrs 2/23/1828 S
COVER George's colored man 2/27/1828 S
TAYLOE John 3/1/1828 S
MAFFITT William 3/4/1828 M
McCALL Catherine 3/10/1828 M
LUPTON Mrs 3/13/1828 W
FISH Francis 3/14/1828 W
BELT Humphrey 3/14/1828 S
MAURY Mrs R B 3/17/1828 M
DAVIS Gideon's child 3/17/1828 W
GRAY H N's colored girl 3/18/1828 S
BRADLEY Barbara (colored woman) 3/22/1828 S
BROWN Miss M A 3/24/1828 W
ASHTON Daniel 3/24/1828 S
McCLISH Mrs's child 3/27/1828 M
DOYLE Anna A 3/27/1828 W

COUNTEE Airy's child (colored) 4/2/1828 S
LYONS John's sister 4/3/1828 M
SHOEMAKER David Jr 4/4/1828 W
WARNER Mrs 4/10/1828 S
DICKSON John's child 4/10/1828 W
JONES John 4/11/1828 W
KNIGHT Mr 4/12/1828 S
MILBURN John 4/21/1828 S
TERRY Andrew's child (colored) 4/25/1828 S
DOVER Sandy (colored) 4/25/1828 S
DADE Elizabeth 4/27/1828 W
NICHOLLS Isaiah 5/7/1828 W
MAGUIRE Hugh 5/8/1828 M
DORSEY Lettie's child (colored) 5/11/1828 S
GANNON Peter 5/13/1828 W
HOMAN Benjamin's child 5/15/1828 M
EVANS Cadwalder's child 5/18/1828 M
ROUNDS Ezeikel (colored) (don't know him) 5/19/1828 S
DODSON Sophia (colored woman) 5/22/1828 S
JACKSON Philip's child (colored) 5/25/1828 S
WIMSETT John 5/30/1828 S
HARRISON George's child 6/?/1828 S (before 6/7/1828)
BRYANT Mary's child (colored) 6/7/1828 S
CASSIN James 6/12/1828 M
LYLES Lewis 6/17/1828 S
GOLDSMITH Jerry (colored man) 6/21/1828 S
NOWLAND Thomas's child 6/22/1828 W
CRUETT Robert's child 6/24/1828 S
NIXDORFF Tobias's colored child 6/25/1828 S
HARDEN William 6/25/1828 W
BEALL Mrs Elizabeth 6/28/1828 M
RENNER Daniel's Gilbert 6/28/1828 S
JONES Mrs's child 7/4/1828 S
SHREVES Samuel 7/5/1828 W
LOVE Thomas R's father 7/8/1828 W
GRAY Prince (colored man) 7/9/1828 S
HOLTZMAN Eli 7/10/1828 W
WRIGHT John 7/13/1828 W
DAVIS Thomas Doctor 7/13/1828 M
BROOME George 7/17/1828 W
KURTZ David's child 7/21/1828 S
PINDELL Mr 7/23/1828 S

THORNTON Sarah 7/24/1828 S
BUTLER Joseph's child (colored) 7/25/1828 S
OTT Anne 7/25/1828 M
RATCLIFFE Joseph's child 7/29/1828 M
SWANN Nathan's child 8/1/1828 W
PUMPHREY Lloyd's child 8/2/1828 W
SMITH Clement's overseer 8/2/1828 S
McPHERSON Henry's colored child 8/2/1828 S
CARSON Mrs 8/4/1828 S
HARVEY James's child 8/7/1828 S
SHECKELL Levi's child 8/8/1828 S
DOLF Mrs 8/11/1828 S
SMART John's child 8/14/1828 W
OVERTON John (colored man) 8/14/1828 S
TERRY Andrew's daughter (colored woman) 8/15/1828 S
DAWSON Mrs Thomas 8/25/1828 M
GRANT W V's child (colored) 8/27/1828 S
BUTLER Samuel's wife (colored) 8/27/1828 S
MATTHEWS Henry's child 8/27/1828 M
HEARD Mr's child 8/28/1828 S
DIXON Miss (Robert Stony's pseudo wife) 8/31/1828 S
MILES William 9/7/1828 S
BROWN Daniel's daughter 9/12/1828 W
LUCAS Bennet's daughter 9/15/1828 S
DAWSON Thomas's mother 9/16/1828 W
WILLIAMS James 9/18/1828 W
BONN James 9/24/1828 S
SOMMERS John 9/27/1828 M
COLLINS Rebecca 9/28/1828 W
ITURBIDE Miss 10/2/1828 M
SEDGWICK Harriet 10/4/1828 S
DARNALL Jacob 10/11/1828 S
JONES Mr T W 10/11/1828 M
KIRKPATRICK Mrs 10/12/1828 S
HARDY Elizabeth 10/12/1828 W
STULL John's colored child 10/12/1828 S
GRAY George's wife 10/16/1828 W
SYLVESTER Mr's child 10/16/1828 W
TAYLOE Mrs's colored boy 10/16/1828 S
DEAN Charles's colored man 10/20/1828 S
MOXLEY Samuel's colored man 10/20/1828 S
BECRAFT William's son (colored) 10/31/1828 S

RATCLIFFE Mary 11/4/1828 M
MILLER Anna Maria 11/7/1828 W
WILLIAMS Jeremiah's colored boy 11/8/1828 S
HENDERSON R H's son 11/13/1828 M
GRAY Henry's child (colored) 11/18/1828 S
REINTZEL Daniel 11/19/1828 W
CARMICHAEL Alexander 11/20/1828 S
ADAMS George A's child 11/21/1828 W
INGEL Thomas 11/24/1828 S
BALCH Elizabeth 11/26/1828 M
ENO Mrs 11/30/1828 W
REDMAN Catherine 11/30/1828 M
Libby (colored woman) 12/8/1828 S
LEACH John 12/10/1828 M
TIMS Mr 12/11/1828 W
EDMONDSON Mrs's Raphie 12/21/1828 S
WATKINS Stephen 12/25/1828 S
BRENT W L's colored woman 12/28/1828 S
KING Mrs Ignatius 1/6/1829 S
HUSLER J T 1/6/1829 S
ADAMS George A's mother 1/6/1829 W
JACKSON John's child (colored) 1/6/1829 S
BEAN Mr's sister 1/7/1829 S
SMITH Thomas's child (colored) 1/7/1829 S
SEWALL Clement 1/8/1829 W
OULD Robert's colored boy 1/8/1829 S
JONES Godfrey 1/9/1829 W
KENGLEY Lewis 1/11/1829 W
NEALE John (colored man) 1/12/1829 S
LYONS Mrs (tobacconist's mother) 1/14/1829 W
WALKER Ann 1/16/1829 S
ROBERDEAU Isaac 1/17/1829 M
A colored man near Colonel Bomford's 1/21/1829 S
MILLARD Mary's daughter 1/28/1829 S
BOUCHER Alexander 1/31/1829 S
WHITE Josabed 2/2/1829 W
NICHOLS I 2/2/1829 W
JONES James C 2/4/1829 W
CASSIN Stephen's colored woman 2/7/1829 S
WEDLOCK Samuel's child (colored) 2/10/1829 S
BRANNEN James 2/18/1829 S
PARSONS William's child 2/22/1829 W

BEAN Captain 2/27/1829 S
SEDGWICK H's child at Paget's 2/28/1829 S
George, that died at Moxley's (colored man) 3/4/1829 S
SPEAKMAN Mr's child 3/8/1829 S
CLARK Samuel's child 3/10/1829 S
NICHOLSON Thomas 3/14/1829 M
HOWARD John's wife 3/16/1829 S
HOWARD John's wife's mother 3/16/1829 S
RAY Mr, a boatman 3/17/1829 W
BALCH Hezekiah 3/18/1829 M
JAMES John's child 3/19/1829 W
SCOTT S C's child 3/24/1829 M
GRAHAM Mrs 3/27/1829 W
McDOWELL Mrs 4/1/1829 S
ROSE Mrs 4/2/1829 W
WILSON John 4/7/1829 W
SPENCER, Doctor's son that died at Holbrook's 4/8/1829 W
SCOTT James's son (Washington) 4/10/1829 S
SYMINGTON Peter's child 4/12/1829 S
PEARS Aquila 4/12/1829 S
ADAMS Isaac 4/12/1829 W
BROOKS Eliza's child 4/17/1829 S
BRUMLEY James 4/17/1829 S
A Colored man that was drowned 4/18/1829 S
TAYLOR Nelly's child (colored woman) 4/27/1829 S
HUGHES Jane 4/28/1829 M
BISHOP Richard 4/29/1829 W
BOARDMAN Mrs 4/29/1829 W
BARNES William 5/2/1829 W
HODSON Zarobable 5/3/1829 W
CROW John's child 5/8/1829 W
SCOTT James (Washington) 5/10/1829 S
RITTENHOUSE Mrs 5/10/1829 M
JACKSON Ann 5/11/1829 M
BOYD Robert's child 5/11/1829 W
NOLAND Mrs 5/13/1829 S
PERLEY Mr 5/14/1829 S
FENWICK Mrs 5/18/1829 W
DODGE Francis's colored man 5/22/1829 S
MAYHUE Jonathan 5/22/1829 S
SPALDING Mr 5/24/1829 S
DUVALL R 5/25/1829 S

STROMAN Mrs's child 5/26/1829 S
A drowned man 5/28/1829 S
DAUGHTY Peter 6/11/1829 S
NICHOLSON George 6/13/1829 S
CARTER Jacob's child 6/15/1829 W
HOWARD Mr's child 6/16/1829 S
A man that died at Thomson Hacy 6/20/1829 S
BATT Mrs 6/26/1829 S
KING James's child 6/28/1829 S
LOUNDS Mrs 7/7/1829 M
GUMBLE Mary 7/8/1829 S
DAVIDSON John (colored man) 7/8/1829 S
TYLER John 7/11/1829 S
Old Luke's wife (colored woman) 7/13/1829 S
JENKINS Nancy 7/13/1829 S
STEWART Mary 7/14/1829 S
BEVAN Jerome's child 7/15/1829 W
FREEMAN John D's woman 7/16/1829 S
BARNES George's wife (colored woman) 7/17/1829 S
BARRETT William D 7/19/1829 M
LANHAM Mr's child 7/21/1829 S
REGEN Henry's child 7/21/1829 W
COKLEY Aaron's child (colored man) 7/23/1829 S
MINIGHIN Robert 7/23/1829 S
JAY Julia's child (colored woman) 7/26/1829 S
DANDRIDGE William's child (colored man) 7/26/1829 S
COKLEY Hanson (colored man)'s child 7/26/1829 S
LUCAS John's child 8/1/1829 S
HIGDEN Mrs 8/6/1829 S
TABLER John's child 8/6/1829 W
VANDERHOOF Daniel 8/10/1829 W
NOLAND Patrick 8/10/1829 S
WILLIAM Lieut.'s child 8/10/1829 M
SNIDER Mr's grandchild 8/12/1829 S
ENGLISH David's colored child 8/12/1829 S
HAUSE Alfred 8/10/1829 S
HYDE Mrs 8/10/1829 W
ROLLINGS William's child 8/13/1829 S
GODDART Thomas's child 8/13/1829 W
REED James 8/14/1829 W
SHAW Lemuel's colored child 8/17/1829 S
NICHOLSON Mrs's child 8/20/1829 W

SAMSON James 8/21/1829 S
DAVIDSON Lieut's child 8/24/1829 M
LANG William's child 8/25/1829 W
NICHOLSON Samuel's child 8/25/1829 S
SEMMES James 8/26/1829 W
PUMPHREY Lloyd's child 8/27/1829 W
BRYANT Mr's child 8/28/1829 S
LANHAM Aquila 8/28/1829 M
LANHAM Eliza 8/28/1829 M
LANHAM Mareia 8/29/1829 M
LEVERET Mr 8/29/1829 W
LINNEY (colored woman) 8/29/1829 S
HARBAUGH B's child 8/30/1829 S
RYAN Patrick 8/31/1829 S
FEW Mrs 9/3/1829 W
HURDUL John 9/3/1829 S
POWER Frederick's child 9/3/1829 S
BURNS Patrick 9/3/1829 M
BRYANT Mr's child 9/4/1829 S
HOLLY Ruben (colored man) 9/4/1829 S
FEELING Steven's child 9/4/1829 S
KEMP Mr's child 9/4/1829 S
ADAM Mrs's child 9/6/1829 S
SMITH Josias's sister's child (colored woman) 9/6/1829 S
ABBOTT John's colored child 9/6/1829 S
DAILY George 9/7/1829 S
CONNER William's father 9/7/1829 S
GANNON Mrs 9/10/1829 W
BRADY Michael 9/10/1829 S
RUSSELL Bill's child 9/13/1829 S
GANNON Michael's child 9/15/1829 W
DONNOLSON John's son 9/18/1829 W
JONES Edward 9/18/1829 M
MORRIS Mrs 9/20/1829 S
JONES Mrs's child 9/20/1829 S
ROBERTSON Lamkin's child 9/20/1829 S
A colored child at Letty Springs 9/21/1829 S
CAMPBELL Mashack's child 9/21/1829 S
SNYDER Mr's daughter 9/25/1829 S
O'DONNALL Hugh's mother-in-law 9/30/1829 S
RITCHIE Mrs 10/1/1829 W
PAGET William's child 10/1/1829 S

HOLTZMAN George's child 10/3/1829 M
FRUTER Beckey 10/9/1829 S
STULL J J's colored woman 10/9/1829 S
RAGON Richard's wife's mother 10/11/1829 S
COOPER Ann's child (colored woman) 10/13/1829 S
NEAL James 10/15/1829 S
FENDLE Miss at Dr Kent's 10/20/1829 M
RUNNALDS Mr 10/19/1829 S
BRYANT Dennis 10/26/1829 S
RAGON Bazil 10/28/1829 W
REACH William's child at the foundry 10/28/1829 S
John that died at Mrs Folio 11/2/1829 S
WHITLAW John's child (colored man) 11/2/1829 S
BLACK Mr's child 11/5/1829 S
MANTIGUA Capt. 11/6/1829 S
CLARK Mrs's colored child 11/6/1829 S
GREEN Cely (colored woman) 11/11/1829 S
HOLTZMAN John's child 11/11/1829 W
KENDRICK Benjamin 11/15/1829 S
BURNET C A (colored man) 11/16/1829 S
DUGGALL Daniel's child 11/18/1829 S
McELAVNAY Thomas 11/21/1829 S
STULL J J's colored child 11/22/1829 S
MOXLEY Horatia 11/22/1829 W
MAGRUDER Lewes 11/23/1829 S
KERLY William 11/27/1829 S
THOMAS Mrs 11/29/1829 W
Old Jenney 11/29/1829 S
GORDEN Mr's colored child 12/4/1829 S
RITTER Peter's colored child 12/4/1829 S
FREEMAN Mr's child 12/5/1829 S
JASON Mrs 12/5/1829 S
CARROLL Cassey's mother 12/5/1829 S
WASHBURN Daniel 12/6/1829 W
CONNELY Michael 12/12/1829 S
SPRIGG Richard 12/12/1829 S
FRYE Mrs 12/12/1829 W
HAMBLETON Rody (colored man) 12/20/1829 S
DAWSON Robert's child 12/20/1829 S
KNOX Mr 12/26/1829 S
NORMAN Patrick's child (colored man) 12/24/1829 S
THOMSON Rachel 12/29/1829 W

ADAMS Nancy 1/4/1830 S
BROWN Betsey (colored woman) 1/4/1830 S
PUMPHREY Lloyd's child 1/7/1830 S
FRENCH John (colored man) 1/8/1830 S
TOOLEY Thomas 1/9/1830 S
BUTLER Nace (colored man) 1/14/1830 S
MASON Ann (colored woman) 1/15/1830 S
FRYE Mr's child 1/15/1830 S
WILLIAMS Mr's child 1/16/1830 S
RUSSELL Judson's brother 1/18/1830 S
EVERETT Mrs's child 1/20/1830 S
CONNER William's child 1/21/1830 W
DONOVER Michael 1/21/1830 S
FANAGAN John 1/23/1830 S
BAKER John W's colored man 1/27/1830 S
HENDERSON John D 1/27/1830 W
SMITH David 1/29/1830 S
DAVIS's child (colored) 1/29/1830 S
MICKUM William 1/29/1830 S
CORCORAN Thomas Senr 1/29/1830 M
GREENTREE Matthew 1/29/1830 M
RENNER Daniel 1/30/1830 M
GANNON James 1/31/1830 W
NICHOLSON Mrs 2/1/1830 M
HAWKINS Bill (colored man) 2/3/1830 S
BROTHERTON John's child 2/4/1830 W
COLE Horatio's wife 2/5/1830 S
BARRY Robert's child 2/6/1830 W
LOVE Mr 2/7/1830 S
CALDER Elizabeth 2/8/1830 M
JARVIS John 2/9/1830 S
CASSIN Mrs's colored woman 2/9/1830 S
BAUKMAN's child 2/10/1830 S
HACKLEY Nancy's child 2/15/1830 S
MURDOCK John 2/17/1830 W
TILLEY Henry W's child 2/19/1830 M
TUCKER Enoch's child 2/19/1830 M
McGINNIS Mrs 2/20/1830 S
A drowned man 2/24/1830 S
POWELL Mrs 2/25/1830 S
FREEMAN Nace's daughter 2/25/1830 S
POWERS Edward 2/26/1830 S

HUBBARD Dyer's daughter 2/27/1830 S
OSBOURN Richard's child 2/27/1830 M
O'NEALE Mrs 3/1/1830 W
FRENCH Mariamne's colored man 3/1/1830 S
HALL Thomas 3/3/1830 S
CLARK Daniel's colored man 3/3/1830 S
WALKER Edward's child 3/3/1830 S
SOUTHERON Susannah's woman 3/3/1830 S
ADDISON Walter D's son Francis 3/5/1830 M
KROUSE Everard's child 3/10/1830 W
WILBERTON Hiram 3/13/1830 S
SHORTER Philip's child 3/14/1830 S
GRAHAM William (colored man) 3/15/1830 S
SULLIVAN John 3/15/1830 S
BOYE Herman 3/21/1830 M
MITCHELL Mrs 3/22/1830 W
KING Ignatius's father 3/22/1830 S
CARROLL Roger 3/22/1830 S
LAY Richard's son 3/25/1830 W
BROWN Statia 3/26/1830 S
WOODWARD Thomas's child 3/26/1830 M
SMALLWOOD Lewis (colored man) 3/27/1830 S
PERRY Mrs's child 3/27/1830 S
TURNER Thomas's child 4/1/1830 M
McDONALD William (colored man) 4/2/1830 S
LEUCAS John's wife 4/3/1830 S
CAMPBELL Mr 4/4/1830 S
A drowned man 4/4/1830 S
LINKINS Henry's child 4/5/1830 S
WOODWARD Thomas's child 4/5/1830 M
JOHNS Richard 4/5/1830 M
PEARCE Ignatius's child 4/5/1830 S
DALAWAY Capt's son 4/5/1830 S
TURNER Thomas's colored child 4/5/1830 S
BAKER John W's colored man 4/6/1830 S
ESSEX James F's mother 4/9/1830 M
HARROT Leonard (colored man) 4/13/1830 S
SHEAKMAN Mr's child 4/13/1830 S
ADAM William's wife 4/15/1830 S
TRAVERS Nicholas's child 4/18/1830 W
TOWNLEY James's child 4/19/1830 M
MULLIN John's child 4/21/1830 S

FAHE Mrs 4/22/1830 W
A Man at Colburn's 4/22/1830 S
WITHERS E D's colored woman 4/25/1830 S
A Child at Mrs Simmons 4/27/1830 S
McGENTISS William 4/28/1830 S
TURNER Nathan (colored man) 4/29/1830
McCHESNEY David's child 5/1/1830 M
SIMMONS Mrs's grandchild 5/1/1830 S
FREEMAN Mrs 5/3/1830 W
PLATER Thomas 5/3/1830 M
FREEMAN Nace's child (colored) 5/4/1830 S
PATTERSON Edgar's daughter 5/5/1830 M
SHAAFF Mrs's colored child 5/9/1830 S
DUNLOP R P's colored child 5/9/1830 S
BRONAUGH William's child 5/9/1830 W
REVEL James 5/12/1830 S
BUSSARD Daniel 5/14/1830 M
HILTEN Thomas's son 5/21/1830 M
MITCHELL Judson's child 5/21/1830 W
FOWLER Mrs 5/21/1830 S
GETTY Robert's child 5/21/1830 S
FELSON Jane (colored woman) 5/22/1830 S
FRENCH's Isaac's twin 5/27/1830 S
Sarah (orphan child) 5/29/1830 S
LANHAM Marcia's colored woman 5/29/1830 S
McCARTHY Mr's child 6/1/1830 S
BUCHANAN John 6/1/1830 W
O'DONOGHUE Timothy's child 6/2/1830 W
TRAVERS Sarah's colored child 6/5/1830 S
RYAN Patrick's child 6/5/1830 S
HUDSON Mr's child 6/6/1830 S
GERRY James's child 6/9/1830 S
BRUSH Mr 6/11/1830 W
HIGDON Joseph 6/13/1830 S
CASSIN Mrs 6/15/1830 M
ROBERTSON H B's child 6/18/1830 W
STULL John J's child 6/20/1830 M
WARD George 6/20/1830 W
CROW John's child 6/20/1830 W
SWEENEY George's child 6/20/1830 S
Mary Ann, a colored woman at R Hodge's 6/20/1830 S
O'DONOGHUE Timothy 6/25/1830 W

PARKER Thomas's father 6/26/1830 W
McMAHON Roger 6/26/1830 S
Jacob's child 6/27/1830 S
CONNELLY Bridget 7/1/1830 W
ROBERTSON John's daughter 7/2/1830 W
McMULLINS Patrick 7/3/1830 S
COLE Polly's husband 7/3/1830 S
FLEET Thomas's child (colored) 7/7/1830 W
WINEMILLER Mrs 7/12/1830 W
COLLINS Nancy 7/14/1830 S
CROSSEN Mrs 7/14/1830 S
HOOPER Sally 7/17/1830 S
O'DONOGHUE John 7/17/1830 S
CONNELL William 7/18/1830 S
REINTZEL Samuel's child 7/18/1830 W
KAHOE Patrick 7/20/1830 S
RIESE Mr's child 7/20/1830 S
HOLAHAN Andrew 7/21/1830 S
ROBINSON Mr 7/21/1830 S
ROACH James 7/21/1830 S
MURRAY Michael 7/21/1830 S
SCOTT Mrs's child 7/21/1830 S
RYAN Richard's child 7/21/1830 S
HORROGON John 7/22/1830 S
VALLY Mr 7/22/1830 W
SHIPLEY Mrs's daughter 7/22/1830 S
SHAHAN Mr 7/23/1830 S
MULLIGAN Thomas 7/23/1830 S
GRADY John 7/23/1830 S
COLFER Andrew 7/23/1830 S
THACKER James's child 7/23/1830 W
MATTHEWS Allen's child (colored) 7/23/1830 S
SCOTT Jessee 7/23/1830 M
HAMILTON Robert 7/24/1830 S
DAVIS Gideon's child 7/24/1830 W
PROCTOR Polly (colored woman) 7/25/1830 S
FAGAN Daniel 7/25/1830 W
CURDY Michael 7/26/1830 S
A Man at Foy's 7/26/1830 S
HART Thomas 7/26/1830 S
BROWN Gus's colored man 7/26/1830 S
Richard, blacksmith 7/26/1830 S

KLEIBER Mrs 7/26/1830 W
MAHANEY Matthew 7/27/1830 W
MANKIN Henry 7/27/1830 S
SKIDMORE George 7/27/1830 S
BIAS Cook 7/27/1830 S
WEDLOCK Sam's child, colored 7/27/1830 S
DAVIS Augustus's child 7/27/1830 S
FENDLE Michael's child 7/27/1830 S
MALADY Thomas 7/27/1830 S
KIRBY Michael 7/27/1830 S
BAKER Zach's colored woman 7/28/1830 S
SUPPLE Pat 7/29/1830 S
LEVIS Edward's child 7/30/1830 W
HAW Mrs 8/1/1830 M
SIMPSON Sam (colored man) 8/4/1830 S
DOUGHERTY Mary 8/5/1830 W
COX John's colored child 8/5/1830 S
RENNER Christian's child 8/6/1830 S
GIBSON Charles 8/6/1830 S
GRAHAM George 8/9/1830 M
THOMPSON William 8/9/1830 M
WHARTON James 8/10/1830 W
LINKINS James 8/10/1830 W
COSTELAN James 8/10/1830 S
HARRIS John's child 8/10/1830 W
CLARKE William's child 8/12/1830 S
MOXLEY Samuel's colored child 8/14/1830 S
MAGRUDER Thomas 8/15/1830 M
MANTZ Isaac 8/15/1830 W
LYNCH Michael 8/16/1830 S
ROSS Richard's nephew 8/16/1830 M
SHANLEY Patrick 8/17/1830 S
HUSLER Sarah 8/17/1830 S
DUFFY Matthew's mother 8/19/1830 W
CAIRNS Stephen 8/19/1830 S
WILKINS Mr 8/19/1830 S
A Child 8/19/1830 S
BOWIE Mrs John 8/20/1830 M
SCOTT Mr William A's wife 8/20/1830 W
LONG Margaret 8/20/1830 S
KERWAN Richard 8/22/1830 S
GEESLIN Mr's daughter 8/22/1830 W

A Child 8/22/1830 S
MULLIN Mr's child 8/23/1830 S
MUDD Bennett 8/24/1830 S
CURRAN Nicholas's child 8/25/1830 S
CORCORAN Michael 8/27/1830 S
MORGAN John's child 8/27/1830 W
CHANNY Jeremiah 8/28/1830 S
SPARROW John 8/31/1830 W
THRELKELD John 8/31/1830 M
MASON Joseph's child (colored) 9/1/1830 S
MURPHY Charles's child 9/3/1830 S
DORIS Bernard 9/3/1830 S
HURLEY Morris 9/4/1830 S
GALVIN Mrs 9/4/1830 S
HARTNES Daniel's child 9/5/1830 S
EASTON William 9/5/1830 S
CREALIN Daniel 9/7/1830 S
McCARTY John 9/7/1830 S
CORNWALL John B's child 9/7/1830 W
PENDELL Mrs's child 9/8/1830 S
CLARK John D's child 9/8/1830 M
John ----- 9/8/1830 S
WOODS Mr's child 9/8/1830 S
CLAGGETT Mrs 9/8/1830 M
DEAKINS Miss 9/11/1830 M
RILEY Joseph 9/11/1830 S
FLEET Wash 9/12/1830 S
BLADEN A D's child 9/12/1830 W
ADDISON Henry's colored child 9/12/1830 S
DRAKE John 9/14/1830 S
DELANY Matthew's sister 9/14/1830 W
BAKER John W's colored boy 9/16/1830 S
JONES R 9/16/1830 S
WELCH David 9/16/1830 S
NIXDORFF Mrs 9/16/1830 M
FLINN Matthew 9/16/1830 S
CROSS Colonel Joseph 9/17/1830 M
GRAY John B's child 9/18/1830 W
BUSEY Samuel 9/18/1830 W
MAHORNEY Daniel 9/18/1830 S
THOMAS Richard's wife 9/21/1830 S
A Man at Murphy's 9/21/1830 S

PAGE George 9/21/1830 S
GATES John 9/25/1830 S
NICHOLLS I S's child 9/26/1830 S
HIGGINS Thomas 9/27/1830 S
FOWLER Thomas 9/28/1830 S
WARDELL S's sister's child 9/28/1830 S
DOUGHERTY Charles 9/29/1830 W
ORR Mrs 9/29/1830 W
DALEY Thomas 10/2/1830 S
WARREN Benjamin 10/2/1830 S
WELCH Michael 10/2/1830 S
WOODS Charles's wife 10/3/1830 W
FOWLER Mrs's child 10/3/1830 S
DUNAVEN John 10/4/1830 S
DUNBAR (colored man) 10/4/1830 S
KELLY Mr's child 10/5/1830 S
SHOEMAKER George's child 10/5/1830 W
SNOWDEN Mrs 10/6/1830 W
NELSON Mrs William 10/6/1830 W
PAYNE Jacob's daughter 10/7/1830 W
LIGHTFOOT Mrs 10/7/1830 S
ANGEL Mrs's child 10/7/1830 S
ALLEN Dennis 10/8/1830 W
HARVEY James's colored man 10/8/1830 S
BALL Mrs 10/8/1830 S
HICKEY John 10/8/1830 S
DUN Ed 10/8/1830 S
CRUTTENDEN Joel's colored woman 10/10/1830 S
KENNY Patrick 10/10/1830 S
MURPHY Daniel 10/10/1830 S
HOLLY Drady (colored woman) 10/12/1830 S
TENNESON I's colored man 10/16/1830 S
A crazy man 10/16/1830 S
BAKER Z's colored man 10/16/1830 S
SOUTHALL Daniel 10/16/1830 M
CRONEY Francis 10/17/1830 S
KIRBY Charles 10/19/1830 S
SEWALL Mrs (Virginia) 10/21/1830 W
WITHERS E D's child 10/21/1830 S
STEVENSON Mrs' daughter 10/21/1830 S
McCARTY John 10/22/1830 S
PERRY Benjamin's child 10/25/1830 S

SHAY John 10/26/1830 S
A Man found in street 10/27/1830 S
A Child 10/28/1830 S
WARREN William 10/29/1830 S
TURVEY William 11/2/1830 S
HOMILLER Michael 11/2/1830 W
GLISSON William 11/3/1830 S
DIGGES Mr Nelson 11/6/1830 S
ROBERTS Henry 11/7/1830 W
DEAKINS Sarah A 11/7/1830 S
MALONEY Mrs 11/7/1830 S
WILLSON Mrs E 11/8/1830 S
RIND Mrs Samuel 11/9/1830 M
CRAWFORD Sarah's colored woman 11/10/1830 S
ROBINSON James 11/11/1830 S
McDONOUGH Charles 11/14/1830 S
BUTLER Mrs's child 11/14/1830 S
PORTER Dorey 11/18/1830 S
BUTLER Mrs's child 11/24/1830 S
COLTER Patrick 11/24/1830 S
CONWAY Owen 11/25/1830 S
WILLIAMS Mrs's child 11/25/1830 W
CORCORAN John's child 11/25/1830 S
EASTON William 11/29/1830 W
KUHN Joseph L's child 11/30/1830 M
TURNER Dennis 11/30/1830 S
HENNEGER John 12/2/1830 S
CRAMPHIN Thomas 12/3/1830 M
CRAWFORD Mrs's colored man George 12/4/1830 S
MURPHY John 12/4/1830 S
KIRK A M 12/9/1830 S
FITZ Thomas's child 12/9/1830 S
WHELAN William 12/11/1830 S
KUHN Mrs Catherine 12/12/1830 M
RABBIT Thomas's child 12/13/1830 W
SHANAHAN Timothy 12/13/1830 S
BUTLER Mrs 12/17/1830 S
DONNEDY Dennis 12/17/1830 S
DAVIS Mr 12/18/1830 S
BENDER Mrs 12/18/1830 S
JACKSON Mr's child 12/18/1830 S
BELT Mrs 12/19/1830 W

WELLS Richard's child 12/19/1830 S
ADAMS Thomas Jr 12/20/1830 S
KAVANAUGH Andrew 12/20/1830 S
WOOD Basil's mother 12/24/1830 S
SHAW Charles T 12/26/1830 W
TOODY Michael 12/27/1830 S
NELSON Thomas 12/29/1830 W
HAYES Peter 12/29/1830 S
SMITH Robert 12/30/1830 M
GODDARD John B 1/1/1831 M
HUNT Daniel (colored man) 1/1/1831 S
NORMAN William (colored man) 1/1/1831 S
JONES Mrs 1/5/1831 S
A Child at Poor House 1/8/1831 S
WIDDOWS Isaac 1/9/1831 S
SMITH Thomas 1/11/1831 S
PLATOR (colored man) 1/12/1831 S
NUGENT Eli (colored man)'s child 1/15/1831 S
CUSTARD Jacob's child 1/16/1831 S
ROBERTSON Mary 1/17/1831 W
QUEEN Samuel 1/18/1831 W
MACOMB Alexander Senr 1/20/1831 M
GALLAGHER Mrs's child 1/20/1831 S
GANTT Miss 1/22/1831 M
CRAWFORD Mrs's mother 1/23/1831 M
BOOTES Samuel's grandchild 1/24/1831 M
DRUMMOND Cornelius's child 2/4/1831 S
McKIMM John 2/6/1831 S
SCOTT Mrs's colored child 2/9/1831 S
REED William (colored man) 2/9/1831 S
CLARK Samuel's child 2/12/1831 W
CURRANT Peter's wife 2/12/1831 S
GROSS Francis's child 2/15/1831 W
LONG Madison's wife 2/15/1831 S
CLEMENTS Bennet's son 2/16/1831 W
SIMMONS Robert 2/17/1831 S
PRATER Mrs 2/22/1831 S
A Man at Poor House 2/22/1831 S
REMMINGTON J A 2/22/1831 W
WARFIELD Doctor's Mordecai 2/27/1831 S
James at Poor House 2/28/1831 S
WALLACE Margarett 2/28/1831 M

GODY William 3/13/1831 S
NICOLLS I S's child 3/16/1831 M
LIBBY William 3/17/1831 W
OLIVER Mrs 3/20/1831 W
A Man at Poor House 3/25/1831 S
SCOTT Mrs J's colored child 3/26/1831 S
SCOTT Allen's colored child 3/27/1831 S
A Man at Poor House 3/29/1831 S
SMITH Josias's sister's child 4/2/1831 S
DOONAN Michael 4/4/1831 S
JACKSON Samuel 4/6/1831 S
FEARSON J N's child 4/11/1831 S
CROPLEY Samuel's child 4/13/1831 W
ADDISON Henry's colored woman 4/14/1831 S
HAYDEN Miss 4/14/1831 S
COATS Mrs's colored girl 4/16/1831 S
THOMPSON James's colored girl 4/16/1831 S
WELSH Hugh 4/17/1831 S
MORSELL Mrs J S 4/19/1831 M
SCOTT Sabrett E's child 4/20/1831 M
MARCY Thomas's colored woman 4/20/1831 S
NEVINS Mr 4/22/1831 W
WILLIAMS Mrs's child 4/24/1831 S
WHITE John's child 4/24/1831 W
BRYANT William's child 4/24/1831 S
LATIMER Marcus 4/26/1831 W
HOLLY Reuben (colored man) 4/27/1831 S
KNOWLES Mrs 4/27/1831 W
DAVIS Richard's son 4/28/1831 M
WHITE John's child 5/1/1831 W
DANNELLS A 5/3/1831 S
LITTLEJOHN A S's child 5/6/1831 W
EDELIN Matilda's child 5/7/1831 S
AVERY Joseph 5/8/1831 W
WOODWARD Sedley's child 5/10/1831 W
RAGAN Ed 5/16/1831 S
CLARK Sophia (colored woman) 5/16/1831 S
KING John A's colored man 5/20/1831 S
JACKSON Joseph 5/22/1831 W
A Colored Child 5/26/1831 S
LAW John 5/30/1831 S
MACOMB 6/5/1831 M

ADDISON Mr's John 6/9/1831 S
POST Peter L 6/17/1831 S
CHEW Samuel's daughter 6/18/1831 M
DONALDSON William's child 6/20/1831 S
GODDARD Thomas's child 6/25/1831 W
BROONS Mrs's Ned 6/25/1831 S
RITCHIE John 6/27/1831 M
COLEMAN Ann's child 6/28/1831 S
FREEMAN John D's William 6/28/1831 S
DAWSON Robert's child 6/29/1831 S
WATKINS W W's child 6/30/1831 W
COLE L 6/30/1831 S
ARDREY John 6/22/1831 S
STAUNTON Richard's child Alexander 7/1/1831 M
RENNER John's child 7/4/1831 S
SHAAFF Mrs's colored child 7/6/1831 S
WILLIAMS Charles (colored man)'s child 7/7/1831 S
ALLEN Mrs 7/7/1831 S
ROBERTSON Kitty (colored woman)'s sister 7/10/1831 S
WITHERS E D's colored man 7/10/1831 S
CLARK John D's child 7/12/1831 M
HUTCHINS F's child 7/12/1831 S
WHELAN Mr's mother-in-law 7/12/1831 S
SIM Mrs Thomas 7/13/1831 M
BURK Thomas 7/14/1831 S
GRIMES Mr's child 7/14/1831 S
RENNELLS Mrs's child 7/17/1831 S
WALLER William's child 7/18/1831 S
GRAVES Mr's child 7/20/1831 S
GAITHER George R's child 7/20/1831 M
BARBER J 7/26/1831 W
COX John's colored child 7/26/1831 S
DAVIS Samuel (colored man)'s brother 7/27/1831 S
BROWN John 7/28/1831 S
SKIDMORE Jared's wife 7/28/1831 S
Ben (colored man) 7/29/1831 S
HEWS Patrick 7/29/1831 S
BALL Mrs of Virginia 7/30/1831 S
POWERS Frederick's child 7/30/1831 W
WILLIAMS Nace (colored man)'s child 7/30/1831 S
ATKINSON Mrs's daughter 7/31/1831 M
A Name Unknown at Poor House 8/1/1831 S

HARRISON Mrs C C 8/1/1831 M
NEWTON Mrs's child 8/2/1831 S
GANTT John's colored man 8/5/1831 S
NEWTON John's child 8/6/1831 S
McNERHENNY Mrs 8/7/1831 S
YOUNG Benjamin's child 8/7/1831 M
PHELAN Stephen's child 8/9/1831 S
THOMAS Lewis (colored man)'s child 8/10/1831 S
ELLIOTT Mrs Statira 8/11/1831 W
MASON John Junr's child 8/14/1831 M
CHASE -------- 8/14/1831 S
JONES Thomas's child 8/16/1831 S
WHITNEY -------'s child 8/16/1831 S
CARTER Jacob's child 8/16/1831 W
BEALL Harriette 8/18/1831 W
MINOR George (Wm Minor's son) 8/18/1831 M
MARCY Thomas 8/19/1831 W
JENNIFER Mr 8/20/1831 M
RAIN Lawrence 8/23/1831 S
WOLTZ Henry 8/23/1831 W
ELGIN Hamilton 8/23/1831 W
HAMMET J's child 8/24/1831 S
CARTER Jacob's child 8/24/1831 W
DIFFENBAUGH John M 8/24/1831 W
NELSON Nancy 8/26/1831 S
HUTCHIN Bennet's child 8/26/1831 S
HERBERT Charity's child (colored) 8/26/1831 S
DONALDSON John's child 8/27/1831 W
MORGAN John's child 8/27/1831 W
MORGAN John's child 8/28/1831 W
ROBERTSON Henry B's child 8/29/1831 W
WILLIAMS Rosanna (colored woman)'s child 8/29/1831 S
MOODY ------- 8/30/1831 S
O'DONOGHUE Dennis's child 8/31/1831 W
TYLER Minty 9/1/1831 S
MATTHEWS Rezin (colored man)'s child 9/3/1831 S
WOODWARD Sedley's son 9/3/1831 W
CLEMENTS John's child 9/4/1831 W
ROBERTSON William B 9/5/1831 W
OGLE Horatio 9/5/1831 S
SIMPSON Mrs 9/5/1831 W
WEAVER Michael's child 9/8/1831 S

ERRINGSHAW Thomas 9/10/1831 W
MYER Franklin S's child 9/10/1831 M
BAYLISS Collin's father 9/12/1831 S
BAYLISS Collin's mother 9/12/1831 S
FRENCH Mariamne's colored man 9/12/1831 S
ADDISON Henry's child 9/12/1831 M
HALL William 9/12/1831 W
ELIASON Miss Maria 9/13/1831 M
WILLIAMS Mrs Philip 9/14/1831 M
SIMMONS Elizabeth 9/14/1831 S
WHITNEY William's mother 9/14/1831 W
PORTER William's sister 9/15/1831 S
LOUD Mrs 9/17/1831 S
ROBERTSON Henry 9/17/1831 M
RIDGWAY John F's child 9/18/1831 W
GRIMES Helen (colored woman) 9/18/1831 S
LAY Richard Senr 9/20/1831 M
PARIE Sarah 9/21/1831 S
KIRK Mrs's colored boy 9/21/1831 S
PIERCE Ignatius 9/22/1831 S
MOUNTZ John's colored woman 9/23/1831 S
SUTER Ann 9/24/1831 M
HAW John's colored man 9/24/1831 S
LACY John's child 9/24/1831 S
HAWKINS Milly (colored woman) 9/24/1831 S
ROSS Richard 9/27/1831 M
ROBERTSON Ann's child 9/30/1831 W
THOMPSON Captain John 10/1/1831 M
RITTER Peter's colored child 10/1/1831 S
FOWLER Thomas 10/2/1831 S
HAYDEN Mrs's daughter 10/3/1831 S
SHECKELLS Thomas 10/3/1831 W
HARBAUGH Mr's child 10/4/1831 S
PAYNE John 10/4/1831 S
WILLIAMS George 10/4/1831 S
PLANTS Eliza's child 10/5/1831 S
FETTERS Peter 10/5/1831 M
EDES W H's child 10/7/1831 S
HARVEY James's child 10/8/1831 S
HUTCHENS Susan's child 10/9/1831 W
CORNWALL John B's child 10/9/1831 W
WOODS Joseph's child 10/10/1831 S

SAMON John 10/11/1831 S
DONALDSON William's child 10/11/1831 S
MORGAN John's child 10/19/1831 S
JOHNSON Matthew's son 10/21/1831 S
McMANNERS Ellen's child 10/22/1831 S
BROWN John's child 10/22/1831 S
BEATTY Edmond 10/23/1831 W
ROBERTSON George 10/23/1831 W
DONALDSON William's son 10/25/1831 S
COOPER Lieutenant's child 10/25/1831 M
BOWIE Walter B 10/23/1831 M
KING Andrew's child 10/27/1831 S
FORD Lewis (colored man)'s child 10/28/1831 S
McILHANEY Mr's child 10/28/1831 W
LINAHAN John 10/29/1831 S
FORD Lewis (colored man)'s child 11/2/1831 S
SHECKELLS Mrs 11/6/1831 S
ABBOTT John's colored boy 11/8/1831 S
Sister Charity, a nun 11/8/1831 S
WATSON Mrs Jane 11/9/1831 W
GRIMES Thomas's child 11/11/1831 S
HARRIS Peter (colored man) 11/13/1831 S
HILLARY N D 11/28/1831 S
TURNER Billy (colored man)'s wife 12/1/1831 S
JACKSON ------ 12/2/1831 W
COX John's Harry 12/8/1831 S
DICKSON James 12/10/1831 S
GOOD William's niece 12/10/1831 M
THOMAS Henry's child 12/11/1831 S
SMITH Doctor Clement 12/12/1831 M
THOMAS Lewis (colored man)'s grandchild 12/13/1831 S
JOHNSON Richard 12/14/1831 S
EDDS John 12/14/1831 M
JOHNS Mrs Mary P 12/16/1831 W
HARVEY James's child 12/16/1831 S
BUTLER Abram (colored man) 12/16/1831 S
STEVENSON Mrs 12/17/1831 W
BROWN John's child 12/17/1831 M
ORME Jeremiah's child 12/19/1831 W
SMITH Mrs's child 12/21/1831 S
GORDON Mrs 12/23/1831 S
MURDOCK Mrs 12/25/1831 W

SMITH Mrs 12/25/1831 S
BUTLER John (colored man) 12/26/1831 S
McPHERSON Daniel 12/27/1831 W
WINTER Mary C 12/30/1831 M
WILLIAMS James (colored man)'s son 12/30/1831 S
COLLINS George 12/30/1831 S
SUTER Alexander's daughter 1/3/1832 W
BARNES Alexander (colored man) 1/5/1832 S
RICHARDSON Jessee (colored man) 1/5/1832 S
COLLINS Edward's child 1/6/1832 S
HOLT John R 1/7/1832 M
LINKINS Mrs Henry 1/8/1832 W
BRONAUGH William's child 1/9/1832 W
KING Mrs Charles 1/14/1832 M
FREEMAN Jack 1/16/1832 S
CROW John's child 1/16/1832 W
HEBRON Andrew (colored man)'s child 1/16/1832 S
HANSON Mr 1/22/1832 W
WOOLLAND Mrs 1/24/1832 S
Minty 1/26/1832 S
LINTHICUM O M's child 1/30/1832 W
LINKINS Henry 2/3/1832 W
COVER George's brother 2/4/1832 S
GOODRICK William's mother 2/5/1832 S
RIFFLE G 2/7/1832 S
FLORIS Mrs 2/14/1832 W
HOLTZMAN Thomas's child 2/27/1832 W
HOLLIDAY William's wife 3/3/1832 W
LITTLEJOHN Alexander's child 3/3/1832 S
MOUNTZ Mrs (the old lady) 3/5/1832 W
SHORTER Jessee (colored man)'s wife 3/6/1832 S
CLAXTON Mrs John 3/11/1832 W
YOUNG Mrs 3/14/1832 S
LINKINS Sarah (colored woman) 3/19/1832 S
GOODRICK William 3/19/1832 W
COLBECK Josiah (colored man) 3/20/1832 S
ROBERTSON Peggy (colored woman) 3/21/1832 S
GREEN Robert 3/23/1832 S
WILSON Henry G's child 3/26/1832 W
NUGENT Eli (colored man)'s wife 3/26/1832 W
OVERTON Richard (colored man) 3/28/1832 S
SEMMES Joseph 3/29/1832 W

THAW William 4/4/1832 M
O'BRIAN Mrs 4/4/1832 W
COMPTON John S 4/4/1832 W
BRAAFORD William (colored man) 4/7/1832 S
HOLTZMAN John's child 4/11/1832 W
MAGEE John's child 4/13/1832 S
SIFFORD Miss 4/14/1832 S
CURRAN William 4/15/1832 W
TAYLOR Mrs 4/15/1832 W
DOUGHTY William's daughter Ellen 4/27/1832 M
BALTZER John's child 4/30/1832 W
THAW Benjamin 5/2/1832 M
Old Semmus (colored woman) 5/7/1832 W
BUTLER Nace (colored man)'s sister's child 5/12/1832 S
RINGGOLD Miss Sophia 5/15/1832 M
WEBSTER Samuel P's colored child 5/15/1832 S
McINTIRE Mrs's child 5/15/1832 S
Unknown (at F S K) 5/16/1832 S
LEWIS Anthony 5/23/1832 S
An old colored man 5/23/1832 S
A child at Billey's 6/6/1832 S
MAGRUDER Thomas 6/6/1832 M
LAIRD Mrs William 6/9/1832 M
SMOOT Mrs's Milly 6/10/1832 S
PEAKE Mr's child 6/16/1832 S
HAW John's William (colored man) 6/17/1832 S
A Child at Poor House 6/18/1832 S
SCOTT Mrs William (Montgomery County) 6/20/1832 W
HILL Catharine 6/21/1832 S
FRENCH Mrs 6/23/1832 S
LINGHAM Mrs Janette 6/29/1832 S
WELLS Richard's child 6/30/1832 M
WARD John's child 7/9/1832 S
BROWN Betsy (colored woman)'s child 7/12/1832 S
HUDSON Samuel's child 7/13/1832 S
WATERS Thomas G's colored man 7/19/1832 S
OULD Robert's son 7/23/1832 S
HURDLE Noble's son 7/24/1832 W
CLARK William's child 7/27/1832 S
REINTZLE Samuel's child 7/27/1832 W
DUNN James C's colored child 7/30/1832 S
MAGRUDER Mrs's child 8/2/1832 S

FULLALOVE James's child 8/2/1832 W
JONES John's child 8/2/1832 W
MATTHEWS Henry's child 8/5/1832 M
WILLIAMS George (colored man) 8/5/1832 S
POWERS Alexander 8/7/1832 S
WILLSON Jeffry (colored man) 8/12/1832 S
STAHL Jacob's child 8/12/1832 S
NEWTON Mrs's child 8/13/1832 S
DUVAL Miss (P G Co) 8/14/1832 W
HARTMAN Mrs's son 8/14/1832 W
BRYANT Mr's child 8/15/1832 S
BADGER Alfred M's child 8/15/1832 W
SMITH William (colored man) 8/18/1832 S
DUNLOP R P's colored boy 8/19/1832 S
ALLEN Mrs's child 8/22/1832 W
COLE Horace (colored man) for ------ 8/24/1832 S
TENNISON Joshua 8/24/1832 M
LOWNDES Francis's colored child 8/25/1832 S
BUTLER Ann (colored woman) 8/26/1832 S
STULL John J's colored woman 8/26/1832 S
TAYLOR Winder's child 8/26/1832 W
DOYLE Francis's child 8/27/1832 W
ROLLINGS Thomas (colored man) 8/28/1832 S
BUTLER James (colored man) 8/28/1832 S
GLASSCO John (colored man) 8/28/1832 S
BRAWNER Mr's colored boy 8/28/1832 S
BARRY Robert's colored man 8/29/1832 S
RYE Mr's child 8/29/1832 S
McINTIRE ------ 8/31/1832 S
EDMONDSON Mrs's son 8/31/1832 W
SCHELL Seth 9/1/1832 W
BRUNETT Mrs 9/2/1832 S
MORRISON Miss 9/3/1832 M
FORD Peggy (colored woman) 9/3/1832 S
RIDGEWAY John 9/3/1832 W
DAVIDSON John's child 9/3/1832 M
JENKINS Dennis 9/3/1832 S
O'NEAL Theodore 9/4/1832 W
Old Frank (colored man) 9/4/1832 S
BROWN John's child 9/5/1832 W
OVERTON Susan (colored woman) 9/5/1832 S
LYLES Mrs 9/6/1832 S

ERSLING George 9/7/1832 S
CROPLEY Samuel's child 9/7/1832 W
CARROLL Frank 9/7/1832 S
MATTINGLY Susan 9/7/1832 S
GUSTINE Joel's colored man 9/7/1832 S
BIRTH James's colored man 9/7/1832 S
FEARSON Joseph 9/7/1832 W
ESPY William 9/7/1832 W
OWENS Mrs Mary 9/7/1832 M
BROOKS Harriett 9/7/1832 S
COOK David 9/8/1832 S
RIDGEWAY Mrs's child 9/8/1832 S
GORDON Mr's colored child 9/8/1832 S
GIBSON Mrs 9/9/1832 S
HULL William 9/9/1832 W
HURDS Mrs (colored woman) 9/9/1832 S
WOODWARD Sylvester 9/9/1832 S
FEARSON Mrs's colored man 9/10/1832 S
BROWN Mrs 9/10/1832 S
SHAAFFER George 9/11/1832 S
A Colored woman (at hospital) 9/11/1832 S
TWINE William (colored man) 9/11/1832 S
BELL Nancy (colored woman) 9/11/1832 S
GRAY William 9/11/1832 S
WHELAN Mrs Rebecca 9/11/1832 W
HAW John S 9/12/1832 M
CARTWRIGHT ------ 9/12/1832 W
WARING Henry's colored man 9/13/1832 S
HEYER J 9/13/1832 S
WOODS Joseph's wife 9/13/1832 W
MITCHELL Matthew 9/13/1832 W
BIRD Mary A 9/14/1832 S
WATERS Thomas G's colored man 9/14/1832 S
THOMSON John 9/14/1832 M
CLARK Edward's colored man 9/14/1832 S
Samson (colored man)'s wife 9/14/1832 S
RITCHIE William 9/15/1832 W
NOLAN Thomas's child 9/15/1832 W
BARNES George (colored man)'s wife 9/15/1832 S
REEDER Thomas 9/15/1832 S
BRUNNER Mr's child 9/16/1832 W
CURTIS Rachael 9/16/1832 S

SIM Doctor Thomas 9/16/1832 M
THOMSON Miss Isabella 9/17/1832 M
BOGENRIEFF Mrs 9/17/1832 W
BOLIN Joseph (colored man)'s mother-in-law 9/17/1832 S
LOVEJOY Zedekiah 9/18/1832 W
GROSS Thomas (colored man)'s son 9/18/1832 S
SLYE Mrs Thomas G 9/18/1832 S
ROBERTSON Charles (colored man) 9/20/1832 W
BENNET Catharine's colored woman 9/20/1832 S
TILLEY Henry's colored woman 9/20/1832 S
HAMBLY James 9/20/1832 W
DAVIDSON L G's child 9/20/1832 M
ELIASON John 9/20/1832 M
EDWARDS Miss 9/20/1832 M
REINTZLE Mrs Daniel 9/20/1832 M
BAKER Miss Eliza Ann 9/21/1832 M
COXE Richard S's child 9/21/1832 M
GOLDING Samuel 9/21/1832 S
ALLEN Elijah 9/21/1832 S
KING Mary Emily (F King's child) 9/21/1832 M
BARRY Robert 9/22/1832 W
LUCAS Harrison 9/22/1832 S
FEARSON S S's colored woman 9/22/1832 S
HARRY John's colored child 9/22/1832 S
ENGLISH David Senr's colored woman 9/22/1832 S
NORRIS Mrs's child 9/23/1832 S
RAGON Richard 9/23/1832 W
WHELAN Thomas's father 9/23/1832 W
JOHNSON John's child 9/23/1832 S
BURGESS John (colored man) 9/23/1832 S
NORRIS Mrs's child 9/24/1832 S
THOMPSON James (colored man) 9/25/1832 S
UPPERMAN Henry's colored man 9/26/1832 S
ROBERTSON Henry B's child 9/26/1832 W
RIDGEWAY Mrs's child 9/26/1832 W
CLARK Mrs Edward 9/27/1832 W
DAWSON Thomas's child 9/27/1832 W
GRAHAM Mrs Jane's son James 9/30/1832 M
SLYE Robert A 10/2/1832 M
BOWIE William (deceased)'s son 10/2/1832 M
SMOOT Walter's colored woman 10/2/1832 S
Dorsey (colored man) 10/7/1832 S

EASTON ------ 10/7/1832 S
GOOD Thomas G's child 10/8/1832 M
FORREST Mrs's colored man 10/8/1832 S
DUVAL Mrs A C 10/8/1832 M
JEFFERSON William 10/9/1832 S
FEARSON Mrs's colored man 10/9/1832 S
BRADLEY Mr's child 10/9/1832 S
SMITH Clement's colored woman 10/9/1832 S
PUMPHREY Lloyd's child 10/12/1832 W
YOUNG Thomas 10/12/1832 W
CHEW Walter's child 10/15/1832 M
BROWN W's child 10/17/1832 S
McPHERSON Henry's colored woman 10/19/1832 S
WALLAN Mr 10/20/1832 W
RYE Mr's child 10/21/1832 S
CUSTIS G W P's colored man 10/21/1832 S
JOHN Mrs's colored man 10/24/1832 S
STURTEVANT Seth's colored man 10/27/1832 S
RATCLIFFE George's child 10/28/1832 W
THOMPSON Mrs's colored man 10/28/1832 S
MASON Mary (colored woman) 10/31/1832 S
McNERHENNY John 10/31/1832 W
DAVIDSON Lewis G 11/2/1832 M
BOWEMAN Charles's child 11/5/1832 S
MORTON Miss Isabella 11/6/1832 W
BURKHARD W's child 11/6/1832 S
LYLES Semos (colored woman)'s child 11/7/1832 S
FEARSON J N's child 11/8/1832 S
PATTERSON Miss 11/8/1832 M
LINKINS Hope 11/8/1832 S
CRUIT John L's child 11/11/1832 W
SAYERS James's wife 11/13/1832 W
VANNESSEN Mrs Peter 11/13/1832 M
BOGENRIEFF Valentine 11/14/1832 W
ROSS William's wife 11/14/1832 S
BOOTH Mrs 11/15/1832 W
SHAW John's child 11/18/1832 S
GOUGH Miss 11/18/1832 M
RICHEY Mrs's daughter 11/23/1832 W
RICHEY Mrs's son 11/24/1832 W
SMITH Clement's colored woman 11/24/1832 S
BEALL Aquilla 11/25/1832 S

ROSATER Thomas's wife 11/27/1832 S
PYFER Henry's child 11/29/1832 M
CARBERRY Lewis's son Thomas 12/4/1832 W
LAMBERT Edward 12/5/1832 M
Two Children, names unknown 12/5/1832 S
ADDISON Henry's colored girl 12/6/1832 S
COMPTON Mrs's child 12/8/1832 S
TRACY Mr's child 12/8/1832 S
RANNALS Jessee (colored man)'s child 12/10/1832 S
LINTHICUM Otho M's children (two) 12/12/1832 M
HELM Mrs Joseph 12/13/1832 M
CLARK William 12/16/1832 S
LINTHICUM Otho M's child 12/17/1832 M
MORRIS Miss (at Academy) 12/17/1832 M
WARING Miss Susan 12/19/1832 M
ENGLISH David's colored woman 12/23/1832 S
BERRY Zachariah's child 12/24/1832 M
GARDINER Mr's child 12/27/1832 S
DUNN James C's colored girl 12/28/1832 S

ALPHABETICAL LISTING

----- Mrs 12/8/1821 S
----- Mrs's child 8/3/1823 S
A black child 6/13/1819 S
A black child 12/2/1812 S
A black child (Watt Spokes) 6/8/1812 S
A black child 1/26/1819 S
A black child 5/25/1815 S
A black man at Landes 12/18/1814 S
A black child at Mr Langs 8/16/1815 S
A black child at Mrs Villard's 3/19/1818 S
A black man 6/2/1819 S
A black man that died at J. Brown's 9/15/1812 S
A black woman at Duports 8/21/1815 S
A black woman 7/24/1818 S
A black woman that died at Langs 12/31/1812 S
A boatman 9/7/1823 S
A captain of G W P Custis's vessel 5/20/1815 S
A child 10/28/1830 S
A child 12/20/1809 S
A child 2/23/1826 W
A child 6/25/1826 S
A child 8/19/1830 S
A child 8/22/1830 S
A child at Mrs Shiveley's 8/14/1824 S
A child at Poor House 1/8/1831 S
A child at Poor House 6/18/1832 S
A child at Mrs Simmons 4/27/1830 S
A child at E Patterson's factory 11/17/1817 S
A child at Billey's 6/6/1832 S
A child at Josias Smith (colored man)'s 7/20/1825 S
A child in the country 1/12/1818 s
A child that died at L Hill's 7/3/1820 M
A child that died at Gunn 8/31/1820 S
A child that Nancy Pool nursed 8/14/1815 S
A colored boy 5/27/1826 S
A colored child 8/5/1809 S
A colored child at Letty Springs 9/21/1829 S
A colored child 4/21/1818 S
A colored child at H Addison's 12/17/1823 S

A colored child 5/26/1831 S
A colored man at C. Shorter's 4/19/1815 S
A colored man near Colonel Bomford's 1/21/1829 S
A colored man that was drowned 4/18/1829 S
A colored man 8/13/1826 S
A colored man 5/9/1826 S
A colored man's child 9/29/1817 S
A colored woman at Mr McGill's 9/17/1824 S
A colored woman at poor house 4/21/1827 S
A colored woman 7/9/1818 S
A colored woman (at hospital) 9/11/1832 S
A colored woman at Gideon Davis's 3/4/1823 S
A colored woman at T Beck's house 10/24/1823 S
A colored woman 7/5/1825 S
A colored woman at James Wharton's 11/11/1825 W
A colored woman 4/5/1826 S
A crazy man 10/16/1830 S
A drowned child 6/27/1824 S
A drowned colored man 9/14/1827 S
A drowned colored man 2/19/1828 S
A drowned man 4/4/1830 S
A drowned man 2/24/1830 S
A drowned man 5/28/1829 S
A drowned man 7/15/1824 S
A drowned man 6/1/1821 S
A foundling at Havenlar 8/9/1822 S
A foundling child 8/3/1824 S
A foundling child 12/1/1825 S
A man at Tenlytown (Noveres) 1/4/1828 S
A man at Colburn's 4/22/1830 S
A man at Murphy's 9/21/1830 S
A man at Poor House 3/25/1831 S
A man at Poor House 3/29/1831 S
A man at Foy's 7/26/1830 S
A man at Poor House 2/22/1831 S
A man drown'd at the falls 10/1/1817 S
A man found in street 10/27/1830 S
A man per Mr Custis 5/21/1823 S
A man that died at Mr Dyer's 2/2/1820 S
A man that was drowned 5/28/1817 S
A man that was drowned 7/29/1816 S
A man that died at Thomson Hacy 6/20/1829 S

A man that came down the river 6/8/1812 S
A man that died at Mr Chrten 10/2/1816 W
A Name Unknown at Poor House 8/1/1831 S
A Negro 4/9/1819 S
A Negro child at McCandlass's 7/22/1825 S
A Negro child at McCandlass's 7/20/1825 S
A Negro Woman 9/6/1813 S
A ---- Over the river got by Mr Lawrence 1/16/1821 S
A pauper at William Turner's 2/4/1824 S
A sailor 5/26/1821 S
A stranger 9/9/1820 S
A woman at Spalding's 10/27/1821 S
A woman drowned near the Falls Bridge 5/12/1812 S
A woman that died at Graces 11/21/1816 S
An old colored man 5/23/1832 S
Agnes (colored woman) 3/11/1824 S
Ana (colored woman)'s child 7/9/1817 S
Andrew 1/16/1815 S
Aunt Lucy 1/19/1818 W
Ben (colored man) 7/29/1831 S
Candis's son 7/4/1822 S
Candis's son in law 5/13/1814 S
Care (colored woman)'s mother 3/4/1823 S; see also Letcher
Cassey (colored woman) 6/15/1825 S
Chaves, a black man 8/7/1812 S
Clare's mother (colored woman) 6/10/1823 S
Collins 3/5/1807 S
Cyrus 7/27/1820 S
Cyrus's wife 11/24/1812 S
Dennis ------'s black boy 7/8/1810 S
Dodd (Colored woman) 4/29/1821 S
Dorsey (colored man) 10/7/1832 S
George a black man's child 7/7/1813 S
George that died at Moxley's (colored man) 3/4/1829 S
George's daughter (colored woman) 10/3/1821 S
George's child 7/31/1820 W
George's wife 8/30/1816 S
Grace (colored woman) 1/20/1821 S
Hanson (colored man)'s child 5/12/1825 S
Harriet's child (colored) 6/26/1826 S
Hercules (Clagett's colored man) 4/27/1827 S
Hercules (colored man) 6/1/1825 W

Hercules's child 9/22/1820 S
Jacob's child 6/27/1830 S
James at Poor House 2/28/1831 S
James 4/29/1820 S
James 9/21/1818 S
Jane 6/15/1818 S
John ----- 9/8/1830 S
John 3/12/1818 S
John that died at Mrs Folio 11/2/1829 S
Kitty (colored woman) 11/15/1821 S
Letitia's child 4/15/1819 S
Levi's child 9/9/20/1814 S
Levi's father in law a colored man 4/14/1814 S
Linney (colored woman) 8/29/1829 S
Lucy 3/22/1821 S
Mama Betty 3/10/1812 S
Maria's child 7/18/1818 S
Mary Ann, a colored woman at R Hodge's 6/20/1830 S
Mary (a colored woman)'s mother 10/9/1816 S
Miles a black man's child 8/26/1820 S
Milly's child 9/25/1820 S
Minty 1/26/1832 S
Minty 3/10/1813 S
Nancy (colored woman)'s father 11/10/1821 S
Nancy a black woman's child 8/13/1812 S
Nancy's child 8/30/1818 S
Ned (colored man)'s child 3/2/1825 S
Negro Beale 1/29/1825 S
Negro Celia 1/25/1825 S
Negro Dolly 10/18/1813 S
Negro Rachel (Hackey) 8/9/1825 S
Negro child 10/2/1802 S
Negro Hatfield 1/19/1812 S
Negro Joseph 5/23/1820 S
Negro Macy's child 2/21/1812 S
Old Cissay 2/4/1820 S
Old Davy's wife 3/31/1817 S
Old Frank (colored man) 9/4/1832 S
Old George (gravedigger) 8/10/1805 S
Old Harry 11/25/1824 S
Old Jenney 11/29/1829 S
Old Kit's grandchild 12/16/1826 S

Old Kitty 2/16/1818 S
Old Luke's wife (colored woman) 7/13/1829 S
Old McDaniel 2/8/1820 S
Old Sam 12/6/1823 S
Old Semmus (colored woman) 5/7/1832 W
Old Tom 3/21/1820 S
Patience (Negress) 5/18/1811 S
Priscilla's child 6/1/1818 S
Richard, blacksmith 7/26/1830 S
Richard 7/12/1819 S
Safa child 4/20/1813 S
Sally (colored woman) 5/15/1823 S
Samson (colored man)'s wife 9/14/1832 S
Sarah (orphan child) 5/29/1830 S
Sarah 11/29/1827 S
Sister Charity, a nun 11/8/1831 S
Statia a black woman 2/15/1815 S
Susan 12/22/1826 S
Theresa (colored woman) 3/28/1823 S
Thomas (colored man)'s child 1/17/1822 S
Thomas's child (a colored man) 2/28/1815 S
Thomas's child (a black man) 10/5/1812 S
Two Children, names unknown 12/5/1832 S
Unknown (at F S K [Francis Scott Key}) 5/16/1832 S
Unknown 11/7/1800 S
Unknown 5/14/1800 S
Unknown 9/1/1796 S
ABBOT John's child 9/4/1819 M
ABBOT John's child 9/21/1820 M
ABBOT Mr's child 8/25/1803 W
ABBOTT John's black child 8/17/1818 S
ABBOTT John's child 12/7/1810 M
ABBOTT John's colored boy 11/8/1831 S
ABBOTT John's colored child 8/28/1826 S
ABBOTT John's colored child 9/6/1829 S
ABBOTT Mr's colored child 9/20/1826 S
ADAM Mrs's child 9/6/1829 S
ADAM Thomas's chld 7/5/1802 S
ADAM William's wife 4/15/1830 S
ADAMS Betsey 1/31/1826 s
ADAMS Chas 8/11/1825 S
ADAMS George A's child 11/21/1828 W

ADAMS George A's mother 1/6/1829 W
ADAMS Hannah 1/21/1823 W
ADAMS Henry's child 10/6/1820 S
ADAMS Isaac 4/12/1829 W
ADAMS Isaac's child 8/8/1813 S
ADAMS John for ----- 10/30/1810 W
ADAMS John Q's child 6/23/1806 M
ADAMS Mary 5/27/1818 S
ADAMS Miss's child 5/12/1826 W
ADAMS Mr 12/22/1817 S
ADAMS Mrs 9/3/1813 W
ADAMS Nancy 1/4/1830 S
ADAMS Thomas Jr 12/20/1830 S
ADAMS Thomas's black woman 2/1/1814 S
ADAMS Thomas's child 7/26/1806 W
ADAMS William 9/5/1809 W
ADDISON Henry's child 9/12/1831 M
ADDISON Henry's child 12/23/1823 M
ADDISON Henry's child 2/6/1824 W
ADDISON Henry's child 7/24/1825 W
ADDISON Henry's colored girl 12/6/1832 S
ADDISON Henry's colored woman 4/14/1831 S
ADDISON Henry's colored child 9/12/1830 S
ADDISON John 10/17/1799 W
ADDISON Mr E 6/23/1814 M
ADDISON Mr's John 6/9/1831 S
ADDISON W D's colored woman 8/4/1822 S
ADDISON Walter D's son Francis 3/5/1830 M
ADDY Mr 1/21/1800 W
AIKINS Mr's wife 8/19/1826 S
AIR John 2/12/1815 S
ALFIND Mr's daughter 11/5/1813 S
ALFRED D 12/21/1820 S
ALLEN Dennis 10/8/1830 W
ALLEN Elijah 9/21/1832 S
ALLEN Mr 3/14/1815 S
ALLEN Mrs 7/7/1831 S
ALLEN Mrs's child 8/22/1832 W
ALLEN William's wife 4/24/1819 S
ALLIN William's brother 6/21/1820 S
ANDERSON Andrew 11/9/1816 W
ANDERSON Charlotte (colored woman) 8/13/1824 W

ANDERSON David 4/23/1818 S
ANDERSON Mr 2/16/1817 W
ANDERSON Mr at Whites 9/28/1814 S
ANDERSON Mrs 6/18/1805 W
ANDERSON Philip (colored man)'s child 9/1/1825 S
ANDERSON Samuel's colored man 10/14/1807 S
ANDERSON William 7/9/1827 S
ANDREWS Miss's child 3/18/1823 S
ANDREWS Mr's child 7/28/1806 W
ANDREWS Mrs's child 8/4/1815 W
ANDREWS Mrs's child 9/2/1819 W
ANDREWS Mrs's child 8/13/1817 W
ANDREWSON Samuel 8/14/1817 S
ANGEL Mrs's child 10/7/1830 S
ARDREY John 6/22/1831 S
ARMSTRONG Robert 11/5/1818 S
ARNAY Joseph's lad 11/5/1818 S
ARNAY Mrs 11/18/1821 W
ARNOLD Mr 11/14/1814 W
ARNOLD Mr 7/12/1820 S
ARNOLD Mr's child 4/17/1809 S
ARNY Mr's boy 1/31/1818 S
ASHTON Daniel 3/24/1828 S
ASHTON E's child 2/13/1828 S
ASHTON E's child 10/24/1825 S
ASHTON Margaret .5/3/1826 W
ASHTON Mr's child 10/9/1819 W
ASTAN Peggy's child 9/17/1813 S
ASTON Elizabeth's child 10/31/1811 S
ASTON Peggey's child 11/9/1814 S
ATEASON Mrs 2/27/1817 S
ATKINSON Miss 12/9/1799 W
ATKINSON Mrs for ----- 12/25/1799 S
ATKINSON Mrs's daughter 7/31/1831 M
ATTWATER William C's mother-in-law 3/28/1827 W
ATWATER William C's child 10/10/1821 M
ATWOOD John's child 8/4/1817 W
ATWOOD John's child 7/12/1823 W
AUBERT Henry for ----- 8/9/1803 W
AVARD Mrs's child 8/12/1820 S
AVARD Samson 5/3/1820 S
AVERY Joseph 5/8/1831 W

AYRES Mrs's child 10/26/1823 S
BACCUS Mr's child 9/6/1817 W
BACEN Mrs's child 1/21/1815 S
BACENS Mr's child 1/16/1815 S
BACENS Mrs 1/8/1815 S
BACOCK Mr's son 6/22/1819 S
BADGER Alfred M's child 8/15/1832 W
BAILEY Jessee for ----- 11/14/1810 W
BAILY James C (waterman) 1/23/1825 W
BAILY Jessee's child 7/26/1796 W
BAIN Quentin for ----- 8/2/1806 S
BAIN Quintin for ----- 11/28/1801 W
BAIN Quintin's child 1/30/1802 W
BAIRD Andrew 9/12/1807 W
BAIRD Mrs's child 8/19/1808 S
BAIRN John's granddaughter 9/22/1822 M
BAKER D W's son 6/5/1809 S
BAKER Doctor William 3/22/1812 W
BAKER Doctor's negro man 8/26/1809 S
BAKER J W's colored woman 12/10/1827 S
BAKER John W's colored man 1/27/1830 S
BAKER John W's colored man 4/6/1830 S
BAKER John W's colored boy 9/16/1830 S
BAKER John W's colored man 11/2/1826 S
BAKER John W's colored man 3/30/1826 S
BAKER John's child 7/26/1819 M
BAKER John's child 7/20/1821 M
BAKER John's child 1/27/1824 M
BAKER John's child 1/14/1823 M
BAKER John's man 5/15/1818 S
BAKER John's mother 1/17/1820 M
BAKER John's son 7/9/1814 M
BAKER Mary 12/28/1825 S
BAKER Mary 6/24/1824 S
BAKER Miss Eliza Ann 9/21/1832 M
BAKER Mr's child 4/17/1812 W
BAKER Mr's child 8/2/1810 S
BAKER Mrs 11/21/1826 M
BAKER Nancy 1/26/1825 W
BAKER Polly 8/16/1821 S
BAKER S 2/11/1821 M
BAKER William's child 4/6/1815 M

BAKER Z's child 8/18/1820 W
BAKER Z's child 5/17/1827 W
BAKER Z's colored man 10/16/1830 S
BAKER Zach's colored woman 7/28/1830 S
BAKER ~~Zachariah~~ Mrs 1/19/1815 M
BAKER Zachariah's child 10/5/1826 W
BAKER Zackriah's child 7/3/1819 W
BALCH Elizabeth 11/26/1828 M
BALCH Hezekiah 3/18/1829 M
BALCH Mrs 6/28/1827 M
BALCH Stephen B's child 2/7/1798 W
BALL Aquala 12/1/1814 W
BALL Betsey's child 10/4/1821 S
BALL Lewis 10/11/1821 S
BALL Mr 12/14/1814 W
BALL Mrs 10/8/1830 S
BALL Mrs of Virginia 7/30/1831 S
BALL Richard 7/19/1807 S
BALTZER George 11/23/1813 W
BALTZER George's child 6/6/1810 M
BALTZER John 9/26/1808 M
BALTZER John's child 1/21/1808 M
BALTZER John's child 4/1/1802 M
BALTZER John's child 4/30/1832 W
BALTZER Joseph 12/25/1824 W
BALTZER Mrs 11/29/1825 W
BANISTER Richard's child 8/4/1820 S
BANISTER Richard's child 9/14/1812 W
BANKS John 1/2/1810 M
BANKS John's child 2/19/1804 M
BANKS John's child 10/4/1805 M
BANKS Mrs's child 3/25/1810 S
BANNISTER Richard's child 10/29/1823 S
BANSELL William 2/23/1815 W
BARBARA's child (a colored woman) 9/20/1816 S
BARBER Barna's daughter 7/5/1813 S
BARBER Barney 12/30/1825 S
BARBER J 7/26/1831 W
BARCLAY Mary Ann 12/29/1824 W
BARCLAY Mrs 3/6/1826 W
BARCLEY J D's child 9/1/1821 M
BARKER Andrew's father 7/23/1819 S

BARKER Murray's child 9/3/1818 S
BARKER Thomas a colored man's wife 11/28/1816 S
BARKLEY John's child 7/7/1820 M
BARLOW Mrs 6/1/1818 M
BARN Ann's child 1/26/1821 S
BARN Nancy's child 8/10/1815 S
BARN Ned's child 7/28/1818 S
BARNES Alexander (colored man) 1/5/1832 S
BARNES George (colored man)'s wife 9/15/1832 S
BARNES George's wife (colored woman) 7/17/1829 S
BARNES John 2/13/1826 M
BARNES Lucy's child 8/13/1816 S
BARNES Mathew 3/9/1813 S
BARNES Mr's child 8/17/1801 M
BARNES Mrs 6/22/1825 W
BARNES William 5/2/1829 W
BARNES's Frank 2/21/1824 S
BARNS Nancy 1/7/1818 S
BARNS Ned 8/1/1819 S
BARRETT Mrs 5/1/1819 W
BARRETT William D 7/19/1829 M
BARRY James 1/8/1811 S
BARRY Robert 9/22/1832 W
BARRY Robert's child 2/6/1830 W
BARRY Robert's colored man 8/29/1832 S
BARTLET Isaac's child W
BARWISE Mr's stageman 7/30/1803 S
BARWISE Mr for ----- 10/30/1804 S
BARWISE Mr's child 10/17/1804 S
BASTEN Charles's boy 8/24/1802 W
BASTEN Charles's child 7/18/1802 W
BATT Mrs 6/26/1829 S
BAUGHMAN Mrs 3/12/1827 S
BAUKMAN's child 2/10/1830 S
BAUM Mr's child 9/17/1805 W
BAUTCHER Mr's child 3/10/1822 W
BAYLEY William 3/9/1824 W
BAYLISS Collin's father 9/12/1831 S
BAYLISS Collin's mother 9/12/1831 S
BEADLE A's child 2/10/1828 S
BEAL Samuel 1/7/1820 W
BEALL Ann 4/10/1827 M

BEALL Aquilla 11/25/1832 S
BEALL Aquilla's negro girl 11/28/1801 S
BEALL B W 7/25/1823 W
BEALL Basil 2/18/1824 S
BEALL George 10/17/1807 M
BEALL George for unknown 5/3/1799 M
BEALL Harriette 8/18/1831 W
BEALL Jerry (colored man) 5/4/1827 S
BEALL Joseph S for ----- 2/17/1808 S
BEALL Lloyd for ------ 8/10/1795 S
BEALL Lloyd's child 8/27/1796 S
BEALL Lloyd's child 9/19/1799 S
BEALL M (colored woman) 8/8/1824 S
BEALL Mrs 11/28/1827 S
BEALL Mrs 6/12/1802 W
BEALL Mrs B 9/23/1823 M
BEALL Mrs B's colored child 7/26/1823 S
BEALL Mrs Brook's colored child 9/1/1805 S
BEALL Mrs Elizabeth 6/28/1828 M
BEALL Mrs's colored woman 12/8/1818 S
BEALL Mrs's girl 12/18/1820 S
BEALL N's brother-in-law 10/31/1821 S
BEALL Ninian's black girl 12/8/1815 S
BEALL Ninian's child 10/22/1810 W
BEALL Rinsey 10/11/1820 W
BEALL T B 10/1/1820 M
BEALL Thomas B's John 4/22/1806 S
BEALL Thomas B's colored child 8/30/1808 S
BEALL Thomas for ----- 3/25/1802 W
BEALL Thomas of George 10/6/1819 M
BEALL Upton for a lad 11/8/1806 M
BEALL W B's daughter 8/30/1823 W
BEALL W B's daughter 7/9/1821 W
BEALL William D's colored person 7/30/1801 S
BEALL William D's mother 5/10/1806 W
BEAN Captain 2/27/1829 S
BEAN Mr's sister 1/7/1829 S
BEAN Mrs 10/24/1822 S
BEAN William's child 7/2/1816 W
BEARD Captain's child 7/14/1827 S
BEASLY Mrs 4/25/1822 W
BEATTY Charles 9/17/1804 M

BEATTY Charles A's child 3/1/1798 M
BEATTY Edmond 10/23/1831 W
BEATTY John 1/23/1827 M
BEATTY Kitty 12/23/1812 M
BEATTY Major Thomas's child 8/15/1796 M
BEATTY Thomas 2/28/1815 M
BEATY John 4/15/1815 M
BECK Joseph 1/18/1812 W
BECK Joseph's negro woman 9/9/1810 S
BECK Mrs 6/18/1822 W
BECK Mrs 9/20/1813 M
BECK Mrs Dorcas 10/10/1826 M
BECK Rezin for ----- 3/24/1807 W
BECK Rezin's negro man 9/24/1806 S
BECK Rezin's negro boy 1/3/1807 S
BECK Richard 4/3/1810 M
BECK Richard's child 1/31/1804 M
BECK Richard's child 1/5/1810 M
BECK Richard's colored child 10/28/1807 S
BECK Truman's black girl 9/11/1816 S
BECRAFT William's son (colored) 10/31/1828 S
BEDDO William 3/28/1820 S
BEDDOW James' black man 7/21/1817 S
BEDLEY Mrs's child 3/26/1823 S
BELL Elenor 6/21/1818 M
BELL Nancy (colored woman) 9/11/1832 S
BELL Rachel 6/8/1827 S
BELT Humphrey 3/14/1828 S
BELT James's child 4/16/1827 M
BELT James's child 6/20/1823 M
BELT Joseph S 12/23/1816 M
BELT Mrs (PG Co) 8/7/1825 M
BELT Mrs 12/19/1830 W
BELT Sarah 1/22/1827 M
BENDER Mrs 12/18/1830 S
BENFIELD Mrs 10/6/1818 W
BENNET Catharine's colored woman 9/20/1832 S
BENNET Mr's child 10/19/1823 W
BENNET Mr's child 8/9/1824 W
BENSON L M (sailor) 3/7/1827 S
BENSON Mr's child 1/20/1823 S
BENSON Mrs 10/4/1822 W

BENSON Mrs's child 3/10/1821 S
BENTON Mrs 2/20/1817 S
BENTZ Adam 10/29/1823 S
BERRY Mr 9/15/1820 S
BERRY Mr 9/7/1809 S
BERRY Mr's child 6/19/1815 W
BERRY Mrs 4/15/1815 M
BERRY Mrs 7/21/1817 W
BERRY Zachariah's child 12/24/1832 M
BETTY 4/22/1818 S
BEVAN Jerom's child 9/9/1816 W
BEVAN Jerom's child 8/17/1816 W
BEVAN Jerome's child 7/15/1829 W
BEVERLY Robert's child 2/24/1807 M
BEVERLY Robert's negro child 11/23/1809 S
BIAS Cook 7/27/1830 S
BIAS Cooke's wife 9/2/1819 S
BIAS Cynthia's child 10/25/1823 S
BIAS Pally's child (colored man) 8/11/1821 S
BIAS Smithy (colored man)'s child 9/16/1821 S
BIDDASON Daniel's child 8/25/1818 S
BIGGS Thomas 10/9/1819 S
BIRCHAN Mrs 6/28/1811 W
BIRD Mary A 9/14/1832 S
BIRTH James's child 3/25/1802 W
BIRTH James's colored man 9/7/1832 S
BIRTH James's Ned 6/6/1824 s
BIRTH John 8/26/1818 W
BIRTH Mr's child 3/24/1804 W
BIRTH Mrs 9/27/1818 W
BISHOP Mr's child 1/1/1824 S
BISHOP Mr's child 7/15/1827 S
BISHOP Richard 4/29/1829 W
BLACK Eliza 8/21/1824 S
BLACK Mr's child 11/5/1829 S
BLADEN A D's child 9/12/1830 W
BLAGE Benjamin 2/1/1821 S
BLAGGE John's black child 7/29/1819 S
BLAGGE John's child 9/22/1819 M
BLAGGE Mr's child 6/24/1818 M
BLAGROVE H B's child 1/22/1818 S
BLAGROVE Mr 5/4/1818 W

BLAGROVE William's child 6/10/1816 S
BLAIR Miss 7/24/1821 M
BLAIR William's child 6/22/1824 W
BLANCHARD Doctor's child 10/11/1818 M
BLANCHARD William's child 10/30/1819 M
BLANCHARD William's child 9/29/1806 M
BLUER John 5/2/1812 S
BOAMAN Raphael's child 8/12/1818 S
BOARDMAN Mrs 4/29/1829 W
BOARMAN Mr's child 8/9/1824 W
BOGENRIEFF Mrs 9/17/1832 W
BOGENRIEFF Valentine 11/14/1832 W
BOHRER Abraham for ----- 10/18/1811 W
BOHRER Abraham's child 9/15/1820 W
BOHRER Barbary 1/3/1821 W
BOHRER Jacob's black woman 4/25/1821 S
BOHRER Jacob's son 9/4/1820 W
BOHRER Mrs 5/22/1821 W
BOLIN Joseph (colored man)'s mother-in-law 9/17/1832 S
BOLTON Isaac 10/30/1814 W
BOND Mrs 1/30/1816 S
BOND Thomas (seaman) 5/22/1825 S
BONN James 9/24/1828 S
BOON Arnold's child 3/26/1812 W
BOON Mrs 11/17/1813 W
BOONE Mr 7/4/1818 S
BOOTES Samuel's grandchild 1/24/1831 M
BOOTH Mr 2/22/1820 S
BOOTH Mr's daughter 4/2/1821 S
BOOTH Mrs 11/15/1832 W
BOSSWELL Ben's servant's child 7/29/1824 W
BOSTON Mrs for ----- 8/24/1811 S
BOSWELL Benjamin Senr 4/9/1826 S
BOSWELL Mrs 10/9/1816 W
BOSWELL Mrs 4/13/1820 W
BOSWELL Mrs 8/25/1826 S
BOUCHER Alexander 1/31/1829 S
BOUSCH John C for ----- 9/30/1811 M
BOWEMAN Charles's child 11/5/1832 S
BOWER Eversfield 5/8/1816 M
BOWER James's child 7/17/1822 W
BOWER Thomas's son 1/5/1812 M

BOWIE Alexander's wife 3/30/1801 M
BOWIE Allen 5/22/1803 M
BOWIE Humphrey 11/19/1827 M
BOWIE John 2/19/1825 M
BOWIE Miss Margaret 12/5/1825 M
BOWIE Mrs 5/16/1812 M
BOWIE Mrs 8/14/1819 M
BOWIE Mrs 8/16/1812 M
BOWIE Mrs John 8/20/1830 M
BOWIE Mrs of Bladensburg 1/4/1814 W
BOWIE Robert 1/12/1818 M
BOWIE Thomas (PG County) 10/8/1827 M
BOWIE Thomas 1/30/1823 M
BOWIE Walter B omitted 10/23/1831 M
BOWIE Washington 4/13/1826 M
BOWIE Washington's child 12/28/1813 S
BOWIE Washington's child 9/11/1815 S
BOWIE Washington's child 12/31/1812 S
BOWIE Washington's daughter 8/11/1824 M
BOWIE William (deceased)'s son 10/2/1832 M
BOWIE William 9/11/1826 M
BOWLINE Joseph's wife 8/20/1827 S
BOWMAN Babtist 2/13/1813 S
BOWMAN Mr 12/6/1819 W
BOWMAN Nat's child 9/14/1820 S
BOWN John C's child 3/30/1814 W
BOWYER Mrs's child 9/3/1816 S
BOYD Abraham for ----- 10/27/1804 W
BOYD George's child 7/11/1806 M
BOYD Mr 12/24/1817 S
BOYD Robert's child 5/11/1829 W
BOYD Washington for ----- 11/15/1807 W
BOYE Herman 3/21/1830 M
BRAAFORD William (colored man) 4/7/1832 S
BRADEY Caleb's child 1/9/1828 S
BRADFIELD John's child 12/16/1822 S
BRADFORD William for ----- 12/24/1811 S
BRADFORD Wm's wife's sister 8/31/1819 S
BRADLEY Barbara (colored woman) 3/22/1828 S
BRADLEY Mr's child 5/8/1826 S
BRADLEY Mr's child 10/9/1832 S
BRADLEY Mrs 9/15/1808 M

BRADLEY Thomas 4/4/1824 M
BRADLEY's child (colored) 1/10/1827 S
BRADSHAW Mrs 12/10/1827 S
BRADWELL James's father 8/18/1817 W
BRADY Caleb Senr 11/4/1823 W
BRADY Caleb's child 10/9/1819 S
BRADY Caleb's son 5/12/1817 S
BRADY Michael 8/8/1823 W
BRADY Michael 9/10/1829 S
BRADY Mrs in Virginia 10/16/1823 W
BRANNEN James 2/18/1829 S
BRANNUM Mrs 10/31/1822 S
BRANNUM Mrs 5/26/1812 S
BRAWNER Mr's colored boy 8/28/1832 S
BRAY William 1/24/1814 S
BRENNER Mr's child 9/9/1820 W
BRENT Elizabeth 9/17/1827 W
BRENT Richard 12/31/1814 M
BRENT W L's colored woman 12/28/1828 S
BREWER Joseph's child 9/24/1809 M
BRICE Miss 4/12/1805 M
BRISCO George 4/2/1817 M
BRODHAG Charles F for ----- 10/19/1802 M
BRODWEL James's child 4/16/1817 W
BRONAUGH J W's daughter 2/10/1823 M
BRONAUGH William's child 1/9/1832 W
BRONAUGH William's child 5/9/1830 W
BRONOUGH John W's child 12/7/1808 M
BRONOUGH John's black woman 9/24/1818 S
BROODWELL James's child 4/15/1823 W
BROOK Charles's child 8/17/1816 S
BROOK J B's child 8/31/1817 M
BROOK James B's boy 6/8/1817 S
BROOK James B's woman 3/17/1816 S
BROOK James's black girl 11/17/1818 S
BROOK Joseph's child 10/12/1819 W
BROOK Miss 8/16/1817 W
BROOK Miss Latty 10/12/1815 M
BROOK Miss Mary's negro girl 6/1/1805 S
BROOKE Betsy (colored woman) 9/12/1827 S
BROOKE Thomas 10/8/1824 M
BROOKES Mary 2/9/1827 M

BROOKS Daphne's child (colored) 10/1/1826 S
BROOKS Dafnay (colored man)'s child 9/2/1821 S
BROOKES Daphne (colored woman)'s child 11/23/1823 S
BROOKS Dafney (colored woman)'s child 10/6/1822 S
BROOKS Eliza's child 4/17/1829 S
BROOKS Harriett 9/7/1832 S
BROOKS Joseph's child 8/28/1803 W
BROOKS Mr's black man 2/24/1815 S
BROOKS Mrs 11/26/1821 S
BROOKS Mrs 12/19/1818 S
BROOKS Thomas 12/17/1821 M
BROOKS William 1/27/1822 S
BROOME George 7/17/1828 W
BROONS Mrs's Ned 6/25/1831 S
BROTHERTON John's child 2/4/1830 W
BROW Adam 4/25/1816 S
BROWN Betsey (colored woman) 1/4/1830 S
BROWN Betsy (colored woman)'s child 7/12/1832 S
BROWN Betty 12/20/1826 S
BROWN Catherine 10/12/1825 S
BROWN Charles's child 10/11/1799 S
BROWN Clary a black woman's child 8/13/1812 S
BROWN Clary's son 4/26/1821 S
BROWN Daniel's daughter 9/12/1828 W
BROWN Gus's colored man 7/26/1830 S
BROWN Hen's child 7/28/1824 S
BROWN Henry's child 9/6/1824 S
BROWN James 7/13/1824 S
BROWN James a colored man 12/5/1818 S
BROWN James's child 11/16/1823 S
BROWN Jane's child 12/28/1825 S
BROWN Joel's child 10/4/1806 M
BROWN Joel's child 9/15/1812 M
BROWN Joel's child 7/26/1827 W
BROWN John (colored man)'s relation 1/15/1822 S
BROWN John 7/28/1831 S
BROWN John's child 9/5/1832 W
BROWN John's child 10/22/1831 S
BROWN John's child 12/17/1831 M
BROWN John's child 3/28/1827 W
BROWN Lucy's child 8/30/1815 S
BROWN Milly 6/15/1816 S

BROWN Miss M A 3/24/1828 W
BROWN Mr (stagedriver)'s child 9/25/1816 W
BROWN Mr 2/18/1815 S
BROWN Mr's child 8/10/1801 W
BROWN Mr's child 8/12/1801 W
BROWN Mr's child 5/29/1818 W
BROWN Mr's child 9/5/1815 W
BROWN Mrs 9/10/1832 S
BROWN Mrs Joel 9/16/1827 W
BROWN Nelly's sister 3/10/1817 S
BROWN Parson's wife colored woman 3/18/1815 S
BROWN Sam 3/5/1822 S
BROWN Statia 3/26/1830 S
BROWN W's child 10/17/1832 S
BROWN William (colored man) 4/29/1823 S
BROWN William's child 5/24/1816 S
BROWN Wm 5/18/1819 S
BROWNING Joseph's child 8/25/1804 W
BROWNING Joseph's child 2/12/1807 W
BRUFF Mrs 4/15/1821 W
BRUFF Thomas's child 8/10/1812 M
BRUFF Thomas's child 11/29/1803 M
BRUMBLY Mrs 4/22/1826 M
BRUMLEY James 4/17/1829 S
BRUMWELL Mrs 1/2/1814 W
BRUNETT Mrs 9/2/1832 S
BRUNNER Mr's child 9/16/1832 W
BRUSH Mr 6/11/1830 W
BRUSH Mr's child 6/22/1811 M
BRYAN Mr's child 9/2/1819 S
BRYAN T 10/2/1815 S
BRYANT Dennis 10/26/1829 S
BRYANT Mary's child (colored) 6/7/1828 S
BRYANT Mr's child 8/28/1829 S
BRYANT Mr's child 8/15/1832 S
BRYANT Mr's child 9/4/1829 S
BRYANT Mr's child 8/12/1826 S
BRYANT Mr's wife 8/24/1827 S
BRYANT William's child 4/24/1831 S
BUCHANAN John 6/1/1830 W
BUNNEL Mr's child 7/29/1819 W
BURCH Ann 2/11/1827 W

BURCH James's mother 5/16/1815 W
BURDICK Henry's child 10/2/1816 W
BURGER Richard's child 6/30/1817 M
BURGES Mrs 2/8/1813 M
BURGESS John (colored man) 9/23/1832 S
BURGESS R's black child 5/23/1818 S
BURGESS Richard's child 9/23/1824 M
BURGESS Richard's child 8/24/1825 S
BURGH Mr's child 10/15/1825 S
BURK Thomas 7/14/1831 S
BURKHARD W's child 11/6/1832 S
BURMISTAN Mrs 12/26/1821 M
BURNES David 5/9/1799 M
BURNET C A (colored man) 11/16/1829 S
BURNET C A's boy 6/4/1809 S
BURNET Charles A's child 3/5/1822 M
BURNET Charles A's black woman 4/29/1820 S
BURNET Mrs 1/16/1820 S
BURNETT C A's child 6/3/1810 M
BURNETT Charles A's child 2/1/1809 M
BURNS Mrs 1/29/1807 M
BURNS Mrs' child 7/9/1812 S
BURNS Patrick 9/3/1829 M
BURROWS Mrs 10/5/1823 W
BURRY Nancy 9/29/1810 S
BUSEY J 6/26/1822 S
BUSEY Mrs 3/11/1824 W
BUSEY Samuel 9/18/1830 W
BUSHBY William 7/8/1810 W
BUSSARD Daniel 3/3/1813 M
BUSSARD Daniel 5/14/1830 M
BUSSARD Daniel's Sarah 5/16/1809 S
BUSSARD Philip's child 12/5/1810 M
BUSSARD Philip's child 10/10/1813 M
BUTLER Abram (colored man) 12/16/1831 S
BUTLER Ann (colored woman) 8/26/1832 S
BUTLER Charles 11/1/1827 S
BUTLER Charles's child 8/28/1822 S
BUTLER Charles's child 8/16/1812 W
BUTLER Charles's child 9/10/1815 W
BUTLER Charles's child 11/16/1826 W
BUTLER Dinah (colored woman) 1/7/1827 S

BUTLER Electius's child (colored) 1/14/1828 S
BUTLER Frank 6/16/1816 S
BUTLER Henny (colored woman)'s child 12/24/1825 S
BUTLER Henry (colored man)'s child 1/15/1823 S
BUTLER Henry's child 5/11/1822 S
BUTLER Henry's colored woman's child 5/31/1824 S
BUTLER James (colored man) 8/28/1832 S
BUTLER John (colored man) 12/26/1831 S
BUTLER Joseph's child (colored) 7/25/1828 S
BUTLER L (colored man)'s child 7/16/1822 S
BUTLER Louisa's child 9/1/1818 S
BUTLER Lucy's son 2/15/1814 S
BUTLER Mary (colored woman)'s child 2/14/1824 S
BUTLER Mary 11/27/1820 S
BUTLER Mary 4/28/1822 S
BUTLER Mary's sister 9/25/1818 S
BUTLER Mrs 12/17/1830 S
BUTLER Mrs's child 11/14/1830 S
BUTLER Mrs's child 11/24/1830 S
BUTLER Nace (colored man) 1/14/1830 S
BUTLER Nace (colored man)'s sister's child 5/12/1832 S
BUTLER Nancy 2/14/1817 S
BUTLER P 1/27/1824 S
BUTLER Robert 2/8/1816 S
BUTLER Robert for ----- 8/28/1803 S
BUTLER Sally (colored woman)'s mother 11/26/1821 S
BUTLER Samuel's wife (colored) 8/27/1828 S
BUTLER Sarah (colored woman) 12/1/1825 S
BUTLER Trecy a colored 3/28/1814 S
BUTLER William a colored man 3/9/1815 S
BUTLER's child 3/12/1817 S
CAIN Catharine 1/11/1816 S
CAIRNS Stephen 8/19/1830 S
CALAHAN Mr's child 9/28/1820 S
CALDER Elizabeth 2/8/1830 M
CALDER James's black woman 1/30/1820 S
CALDER William 9/10/1824 M
CALDER William at Kile's 8/31/1821 S
CALDER William's child 9/2/1814 M
CALDER William's child 7/16/1812 M
CALDER William's child 12/10/1815 M
CALDER William's daughter 2/5/1821 M

CALHOON Mrs (colored woman) 12/13/1822 S
CALHOUN William's child 11/4/1823 S
CAMBLE John 12/9/1816 M
CAMBLE Mashake's child 6/25/1812 S
CAMBLE Mrs 3/17/1816 W
CAMPBEL Mr's child 9/29/1810 S
CAMPBELL Com. 11/13/1820 M
CAMPBELL Mashack's child 9/21/1829 S
CAMPBELL Meshac's mother-in-law 1/1/1823 W
CAMPBELL Mr 4/4/1830 S
CAMPBLE Mashack's child 11/5/1813 S
CAMPBLE Miss for a chld 9/26/1811 S
CAMPBLE Mrs 9/25/1813 M
CANNON Mr 11/25/1821 W
CARBERRY Lewis's child 12/26/1825 W
CARBERRY Lewis's son Thomas 12/4/1832 W
CARBERRY Mrs Henry 12/7/1809 W
CARBURY Henry 5/27/1822 M
CARBURY Lewes's child 3/10/1821 W
CARBURY Lewis's child 7/1/1822 W
CARLAN William 7/26/1820 W
CARLISLE Christopher 1/20/1819 M
CARLTON Joseph 5/12/1812 M
CARMAN Mrs 8/9/1816 S
CARMICHAEL Alexander 11/20/1828 S
CARMICHAEL Mrs 2/9/1826 W
CARR John 10/30/1815 S
CARROLL Lucy's child 8/31/1821 W
CARROLL Cassey's mother 12/5/1829 S
CARROLL Frank 9/7/1832 S
CARROLL Roger 3/22/1830 S
CARSON Mr's child 1/1/1817 S
CARSON Mrs 8/4/1828 S
CARTER Betsey (colored woman) 8/10/1824 S
CARTER Jacob's child 8/24/1831 W
CARTER Jacob's child 8/6/1811 S
CARTER Jacob's child 9/7/1803 S
CARTER Jacob's child 8/16/1831 W
CARTER Jacob's child 6/15/1829 W
CARTER Jacob's child 10/14/1807 S
CARTER James 4/5/1823 S
CARTER James's child 1/11/1816 W

CARTER James's relation 6/23/1818 S
CARTER Jane's mother (colored woman) 6/25/1822 S
CARTER Mrs 9/17/1819 W
CARTON Jacob's child 8/26/1817 W
CARTON Louisa 3/24/1817 S
CARTOR Jacob's child 9/5/1812 W
CARTWRIGHT ------ 9/12/1832 W
CARTWRIGHT Joseph's child 12/1/1826 S
CASEY Robert 9/30/1811 M
CASSIN James 6/12/1828 M
CASSIN Mrs 6/15/1830 M
CASSIN Mrs's colored woman 2/9/1830 S
CASSIN Stephen's colored woman 2/7/1829 S
CATON Mr's child 5/6/1812 W
CATON Mr's child 12/31/1814 W
CAUSINE Mr's negro woman 5/10/1809 S
CHANDLER Fanny's child 9/10/1818 S
CHANDLER Mrs's colored woman 10/20/1827 S
CHANDLER W S 5/19/1825 M
CHANDLER W S's black man 1/24/1820 S
CHANDLER W S's black woman 4/17/1818 S
CHANDLER Walter S's son 10/19/1819 M
CHANDLER Walter S's colored woman 11/10/1821 S
CHANDLER Walter S's child 10/4/1804 M
CHANNY Jeremiah 8/28/1830 S
CHAPMAN David 2/8/1826 M
CHAPMAN Henry 12/6/1821 M
CHARLES a colored man's child 12/5/1818 S
CHARLOT's child a black man 8/20/1813 W
CHARRY Mr 6/8/1820 S
CHASE -------- 8/14/1831 S
CHESLEY Mr's child 9/5/1807 W
CHESLEY Mrs 5/21/1823 W
CHESLEY Thomas (colored man)'s wife 11/24/1825 S
CHESTER Mr's child 8/23/1812 S
CHESTER Samuel's child 6/3/1813 S
CHESTER Samuel's son 9/27/1814 S
CHEW Cassy 1/11/1811 W
CHEW Miss (Delphi Mills) 6/26/1825 W
CHEW Mrs 10/17/1815 W
CHEW Philip's wife (colored woman) 4/15/1826 S
CHEW Robt F's child 7/12/1825 W

CHEW Robt's man 2/1/1826 S
CHEW Samuel's daughter 6/18/1831 M
CHEW Walter's child 10/15/1832 M
CHICK Joseph's wife 6/10/1826 S
CHILD, name unknown 4/23/1802 S
CHILDS Cassey 1/29/1815 S
CHILDS Henry 2/9/1812 M
CHILDS Henry's child 8/4/1811 M
CHILY Mrs 11/12/1815 S
CHISHAM John 10/10/1820 S
CHISLEY Zadoc's child 10/6/1819 M
CHORTERS John 6/16/1819 S
CHRIEN Mrs 10/16/1815 W
CHRISTAN Thomas (seaman) 9/25/1825 S
CHUB Nancy (colored woman) 12/31/1821 S
CISEL Mr's child 9/3/1816 S
CISELL Mrs 7/6/1816 W
CLAGETT James's child 12/9/1796 M
CLAGETT Jane's Sally 6/19/1819 S
CLAGETT Mrs' negro woman 7/2/1811 S
CLAGETT Mrs's Charles 10/11/1806 S
CLAGETT Walter 1/14/1801 M
CLAGETT Walter's brother 6/29/1796 M
CLAGGET Jane's woman 8/26/1819 S
CLAGGETT Mrs 9/8/1830 M
CLAGGETT Mrs's black woman 4/12/1813 S
CLAGGETT William 2/26/1825 M
CLARE Benjamin 3/4/1810 M
CLARK Baily 1/11/1816 M
CLARK Daniel 8/4/1815 M
CLARK Daniel's colored man 3/3/1830 S
CLARK Edward's colored man 9/14/1832 S
CLARK Eliza (colored woman) 6/26/1827 S
CLARK Eliza's child (colored) 6/10/1827 S
CLARK George's son 6/11/1820 M
CLARK J D's child 11/25/1816 M
CLARK J D's child 8/31/1817 M
CLARK Jane 4/20/1826 W
CLARK John D's child 7/12/1831 M
CLARK John D's child 9/8/1830 M
CLARK John's son 9/12/1824 S
CLARK Mr 2/14/1827 S

CLARK Mr's child 12/3/1825 S
CLARK Mrs Edward 9/27/1832 W
CLARK Mrs's child 11/3/1827 S
CLARK Mrs's child 10/8/1812 S
CLARK Mrs's colored child 11/6/1829 S
CLARK Samuel's black child 8/16/1820 S
CLARK Samuel's child 2/12/1831 W
CLARK Samuel's child 3/10/1829 S
CLARK Samuel's girl 11/22/1827 S
CLARK Saterlee's child 8/1/1814 M
CLARK Sophia (colored woman) 5/16/1831 S
CLARK Thomas 4/15/1819 M
CLARK Thomas 8/30/1796 M
CLARK William 12/16/1832 S
CLARK William for ----- 5/29/1809 W
CLARK William's child 7/27/1832 S
CLARKE Ann Maria 12/17/1823 M
CLARKE J D's child 9/12/1818 S
CLARKE John D's child 2/18/1824 M
CLARKE Mrs (Samuel's mother) 2/19/1823 W
CLARKE Mrs 1/10/1827 W
CLARKE William's child 8/12/1830 S
CLARKE William's child 6/19/1826 S
CLARKE William's child 3/8/1824 W
CLARKE William's child 9/21/1825 W
CLARKSON Mrs 12/8/1826 S
CLAXTON John 5/16/1818 S
CLAXTON Mrs John 3/11/1832 W
CLEGET Bishop 8/3/1816 M
CLEGET Jane's black woman 8/7/1816 S
CLEGET Mrs 3/18/1815 S
CLEGET Mrs' black man 11/15/1815 S
CLEGGET Mrs 11/24/1813 W
CLEGGET Mrs 11/21/1819 M
CLEMENT John's child 10/7/1827 W
CLEMENTS Benjamin 1/10/1816 W
CLEMENTS Bennet's son 2/16/1831 W
CLEMENTS John's child 9/4/1831 W
CLEMENTS Joseph 11/4/1815 S
CLEMENTS Mr 9/6/1816 S
CLEMENTS Mrs 2/10/1816 S
CLEMENTSON Ed's child 7/22/1825 W

CLEMENTSON Geo Senr 2/19/1826 M
CLEMENTSON Geo's child 9/22/1818 S
CLEMENTSON George Jr 12/9/1826 W
CLEMENTSON George's colored boy 7/7/1825 S
CLEMENTSON John's child 7/27/1827 W
CLINE David's child 11/5/1813 W
CLORIVERE Joseph (priest) 9/30/1826 M
CLOUD Abner's child 3/23/1807 M
CLOXON Mr's child 8/30/1818 S
COAL Jeremiah's mother 6/8/1812 S
COATES James's child 7/29/1803 W
COATS Doctor 2/8/1810 M
COATS Miss 11/7/1818 W
COATS Mrs's colored girl 4/16/1831 S
COBB James D's nephew 9/29/1824 W
COBET Mrs 3/27/1815 W
COBLER James's child 8/18/1821 W
COCKELY Mrs Frances 5/1/1825 W
COGER Mrs (colored woman) 2/18/1824 S
COGSWELL Joseph 12/20/1825 S
COKELY Lewis (colored man) 3/16/1826 S
COKELY Mrs's child 8/4/1825 W
COKLEY Aaron's child (colored man) 7/23/1829 S
COKLEY Hanson (colored man)'s child 7/26/1829 S
COLBECK Josiah (colored man) 3/20/1832 S
COLCLAZER Jacob's child 6/13/1827 S
COLCLAZER Thomas's black child 11/27/1817 S
COLCLAZER Thomas's child 4/20/1816 S
COLCLAZER Thomas's child 7/24/1818 s
COLE (colored man)'s son-in-law 8/23/1821 S
COLE Ambrose (colored) 2/24/1827 S
COLE Beckey 2/9/1815 S
COLE Frank (colored man) 9/13/1827 S
COLE George's child 2/21/1817 S
COLE Hanah's child 9/17/1812 S
COLE Horace (colored man) for ------ 8/24/1832 S
COLE Horatio's wife 2/5/1830 S
COLE L 6/30/1831 S
COLE Negro Stephen 1/23/1812 S
COLE Nelly 2/2/1807 S
COLE Polly's husband 7/3/1830 S
COLEMAN Ann's child 6/28/1831 S

COLEMAN Mrs 2/23/1828 S
COLFER Andrew 7/23/1830 S
COLLINGWOOD Samuel 10/21/1821 W
COLLINGWOOD Samuel's child 8/27/1819 W
COLLINS Ann's child 12/8/1822 S
COLLINS child 8/10/1812 S
COLLINS Edward's child 1/6/1832 S
COLLINS George 12/30/1831 S
COLLINS James's child 9/4/1818 S
COLLINS James's child 8/21/1818 S
COLLINS John's child 7/16/1818 S
COLLINS Joseph S' child 10/24/1816 M
COLLINS Lillemen 5/28/1822 S
COLLINS Mrs 11/24/1826 S
COLLINS Mrs's child 11/4/1822 S
COLLINS Nancy 7/14/1830 S
COLLINS Rachel 9/30/1825 S
COLLINS Rebecca 9/28/1828 W
COLLINS's child 6/24/1819 S
COLTER Patrick 11/24/1830 S
COMBS Mrs 7/27/1813 S
COMPTON John S 4/4/1832 W
COMPTON Mrs's child 12/8/1832 S
CONEGE Mrs 1/25/1816 W
CONLEY John's child 12/3/1806 S
CONLEY Patrick 10/14/1810 W
CONLY John's child 2/9/1810 S
CONNELL William 7/18/1830 S
CONNELLY Bridget 7/1/1830 W
CONNELLY Thos 12/3/1825 W
CONNELY Michael 12/12/1829 S
CONNER Mrs 2/16/1827 S
CONNER Mrs 5/8/1814 S
CONNER Patrick's wife 4/24/1826 W
CONNER Robert's child 12/8/1824 S
CONNER Robert's child 12/5/1826 S
CONNER William's child 1/21/1830 W
CONNER William's father 9/7/1829 S
CONNERS Robert's child 8/30/1821 S
CONNOR Mrs for ----- 8/18/1801 S
CONNTEE Richard 10/11/1820 M
CONROD Godfry's child 1/31/1825 M

CONTEE Mrs 11/14/1821 M
CONWAY Owen 11/25/1830 S
COOK Beck 1/5/1815 S
COOK Charles 12/24/1801 S
COOK David 9/8/1832 S
COOK James 4/17/1798 M
COOK Mr 12/12/1818 M
COOK Mr's black child 2/2/1812 S
COOK Mrs 2/26/1822 M
COOK Thomas's black girl 7/18/1816 S
COOKE John B 8/25/1826 M
COOKE Thomas 8/9/1826 M
COOKENDORFER Leonard 9/4/1823 W
COOKENDORFER Mrs's colored woman 6/28/1826 S
COOLIDGE Miss Peggy 3/4/1814 M
COOLIDGE Samuel 7/31/1812 M
COOPER 11/17/1818 S
COOPER Ann's child (colored woman) 10/13/1829 S
COOPER Lieutenant's child 10/25/1831 M
COOPER Mary's child 10/12/1817 S
COOPER Mrs 10/19/1816 S
COOPER Mrs 5/25/1819 S
COOPER Richard 12/16/1810 S
COPANG Mr 3/24/1819 S
CORCORAN John 11/15/1826 S
CORCORAN John's child 11/25/1830 S
CORCORAN Michael 8/27/1830 S
CORCORAN Mr 10/9/1808 W
CORCORAN Mr's child 9/30/1818 S
CORCORAN Mrs 10/9/1820 W
CORCORAN Mrs 2/1/1827 S
CORCORAN Mrs 6/4/1823 M
CORCORAN Thomas Senr 1/29/1830 M
CORCORAN Thomas's black woman 9/17/1820 S
CORCORAN Thomas's colored child 7/23/1825 S
CORCORAN Thomas's woman 10/28/1825 S
CORNWALL John B's child 10/9/1831 W
CORNWALL John B's child 9/7/1830 W
CORROTHERS G 2/17/1807 S
COSTELAN James 8/10/1830 S
COUNTEE Airy's child (colored) 4/2/1828 S
COUNTEE Dory's girl 7/29/1809 S

COVER Daniel for ----- 10/20/1810 W
COVER George's brother 2/4/1832 S
COVER George's child 12/14/1825 S
COVER George's child 9/7/1819 M
COVER George's colored man 2/27/1828 S
COVER John (colored man)'s child 12/21/1824 S
COVER Miss 8/16/1825 W
COVER Mrs 5/2/1827 M
COVER Richard's child 10/7/1815 M
COX John's child 9/8/1807 M
COX John's child 3/18/1807 M
COX John's colored child 12/22/1808 S
COX John's colored child 7/26/1831 S
COX John's colored child 8/5/1830 S
COX John's Frank 7/27/1805 S
COX John's Harry 12/8/1831 S
COX Mr's child 10/27/1821 S
COX Mrs John 9/12/1807 M
COX William 10/30/1821 S
COXE Richard S's child 9/21/1832 M
COXEN Mr's child 11/12/1821 S
COXEN W's child 2/17/1823 S
COXEN Washington's child 7/10/1818 S
COZENS Doctor's child 9/2/1801 W
CRAGE Robert 12/1/1812 M
CRAGIN Mr's child 1/28/1820 S
CRAIG George 4/19/1815 W
CRAIG George's mother 10/30/1805 W
CRAIG Lewis 9/28/1821 W
CRAIGE Charles 11/20/1815 W
CRAMPHIN Thomas 12/3/1830 M
CRAMPTON Richard for ----- 10/27/1806 M
CRANFORD Mrs (colored woman) 12/8/1821 S
CRANNEL Jesse's child 9/25/1815 M
CRARN E 3/7/1816 S
CRAVEN William's child 1/25/1816 S
CRAVEN William's child 10/24/1820 S
CRAWFORD Mrs's black child 3/27/1817 S
CRAWFORD Mrs's colored man George 12/4/1830 S
CRAWFORD Mrs's mother 1/23/1831 M
CRAWFORD Nathaniel's child 8/30/1800 M
CRAWFORD Sarah's colored woman 11/10/1830 S

CRAWFORD Sarah's colored child 10/4/1823 S
CRAWFORD William 11/28/1816 M
CRAWFORD William's 2 children 12/21/1815 M
CRAWFORD William's Bazil 5/22/1812 S
CRAWFORD William's black woman 7/28/1816 S
CRAWFORD William's black boy 5/10/1813 S
CRAWFORD William's black boy 7/5/1812 S
CRAWFORD William's black child 10/5/1813 S
CRAWFORD William's child 9/3/1809 M
CRAWFORD William's colored child 12/31/1811 S
CRAWFORD William's John 5/9/1806 S
CRAWFORD William's negro child 12/14/1810 S
CREAGER Mrs 4/3/1819 S
CREALIN Daniel 9/7/1830 S
CREEGER Mrs 1/16/1816 W
CRITTENDEN Joel's child 10/7/1819 M
CROMWELL Jessee's child 6/25/1810 W
CRONEY Francis 10/17/1830 S
CROPLEY Samuel's child 4/13/1831 W
CROPLEY Samuel's child 9/7/1832 W
CROSS Colonel Joseph 9/17/1830 M
CROSS Mrs 3/11/1820 M
CROSSEN Mrs 7/14/1830 S
CROW John's child 10/27/1815 W
CROW John's child 6/6/1817 W
CROW John's child 6/28/1825 W
CROW John's child 9/9/1822 W
CROW John's child 1/16/1832 W
CROW John's child 5/8/1829 W
CROW John's child 6/20/1830 W
CROW John's child 9/27/1827 W
CROW John's child 6/23/1826 W
CROWLEY Miss 5/1/1827 S
CROWN S T's child 10/9/1812 S
CROWN Samuel T 12/23/1812 S
CROWN William's child 8/23/1817 S
CRUET Mr 9/19/1821 W
CRUET Mr' child 1/15/1823 S
CRUETT Robert's child 6/24/1828 S
CRUIKSHANK Charles's child 1/14/1825 M
CRUIKSHANK Charles's child 4/9/1823 W
CRUIKSHANK John 11/25/1816 M

CRUIKSHANK John 11/2/1803 M
CRUIKSHANK Mrs's child 11/7/1803 W
CRUIT John L's child 11/11/1832 W
CRUST Henry 10/3/1805 M
CRUTTENDEN Joel's child 7/1/1826 M
CRUTTENDEN Joel's colored woman 10/10/1830 S
CRUTTENDEN Mr's child 3/17/1813 W
CUPPERSMITH Henry 10/28/1815 W
CURDY Michael 7/26/1830 S
CURRAN John 3/5/1807 M
CURRAN John for ----- 9/30/1803 M
CURRAN Nicholas's child 8/25/1830 S
CURRAN William 4/15/1832 W
CURRANT Jane (colored woman)'s daughter 11/22/1821 S
CURRANT Peter's wife 2/12/1831 S
CURTIS Rachael 9/16/1832 S
CUSTARD Jacob's child 1/16/1831 S
CUSTIS G W P's colored man 10/21/1832 S
CUSTIS Mr's man 11/3/1820 S
CUSTIS Mrs's grandchild 4/25/1825 M
CUTTING Nathaniel 3/9/1824 W
DABNEY Mary 7/27/1816 S
DADE Elizabeth 4/27/1828 W
DADE Harry's child 1/3/1828 S
DAILY George 9/7/1829 S
DALANY Mrs 9/28/1819 S
DALAWAY Capt's son 4/5/1830 S
DALENA Matthew 3/9/1815 W
DALEY Thomas 10/2/1830 S
DALTON Tristram's wife 4/19/1799 M
DANDRIDGE William's child (colored man) 7/26/1829 S
DANDRIGE Wm (colored man)'s mother 5/20/1825 S
DANIEL Francis's wife 10/17/1798 W
DANNELLS A 5/3/1831 S
DANOON Mr for ----- 6/2/1810 S
DANT Henry 8/25/1814 S
DANT Mr's child 3/21/1816 W
DARCEY William's black boy 11/17/1814 S
DARNALL Jacob 10/11/1828 S
DASHEALON Miss 9/23/1820 S
DASHIELL Miss S for a girl 9/14/1811 S
DASHIELL Thomas for ----- 4/23/1811 M

DAUGHTY Peter 6/11/1829 S
DAVEY Mrs 12/23/1824 W
DAVIDSON James for ----- 10/17/1806 M
DAVIDSON James's child 10/26/1811 M
DAVIDSON James's child 2/9/1808 M
DAVIDSON John (colored man) 7/8/1829 S
DAVIDSON John's child 9/3/1832 M
DAVIDSON L G's colored man 7/26/1825 S
DAVIDSON L G's child 9/20/1832 M
DAVIDSON Lewis G 11/2/1832 M
DAVIDSON Lewis G's boy 8/2/1824 S
DAVIDSON Lieut's child 8/24/1829 M
DAVIDSON Samuel 8/1/1810 M
DAVIS Amos's child 11/5/1818 S
DAVIS Augustus's child 7/27/1830 S
DAVIS Charles's mother 9/14/1811 W
DAVIS Edward's child 8/15/1812 W
DAVIS George's child 11/3/1819 W
DAVIS Gideon's child 3/17/1828 W
DAVIS Gideon's child 7/24/1830 W
DAVIS James 1/7/1816 W
DAVIS John 2/20/1815 S
DAVIS Maria's child 9/10/1818 S
DAVIS Mr 12/18/1830 S
DAVIS Mr's child 8/5/1817 S
DAVIS Mr's son 8/23/1810 S
DAVIS Mrs 1/16/1814 S
DAVIS Mrs 11/18/1815 M
DAVIS Mrs's daughter 8/9/1815 S
DAVIS Penney 8/18/1814 W
DAVIS Richard's son 4/28/1831 M
DAVIS Sally 8/18/1825 S
DAVIS Samuel (colored man)'s brother 7/27/1831 S
DAVIS Samuel (woman) 2/13/1815 S
DAVIS Samuel's brother 11/15/1821 S
DAVIS Samuel's brother (colored man) 10/20/1821 S
DAVIS Sarah (colored woman)'s child 11/17/1823 S
DAVIS Sarah's child 10/17/1823 S
DAVIS Thomas 7/12/1810 W
DAVIS Thomas Doctor 7/13/1828 M
DAVIS Thomas for ----- 8/23/1800 W
DAVIS Thomas for unknown 12/10/1798 S

DAVIS Thomas's child 9/1/1798 S
DAVIS's child (colored) 1/29/1830 S
DAWES B's colored girl 7/7/1823 S
DAWES Benjamin's child 8/11/1822 W
DAWES Benjamin's child 11/30/1823 W
DAWES Isaac's child 1/30/1809 W
DAWES Mr charged for unknown 7/6/1796 S
DAWES Mrs Ben 9/26/1824 W
DAWS Benjamin's child 11/15/1821 W
DAWS Edward's child 3/8/1817 M
DAWSON Charles 11/2/1822 M
DAWSON Mr's child 7/25/1815 S
DAWSON Mrs Thomas 8/25/1828 M
DAWSON Robert's child 12/20/1829 S
DAWSON Robert's child 6/29/1831 S
DAWSON Thomas's child 9/27/1832 W
DAWSON Thomas's mother 9/16/1828 W
DAY child 10/26/1820 S
DAY Mr's child 10/10/1820 S
DAY Mrs 10/17/1820 S
DAY Mrs 10/26/1820 S
DAYE A 6/10/1821 W
De LONGUERVILLE Mr 7/6/1819 M
DEAKINS Francis 10/29/1804 M
DEAKINS Leonard 6/29/1824 M
DEAKINS Leonard's child 4/18/1812 W
DEAKINS Miss 9/11/1830 M
DEAKINS Mrs 12/11/1821 S
DEAKINS Mrs 2/17/1809 M
DEAKINS Mrs 5/31/1805 M
DEAKINS Sarah A 11/7/1830 S
DEAKINS William 3/5/1798 M
DEAN Charles's colored man 10/20/1828 S
DEAN Felix's child 8/4/1823 S
DEAN Felix's child 10/27/1827 S
DEAN Mr's child 7/29/1817 S
DEAVER Mr's child 8/21/1824 W
DECKER James 10/1/1821 S
DECKER Mrs 8/29/1825 S
DEGGES William's child 2/9/1824 M
DEGIMS Mr 9/13/1804 W
DeKRAFFT Charles 7/25/1804 W

DELAHAY Benjamin's child 12/4/1803 S
DELANY Matthew's sister 9/14/1830 W
DELANY Mrs 11/11/1820 S
DELAPLANE Joseph for ----- 11/14/1810 M
DELLENGER Fredreck 12/17/1815 W
DEMENT Richard's wife 9/25/1826 W
DEMPSY Mr's child (Alexandria) 10/3/1802 M
DeMYER John's child 10/13/1823 S
DENNESON John's child 9/5/1821 W
DENNINGTON Mr 3/31/1825 W
DePLUX Eugene 7/20/1808 M
DEVELIN Daniel 9/19/1804 W
DEVENAY Patrick 3/19/1815 W
DEVERS James's child 8/30/1812 W
DEWES Mr 8/9/1804 M
DICK Jimmy 5/10/1816 S
DICK Thomas (Bladensburg) for ----- 9/28/1802 M
DICKSON James 12/10/1831 S
DICKSON John's child 4/10/1828 W
DICKSON Mrs 7/31/1823 W
DIDENHOOVER Mr 4/13/1824 W
DIFFENBAUGH John M 8/24/1831 W
DIGG Wm's child 8/22/1818 M
DIGGES Mr Nelson 11/6/1830 S
DIGGS Mr 1/14/1806 W
DIGGS Mrs 12/7/1806 W
DIGGS Thomas's woman 5/8/1818 S
DIGGS William's child 7/8/1816 M
DIMENT Richard's mother 10/23/1826 W
DINES Jessee 3/8/1805 W
DINMORE Mr's child 10/16/1799 W
DINMORE Mr's colored person 9/20/1801 S
DINMORE Mr's colored child 9/20/1801 S
DINMORE Richard's child 11/29/1800 S
DITTY John 10/26/1816 W
DIXON James's child 9/2/1819 W
DIXON Miss (Robert Stony's pseudo wife) 8/31/1828 S
DIXON Mr for ----- 12/9/1806 S
DIXON Mrs 5/14/1819 W
DIXON Thomas 2/17/1826 W
DIXON Thomas's child 7/28/1819 W
DIXON William for ----- 4/27/1805 S

DODGE Francis's Abe 3/28/1826 S
DODGE Francis's colored boy 4/26/1825 S
DODGE Francis's colored man 5/22/1829 S
DODSON Sophia (colored woman) 5/22/1828 S
DOLF Mrs 8/11/1828 S
DONALDSON John's child 8/27/1831 W
DONALDSON Mrs 6/4/1823 W
DONALDSON Thomas's wife 6/28/1826 S
DONALDSON William's child 10/11/1831 S
DONALDSON William's child 6/20/1831 S
DONALDSON William's son 10/25/1831 S
DONNEDY Dennis 12/17/1830 S
DONNELSON Mr 3/11/1815 S
DONNOLSON John's son 9/18/1829 W
DONOVER Michael 1/21/1830 S
DOONAN Michael 4/4/1831 S
DORIS Bernard 9/3/1830 S
DORSEY Lettie's child (colored) 5/11/1828 S
DORSEY William H for ----- 11/23/1802 M
DORSEY's Billy's child 9/19/1808 S
DOUGHERTY Charles 9/29/1830 W
DOUGHERTY Mary 8/5/1830 W
DOUGHTY Mr's child 9/15/1801 M
DOUGHTY Mrs (William's mother) 3/7/1810 M
DOUGHTY William's child 8/28/1812 M
DOUGHTY William's colored child 10/25/1805 S
DOUGHTY William's daughter Ellen 4/27/1832 M
DOUGLAS Mr 3/20/1822 M
DOUGLAS Mrs 1/6/1812 S
DOUGLASS Mrs 2/16/1826 W
DOVER Sandy (colored) 4/25/1828 S
DOYLE Anna A 3/27/1828 W
DOYLE Francis's child 8/27/1832 W
DOYNE Joseph 10/17/1821 M
DRAKE John 9/14/1830 S
DRUMMOND Cornelius's child 2/4/1831 S
DUCKER Moses (colored man) 3/10/1825 S
DUCKET Bazil 9/18/1815 M
DUCKET Isaac 7/4/1823 M
DUCKET Miss 5/30/1820 M
DUCKET Miss Mary 5/25/1812 M
DUFFY Brian 12/7/1813 W

DUFFY Brian's child 9/17/1804 S
DUFFY Matthew's mother 8/19/1830 W
DUFFY Wm's chld 8/15/1818 S
DUFIEFF Cherubim 8/7/1826 W
DUFIEFF Mr's child 7/15/1811 W
DUGGALL Daniel's child 11/18/1829 S
DUGLASS Mr's child 8/18/1820 S
DULEY Barton 8/2/1822 W
DULEY Mr for ----- 9/25/1810 W
DULY Mr 10/19/1799 S
DUN Ed 10/8/1830 S
DUN Samuel's child 8/9/1820 W
DUNAVEN John 10/4/1830 S
DUNBAR (colored man) 10/4/1830 S
DUNCAN John 6/27/1816 S
DUNCANSON William M's wife 8/3/1799 M
DUNCASTEL Sally 4/9/1813 M
DUNCASTER Miss Sally's colored child 3/16/1804 S
DUNCASTLE Miss S's colored man 12/21/1811 S
DUNCASTLE Miss S's negro child 6/28/1809 S
DUNCASTLE Miss S's negro child 9/25/1809 S
DUNCASTLE Miss S's negro boy 4/27/1809 S
DUNCASTLE Miss S's negro woman 9/22/1810 S
DUNCASTLE Miss S's colored man 1/24/1809 S
DUNCASTLE Miss S's colored man 4/8/1809 S
DUNCASTLE Miss S's negro child 9/21/1809 S
DUNCASTLE Sarah's colored child 4/24/1806 S
DUNCASTLE Sarah's negro woman 6/2/1806 S
DUNLAP John 11/12/1805 M
DUNLOP George 10/1/1820 M
DUNLOP Henry for ----- 3/17/1807 M
DUNLOP James 3/5/1823 M
DUNLOP James Junr's child 11/2/1820 M
DUNLOP James's child 11/14/1825 M
DUNLOP James's child 11/14/1805 M
DUNLOP R P's colored child 5/9/1830 S
DUNLOP R P's colored boy 8/19/1832 S
DUNN James C's colored child 7/30/1832 S
DUNN James C's colored girl 12/28/1832 S
DUNN Samuel's child 12/3/1826 W
DUVAL Miss (P G Co) 8/14/1832 W
DUVAL Mrs A C 10/8/1832 M

DUVALL Gabriel's negro child 9/14/1810 S
DUVALL Miss (of P G Co) 4/11/1825 W
DUVALL Miss 7/14/1816 W
DUVALL Mrs 4/10/1816 M
DUVALL Mrs's child 1/12/1815 S
DUVALL R 5/25/1829 S
DUVALL William 8/11/1814 W
DUVALL Wm 10/16/1818 W
DYER Aaron 10/5/1814 W
DYERS Mrs 5/27/1819 S
DYKUS Wm's child 8/27/1818 S
EASTERDAY Mrs 2/18/1815 S
EASTON ------ 10/7/1832 S
EASTON Deb's child 11/5/1825 S
EASTON Mr 1/19/1815 S
EASTON William 11/29/1830 W
EASTON William 9/5/1830 S
EATHY George 7/30/1823 W
EATHY George's child 8/17/1820 W
EATHY Hesekiah for ----- 8/16/1805 W
ECKELHART Mr's child 7/2/1816 S
EDDS John 12/14/1831 M
EDELIN Matilda's child 5/7/1831 S
EDES W H's child 10/7/1831 S
EDMONDSON Mrs's Raphie 12/21/1828 S
EDMONDSON Mrs's son 8/31/1832 W
EDMONDSON Thomas 11/20/1824 W
EDMONSON Mr's child 10/12/1818 S
EDMONSON Mrs 8/10/1813 S
EDMUNDSON Miss 6/17/1819 W
EDMUNSON Desham's child 1/31/1817 S
EDMUNSON Edward 4/15/1822 W
EDWARDS Henry's child 11/6/1808 W
EDWARDS John 3/23/1815 S
EDWARDS Miss 9/20/1832 M
EDWARDS Mr's child 9/6/1816 S
EDWARDS Mrs 1/4/1827 W
ELDERKIN Mr's child 1/26/1822 W
ELGIN Hamilton 8/23/1831 W
ELIASON John 9/20/1832 M
ELIASON John Jr 4/30/1821 W
ELIASON John's child 4/21/1810 W

ELIASON John's child 9/3/1808 W
ELIASON John's child 7/30/1817 S
ELIASON John's child 8/30/1808 M
ELIASON Miss Maria 9/13/1831 M
ELIASON Mr's child 10/17/1804 W
ELIASON Mrs 8/6/1817 M
ELIOT Linde 8/5/1817 W
ELLIOTT Mrs Statira 8/11/1831 W
ELLIOTT Mrs's child 8/2/1825 M
ELLIS Hezekiah's child 8/21/1824 S
ELLIS Joshua's child 6/27/1825 S
ELLIS Joshua's child 9/14/1826 W
ELLIS Mrs 5/26/1820 W
ELLIS Mrs's child 10/15/1819 S
ELLIS Mrs's child 9/30/1823 S
ELSY Doctor 6/7/1818 M
ELVIN Mr's child 11/23/1819 S
ELVINS Mr 6/13/1821 S
ELVINS Mr 9/20/1821 W
ENGLISH David for a child 3/30/1800 S
ENGLISH David for ----- 3/30/1800 M
ENGLISH David Jr's child 5/15/1824 S
ENGLISH David Senr's colored woman 9/22/1832 S
ENGLISH David Senr's child 9/14/1821 M
ENGLISH David's colored woman 12/23/1832 S
ENGLISH David's colored child 8/12/1820 S
ENGLISH David's colored girl 12/23/1815 S
ENGLISH David's son Thomas 6/26/1812 W
ENGLISH John 6/4/1807 S
ENGLISH Joseph's child 3/19/1802 S
ENGLISH Mary 5/3/1826 M
ENGLISH Mrs 2/19/1827 M
ENO Edward for ----- 5/12/1798 W
ENO Mrs 11/30/1828 W
ERMANDINGER Jno S 4/29/1825 S
ERRINGSHAW Thomas 9/10/1831 W
ERRINSHAW Mrs 6/18/1823 W
ERSLING George 9/7/1832 S
ESPY William 9/7/1832 W
ESSEX James F's mother 4/9/1830 M
ESTLERMAN Mrs 4/23/1821 W
EVANS Cadwalder's child 5/18/1828 M

EVANS Clarissa's child 7/23/1812 W
EVANS Evan for ----- 9/5/1803 W
EVERET Joseph 9/18/1827 S
EVERETT Mrs's child 1/20/1830 S
EVERSFIELD Mary (colored woman) 10/17/1827 S
EWELL Thomas's child 11/25/1815 M
FAGAN Daniel 7/25/1830 W
FAGAN Daniel's child 2/8/1824 S
FAGAN Mr's child 8/31/1816 S
FAGAN Mr's child 5/21/1823 S
FAGAN Mr's mother-in-law 4/6/1807 S
FAHE Mrs 4/22/1830 W
FAHEY Mr 12/10/1822
FALLS Sally (colored woman) 10/31/1821 S
FANAGAN John 1/23/1830 S
FEARSON J N's child 4/11/1831 S
FEARSON J N's child 11/8/1832 S
FEARSON Joseph 9/7/1832 W
FEARSON Joseph's child 6/14/1822 W
FEARSON Mrs's colored man 9/10/1832 S
FEARSON Mrs's colored man 10/9/1832 S
FEARSON S S's colored woman 9/22/1832 S
FEARSON Wm 10/16/1825 W
~~FECHTIG Lewis R~~ 8/28/1824 M
FECHTIG Lewis R 9/26/1823 M
FEELING Steven's child 9/4/1829 S
FEILD William's girl 8/4/1815 S
FEILDS William 6/18/1817 W
FELIOUS Jacob's black woman 1/19/1815 S
FELSON Alexander's child 2/17/1818 S
FELSON Jane (colored woman) 5/22/1830 S
FENDLE Michael's child 7/27/1830 S
FENDLE Miss at Dr Kent's 10/20/1829 M
FENNECEY James 1/10/1815 S
FENTHAM Mrs for ----- 4/11/1801 W
FENWICK Clara (colored woman)'s child 2/2/1824 S
FENWICK Francis 11/9/1825 S
FENWICK Mrs 2/20/1814 S
FENWICK Mrs 5/18/1829 W
FENWICK Mrs 7/24/1823 S
FENWICK Mrs's ralation 1/22/1814 S
FERGUSON Mr 8/3/1808 S

FETTERS Peter 10/5/1831 M
FEW Mrs 9/3/1829 W
FIELDS Mathew 9/21/1817 S
FINAGAN Benjamin's child 9/25/1803 W
FINNIGAN Mr ("about this time" following 2/21/1796) M
FIPP William 11/3/1821 S
FISH Francis 3/14/1828 W
FISHER Mr's child 10/1/1804 S
FITZ Thomas's child 12/9/1830 S
FITZGERALD Mary's child 8/5/1822 M
FITZGERALD Mr 7/26/1816 M
FITZHUGH Janet 9/23/1819 M
FITZHUGH Mr for ----- 5/18/1802 M
FITZHUGH Richard 5/31/1821 W
FITZHUGH Samuel's child 10/7/1813 M
FLEET Henry (colored man) 3/20/1824 W
FLEET Thomas's child (colored) 7/7/1830 W
FLEET Wash 9/12/1830 S
FLETCHER James's child 7/31/1815 S
FLETCHER James's child 6/23/1826 S
FLINN Matthew 9/16/1830 S
FLONES Charles 12/9/1816 W
FLORIS Mrs 2/14/1832 W
FOLIO Mrs's child 2/6/1823 S
FORD J 4/18/1818 S
FORD James (a black man)'s child 5/1/1814 S
FORD John G's black man 10/18/1818 S
FORD Lewis (colored man)'s child 10/28/1831 S
FORD Lewis (colored man)'s child 11/2/1831 S
FORD Mr 1/1/1817 S
FORD Mr's black woman 5/16/1814 S
FORD Mrs 5/3/1814 W
FORD Peggy (colored woman) 9/3/1832 S
FORMAN Mrs 8/8/1821 W
FORREST Henry 2/25/1826 M
FORREST Henry's child 8/11/1812 M
FORREST Henry's child 6/20/1818 M
FORREST Henry's colored woman 2/4/1824 S
FORREST Henry's woman 8/11/1819 S
FORREST I paid for unknown 5/25/1796 S
FORREST Mrs 7/6/1815 M
FORREST Mrs's colored man 10/8/1832 S

FORREST Mrs's grand child 1/20/1819 M
FORREST Uriah 7/7/1805 M
FORTUNE William's wife's sister 3/11/1824 S
FOSTER Mr 1/15/1812 S
FOWLER Catherine's child 7/18/1825 S
FOWLER Daniel 2/3/1812 W
FOWLER Mr's child 8/31/1824 W
FOWLER Mrs 2/4/1822 W
FOWLER Mrs 5/21/1830 S
FOWLER Mrs's child 10/3/1830 S
FOWLER Thomas 10/2/1831 S
FOWLER Thomas 9/28/1830 S
FOWLER Thomas's child 7/17/1803 S
FOX Bartelton 1/6/1816 W
FOX Ceph 1/6/1816 W
FOX E J 8/8/1821 M
FOX Mary 12/13/1813 W
FOX Mrs 5/3/1819 W
FOX Parmealy 11/9/1816 W
FOX Sally 9/24/1813 W
FOXALL Henry for ----- 3/25/1808 S
FOXALL Henry for ----- 3/17/1808 S
FOXALL Henry for son [John] 1/27/1809 M
FOXALL Henry's ----- 3/7/1804 S
FOXALL Henry's black child 7/23/1815 S
FOXALL Henry's black child 6/27/1813 S
FOXALL Mrs 2/10/1816 M
FRANCIS Mr 10/1/1804 S
FRASIER John's child 5/31/1823 S
FREDERICK's child 9/3/1815 S
FREELOT Mr 8/1/1827 S
FREEMAN Constant 3/1/1824 M
FREEMAN J D's child 8/11/1825 W
FREEMAN Jack 1/16/1832 S
FREEMAN John D's woman 7/16/1829 S
FREEMAN John D's William 6/28/1831 S
FREEMAN Miss Mary 10/23/1827 W
FREEMAN Mr's child 12/5/1829 S
FREEMAN Mrs 5/3/1830 W
FREEMAN Mrs's black man 12/2/1813 S
FREEMAN Mrs's black woman 7/18/1817 S
FREEMAN Mrs's black child 9/4/1815 S

FREEMAN Nace's child (colored) 5/4/1830 S
FREEMAN Nace's daughter 2/25/1830 S
FREEMAN Robert 10/4/1821 S
FRENCH Charles 12/12/1815 M
FRENCH George for ----- 2/9/1811 M
FRENCH George for ----- 7/9/1809 M
FRENCH George's 2 children 7/5/1815 M
FRENCH James 5/26/1818 W
FRENCH John (colored man) 1/8/1830 S
FRENCH Mariamne's colored man 9/12/1831 S
FRENCH Mariamne's colored man 3/1/1830 S
FRENCH Mr 10/22/1814 S
FRENCH Mr 12/16/1798 M
FRENCH Mrs 11/12/1822 W
FRENCH Mrs 3/12/1806 M
FRENCH Mrs 6/23/1832 S
FRENCH Mrs's black woman 4/4/1819 S
FRENCH Mrs's man 9/1/1823 S
FRENCH's Isaac's twin 5/27/1830 S
FRESH Mr's child 7/30/1809 S
FRESH Mr's child 10/15/1806 S
FRESH William's child 5/15/1811 S
FREZIER Thomas 10/12/1822 W
FRIZE Mr's child 7/7/1813 S
FROST Louisa (colored woman) 6/26/1826 S
FRUTER Beckey 10/9/1829 S
FRYE Daniel's 2 children omitted 3/11/1818 M
FRYE Mr's child 1/15/1830 S
FRYE Mrs 12/12/1829 W
FRYE Nath's child 8/2/1819 M
FULLALOVE James's child 11/26/1818 W
FULLALOVE James's child 8/2/1832 W
FULLALOVE Mr's child 9/25/1819 S
FURGASON Mr 8/14/1821 W
FURGERSON Eleonar's mother (colored woman) 9/6/1826 S
GAINES Richard for ----- 12/17/1808 M
GAITHER Colonel 6/23/1811 M
GAITHER G R's child 2/6/1823 S
GAITHER George R's child 7/20/1831 M
GALLAGHER Mrs's child 1/20/1831 S
GALLASPY Mr 10/17/1804 W
GALRIGHT William's child 1/15/1807 S

GALVIN Mrs 9/4/1830 S
GANNON James 1/31/1830 W
GANNON James for ----- 12/20/1806 S
GANNON James's child 9/29/1812 W
GANNON Michael's child 9/15/1829 W
GANNON Mrs 9/10/1829 W
GANNON Peter 5/13/1828 W
GANTT Fielder 10/12/1824 M
GANTT Henry for ----- 4/25/1800 M
GANTT John's colored man 8/5/1831 S
GANTT Live 9/24/1820 S
GANTT Miss 1/22/1831 M
GANTT T T 5/6/1818 M
GARDINER Mr's child 12/27/1832 S
GARDNER John's child 9/7/1803 W
GARDNER Mr's child 8/2/1802 W
GARDNER Mr's child 2/22/1822 S
GARDNER Thomas 4/14/1822 S
GARRETSON John (colored man)'s child 3/18/1823 S
GARY Everard 1/13/1815 M
GARY Everard's child 7/14/1802 M
GATES John 9/25/1830 S
GEARVIS Mrs 5/7/1812 W
GEESLER Mr's child 10/19/1823 W
GEESLIN Mr's daughter 8/22/1830 W
GEESLING Mrs's child 8/20/1827 W
GELASPY Mr 5/10/1816 W
GEORGE Enoch's child 11/6/1814 W
GEORGE Mrs 2/10/1816 W
GEORGE Thomas 10/16/1818 S
GERMAN Valentine's child 8/25/1823 S
GERNES Henry's child 4/17/1817 S
GERRY Elbridge 11/24/1814 M
GERRY James's child 6/9/1830 S
GETTY Robert's child 5/21/1830 S
GETTY Robt's child 8/2/1824 M
GIBBON Mrs 2/4/1815 W
GIBBON Mrs 8/9/1810 M
GIBBON Thomas's child 6/25/1812 W
GIBBONS Mr's child 9/17/1811 W
GIBBONS Thomas's child 4/4/1811 W
GIBSON Charles 8/6/1830 S

GIBSON John's child 7/29/1819 S
GIBSON John's child 8/4/1816 W
GIBSON John's child 8/3/1818 S
GIBSON Joseph's child 10/5/1826 M
GIBSON Mr 1/9/1817 S
GIBSON Mr's child 6/28/1813 S
GIBSON Mr's child 9/7/1812 W
GIBSON Mrs 12/4/1817 W
GIBSON Mrs 9/9/1832 S
GIBSON Richard's father 5/29/1821 W
GIBSON Samuel 4/16/1825 M
GIBSON William 4/11/1824 M
GILDCREST Mr a soldier 2/16/1815 S
GILDY John 2/16/1815 W
GILES John's child 10/6/1819 W
GILHAM B 3/20/1820 S
GILLIS George's colored child 9/6/1822 S
GITTING Mrs 10/8/1819 W
GITTINGS Miss 8/14/1819 W
GLASCO Sally 1/19/1828 S
GLASSCO John (colored man) 8/28/1832 S
GLEN Mrs's child 10/28/1812 S
GLENN Mrs 6/2/1819 S
GLISSON William 11/3/1830 S
GLOYD Mrs's mother 12/31/1811 S
GLOYD Mrs's son 6/5/1815 W
GOADWIN Mrs's child 9/17/1815 S
GODDARD John B 1/1/1831 M
GODDARD John B's child 9/6/1813 W
GODDARD Thomas's child 6/25/1831 W
GODDART John B's child 10/5/1816 W
GODDART John B's child 7/31/1815 W
GODDART Mr's child 11/23/1816 W
GODDART Mrs 11/18/1819 M
GODDART Mrs 2/26/1816 W
GODDART Thomas's child 8/13/1829 W
GODDERT James's child 12/22/1819 M
GODFREY Mr's mother 5/2/1827 W
GODY Mrs 6/21/1814 W
GODY William 3/13/1831 S
GOLDIN Miss 8/15/1796 M
GOLDING Samuel 9/21/1832 S

GOLDSBOROUGH Charles W's man 8/29/1819 S
GOLDSBOROUGH John 2/2/1815 W
GOLDSMITH Jerry (colored man) 6/21/1828 S
GOOD Thomas G's child 10/8/1832 M
GOOD William's niece 12/10/1831 M
GOOD Wm's black child 8/9/1818 S
GOOD Wm's colored man 9/29/1825 S
GOODRICK William 3/19/1832 W
GOODRICK William's mother 2/5/1832 S
GORDEN Mr's colored child 12/4/1829 S
GORDON Mr's colored child 9/8/1832 S
GORDON Mrs 12/23/1831 S
GOSLER Henry Senr 3/4/1827 W
GOSZLER Anthony 2/12/1815 W
GOSZLER George's child 12/16/1815 W
GOSZLER George's child 2/5/1811 W
GOSZLER George's child 1/13/1825 W
GOSZLER Henry's child 8/10/1805 W
GOSZLER Henry's child 4/15/1808 W
GOSZLER John's child 1/15/1815 W
GOSZLER John's child 10/20/1808 W
GOSZLER Mrs 1/9/1823 S
GOUGH Miss 11/18/1832 M
GOULDING Mr's child 12/1/1817 W
GOULDING Mr's child 12/26/1821 S
GRADY John 7/23/1830 S
GRAHAM George 8/9/1830 M
GRAHAM John's child 12/17/1819 M
GRAHAM Mary 3/11/1819 S
GRAHAM Mr's black man 2/10/1815 S
GRAHAM Mr's child 10/21/1808 S
GRAHAM Mr's child 7/19/1809 S
GRAHAM Mrs 3/27/1829 W
GRAHAM Mrs Jane's son James 9/30/1832 M
GRAHAM William (colored man) 3/15/1830 S
GRAHAM William's child 10/28/1808 S
GRAHAM William's child 10/10/1811 W
GRANT W V's child (colored) 8/27/1828 S
GRANT William (a colored man)'s child 9/27/1816 W
GRANT William (colored man)'s child 2/23/1822 S
GRASON Mrs 7/4/1814 S
GRASON Sally's son 9/21/1815 S

GRASON William's child 9/5/1812 M
GRAVES Mr's child 7/20/1831 S
GRAY Alfred's brother (colored man) William 4/2/1827 S
GRAY George's wife 10/16/1828 W
GRAY H N's colored girl 3/18/1828 S
GRAY Henry's child (colored) 11/18/1828 S
GRAY Hugh's child 8/10/1819 S
GRAY John B's child 9/18/1830 W
GRAY Mr's child 6/15/1816 S
GRAY Mr's child 12/30/1811 S
GRAY Mr's child 1/4/1812 S
GRAY Prince (colored man) 7/9/1828 S
GRAY William 9/11/1832 S
GRAYSON Sally 5/21/1825 S
GREATRAKE L's child 8/4/1823 W
GREAVES John's child 8/13/1818 S
GREEN & ENGLISH for colored person 3/4/1802 S
GREEN Cely (colored woman) 11/11/1829 S
GREEN James (colored man)'s child 5/24/1824 S
GREEN James (colored man)'s child 8/3/1824 S
GREEN James (colored man)'s child 6/10/1823 S
GREEN James 7/1/1820 M
GREEN John's child 9/10/1818 M
GREEN Mrs 11/26/1809 W
GREEN Mrs 2/7/1824 S
GREEN Mrs for ----- 6/30/1806 W
GREEN Robert 3/23/1832 S
GREEN Sally 7/7/1819 S
GREEN Simon 1/14/1824 S
GREEN Wm's child 8/11/1818 S
GREENFIELD Mrs 7/10/1812 W
GREENTREE Matthew 1/29/1830 M
GREENTREE Mrs 3/10/1819 M
GREENWELL Mr's child 8/17/1818 S
GREENWELL Mr's child 9/13/1819 S
GREENWELL Mr's child 10/9/1818 S
GREER James's girl 4/26/1824 S
GREUHM Frederic 12/4/1823 M
GREVER Robert's child omitted 7/21/1817 W
GREY Vincent's child 5/1/1818 S
GREY Wm's wife 7/28/1819 W
GRIFFIN Mr 9/26/1823 S

GRIFFIN Mr's child 2/1/1815 S
GRIFFIN Mrs 10/7/1824 W
GRIFFIN Mrs 8/7/1803 S
GRIFFIN T B's child 8/14/1818 W
GRIFFIN T B's child 3/10/1825 W
GRIFFIN T B's brother 10/6/1819 W
GRIM Mrs 12/2/1821 W
GRIMES Helen (colored woman) 9/18/1831 S
GRIMES John 5/6/1824 S
GRIMES Leonard 9/1/1827 S
GRIMES Michael's child 9/20/1809 W
GRIMES Michael's child 5/26/1810 W
GRIMES Michael's mother 7/2/1825 S
GRIMES Mr's child 7/14/1831 S
GRIMES Thomas's child 11/11/1831 S
GROSS Francis's child 2/15/1831 W
GROSS Jacob 9/1/1821 S
GROSS Jacob 9/29/1814 S
GROSS Mrs 9/25/1811 S
GROSS Thomas (colored man)'s son 9/18/1832 S
GROSS Thomas's child 5/28/1827 S
GROSS Thomas's child 5/21/1827 S
GROSS Thomas's child 9/3/1816 S
GROVES Mrs 6/24/1814 W
GRUMBLE Mr's child 8/22/1818 S
GUEST Job's child 10/9/1825 M
GUEST Job's child 4/1/1826 M
GUEST Job's child 6/20/1825 M
GUINNE David for -----4/21/1807 W
GUMBLE Mary 7/8/1829 S
GUSTINE Ann 4/24/1816 M
GUSTINE Green 1/30/1817 M
GUSTINE Joel's colored man 9/7/1832 S
GUSTINE Robert J's child 2/4/1815 M
GUSTINE Samuel 4/3/1815 M
HACKLEY Nancy's child 2/15/1830 S
HADON John 2/21/1815 S
HAGAN Charles 1/3/1813 S
HAGAN Miss 5/22/1817 S
HAGARTY Mrs's child 7/2/1820 W
HAGERTY John 6/13/1820 W
HAGERTY John's child 2/16/1814 W

HAGERTY John's child 11/30/1816 W
HAGERTY John's child 3/1/1815 S
HAGERTY Mrs's child 10/2/1820 W
HAGNER Peter for ----- 12/21/1801 M
HAGNER Peter's child 12/21/1801 S
HAGON Mrs 1/31/1815 S
HAILE Mrs's child 8/16/1827 W
HALL Brice's child 10/23/1825 W
HALL Brice's child 8/10/1820 S
HALL Edward's man 8/7/1818 S
HALL Elisha 4/1/1821 W
HALL Eliza's child 9/13/1815 S
HALL F M 11/24/1826 M
HALL Flora (colored woman) 5/16/1825 S
HALL Henry Low 5/10/1817 M
HALL Kitty (colored woman) 7/16/1825 S
HALL Miss 3/25/1818 M
HALL Richard 5/19/1815 M
HALL Sally (colored woman) 11/24/1822 S
HALL Thomas 3/3/1830 S
HALL William 9/12/1831 W
HALLAT Mr 9/24/1802 S
HALLENBECK Mrs 7/6/1813 M
HALLENBECK William's child 7/27/1816 W
HALLER David 12/28/1825 W
HALLER Geo W's child 6/1/1825 M
HALLIDAY Mr's child 8/22/1806 S
HALLY Harriot's daughter 12/14/1813 S
HAMBLETON Rody (colored man) 12/20/1829 S
HAMBLY James 9/20/1832 W
HAMILTON Robert 7/24/1830 S
HAMMET J's child 8/24/1831 S
HANDY S W's child 9/1/1817 M
HANSON A C's child 11/4/1813 M
HANSON A C's child 10/23/1813 M
HANSON Mr 1/22/1832 W
HANSON Mrs 12/10/1822 W
HARBAUGH B's child 8/30/1829 S
HARBAUGH Leonard 5/14/1812 S
HARBAUGH Leonard for ----- 8/19/1811 S
HARBAUGH Mr 9/18/1810 S
HARBAUGH Mr's child 10/4/1831 S

HARDEN Mrs 1/12/1815 S
HARDEN Thomas 1/21/1815 S
HARDEN William 6/25/1828 W
HARDIE Robert 11/27/1827 W
HARDIN Edward for ----- 5/25/1804 M
HARDISTAY Mr's child 8/11/1823 M
HARDON Miss 9/13/1822 W
HARDY Elizabeth 10/12/1828 W
HARDY William's child 11/1/1810 S
HARP Aquilla's child 4/1/1818 S
HARP Elizabeth's child 9/6/1822 S
HARP, James' child 1/6/1822 S
HARP, James' child 1/9/1822 S
HARP James's child 1/4/1822 S
HARP Miss's child 7/31/1819 S
HARP Mr's child 1/2/1820 S
HARP Mrs 8/22/1823 S
HARPER Dr's woman 11/5/1818 S
HARPER N 4/9/1819 S
HARRIS James a black man 6/1/1813 S
HARRIS John's child 8/10/1830 W
HARRIS Luke 4/4/1823 W
HARRIS Peter (colored man) 11/13/1831 S
HARRISON Dr. John 3/6/1825 M
HARRISON G's woman 5/1/1819 S
HARRISON George's child 6/?/1828 S (before 6/7/1828)
HARRISON Gus.'s child 9/4/1827 M
HARRISON Gustavus's child 6/10/1823 M
HARRISON Gustavus's child 9/23/1819 M
HARRISON Gustavus's colored woman 11/27/1822 S
HARRISON James 9/5/1803 W
HARRISON Mrs C C 8/1/1831 M
HARRISON Richard for ----- 7/31/1808 M
HARRISON Richard's child 1/15/1803 M
HARRISON Richard's child 2/29/1808 M
HARRISON Richard's child 12/12/1808 M
HARRISON Richard's colored woman 2/21/1801 S
HARRISON Richard's Fredrick 10/9/1803 S
HARROT Leonard (colored man) 4/13/1830 S
HARRY John's colored child 9/22/1832 S
HARRY Mrs 3/14/1824 S
HARSHMAN Mr's daughter 2/9/1810 S

HART John's child 11/8/1813 W
HART John's child 10/28/1814 W
HART John's child 8/30/1816 W
HART John's child 10/2/1821 W
HART Mrs 10/24/1822 W
HART Thomas 7/26/1830 S
HARTLOVE John's child 8/30/1826 W
HARTLOVE Mr's child 8/29/1812 S
HARTLOVE Mr's child 8/31/1811 S
HARTLOVE's child 9/20/1813 s
HARTMAN Mrs's son 8/14/1832 W
HARTNES Daniel's child 9/5/1830 S
HARVEY James's child 10/8/1831 S
HARVEY James's child 12/16/1831 S
HARVEY James's child 8/7/1828 S
HARVEY James's colored man 10/8/1830 S
HAUP Mr's child 7/20/1816 S
HAUSE Alfred 8/10/1829 S
HAVEY Mr's child 12/6/1823 S
HAW John S 9/12/1832 M
HAW John's colored man 9/24/1831 S
HAW John's William (colored man) 6/17/1832 S
HAW Mrs 8/1/1830 M
HAWKINS Bill (colored man) 2/3/1830 S
HAWKINS Charles's child 9/15/1818 S
HAWKINS Charles's child 1/30/1820 S
HAWKINS Chas (colored man) 4/29/1825 S
HAWKINS James 12/9/1825 M
HAWKINS Milly (colored woman) 9/24/1831 S
HAWKINS Mrs 3/20/1805 W
HAWKINS Walter (colored man)'s wife 2/5/1826 S
HAWKINS Walter 1/11/1820 S
HAWKINS Walter's child 2/21/1820 S
HAWKINS Walter's child 6/27/1820 S
HAWKINS William's child 7/15/1816 S
HAYDEN Miss 4/14/1831 S
HAYDEN Mrs's daughter 10/3/1831 S
HAYES Peter 12/29/1830 S
HAYNES Mrs 9/28/1823 M
HAYNES Mrs's servant 9/28/1823 W
HAYNES Staley 4/19/1826 W
HAYSWOOD Mr 1/16/1822 S

HAZEL Henry's child 7/9/1824 M
HEADERSON Nicholas's wife 10/12/1826 S
HEARD Mr's child 8/28/1828 S
HEARD Mrs 10/9/1821 W
HEATH Mr 11/6/1801 W
HEATH Mr's child 11/9/1808 S
HEATH Nathaniel for mother 10/24/1811 W
HEATH Nathaniel's child 10/30/1811 M
HEATH Nathaniel's child 10/28/1811 M
HEBNER Frederic's child 8/16/1823 W
HEBNER Frederick's child 8/19/1820 W
HEBORAN John colored man 9/28/1816 S
HEBORAN Peter's child 11/30/1816 S
HEBRON Andrew (colored man)'s child 1/16/1832 S
HEBRON John's black child 5/31/1818 S
HEDGE Cassey 4/6/1826 S
HEDGE Mr 8/5/1801 S
HEDGES Mrs 5/11/1822 M
HEDGES Nicholas for wife 6/13/1798 M
HEDGES Nicholas's child 3/22/1812 W
HEDGES Nicholas's child 11/3/1806 W
HEDGES Nicholas's child 10/28/1806 W
HEISE John C's child 12/18/1814 W
HEISTER General 3/7/1804 M
HELEN Mr's colored man 7/19/1823 S
HELLEN Walter 10/31/1815 M
HELLEN Walter for ----- 1/1/1811 M
HELLEN Walter's child 9/20/1803 M
HELLEN Walter's child 12/20/1806 M
HELM Mrs Joseph 12/13/1832 M
HEMFLEY Henry 7/27/1821 W
HENDERSON Doctor's child 10/31/1826 M
HENDERSON Doctor's man 7/8/1824 S
HENDERSON John D 1/27/1830 W
HENDERSON John's child 8/31/1815 W
HENDERSON John's child 6/6/1822 W
HENDERSON Mr 10/6/1805 M
HENDERSON Mr 11/16/1796 S
HENDERSON Polly 10/28/1826 S
HENDERSON R H's son 11/13/1828 M
HENDERSON Richard 8/30/1802 M
HENDERSON Sarah's black man 4/7/1820 S

HENDERSON Thomas's child 7/5/1827 M
HENDERSON Thos's child 8/18/1824 M
HENNEGER John 12/2/1830 S
HENOP Mrs for ----- 9/20/1799 W
HENOP Mrs for ----- 10/5/1802 W
HENOP Mrs's child 11/19/1804 S
HENOP Mrs's colored child 3/6/1806 S
HERBERT Charity's child (colored) 8/26/1831 S
HERBERT Francis's child 8/3/1818 W
HERBERT Mrs 4/1/1824 S
HERMANCE Ann 6/9/1822 M
HERN Elizabeth 9/6/1824 S
HERRITSON Elizabeth for ----- 7/25/1806 S
HERRON John 3/3/1816
HERSEY Benjamin for Brown 12/11/1808 M
HERSEY Benjamin's wife 12/29/1802 M
HERSEY J C's child 9/30/1818 W
HERSY John C for ----- 4/20/1810 W
HERSY John C's child 7/21/1810 S
HERVEY Jane 2/20/1825 M
HERVEY Mr's child 9/14/1824 S
HEWES Mrs's child 4/8/1802 S
HEWIT Thomas 4/13/1810 W
HEWS Patrick 7/29/1831 S
HEWSTEN Charles's child 8/22/1809 W
HEYER J 9/13/1832 S
HICKASON John 5/5/1815 W
HICKASON Mr's black man 4/21/1814 S
HICKASON Mr's black woman 4/24/1814 S
HICKEY John 10/8/1830 S
HIGDEN Mr 2/20/1823 S
HIGDEN Mrs 8/6/1829 S
HIGDEN Nelly's child 9/5/1817 S
HIGDON Joseph 6/13/1830 S
HIGDON Mr's child 1/4/1816
HIGDON Mrs 5/16/1821 S
HIGGINS Thomas 9/27/1830 S
HIGHT Mrs 11/2/1813 S
HILL Catharine 6/21/1832 S
HILL Mr 5/13/1818 S
HILL Mr's child 8/13/1818 W
HILL R's child 2/3/1820 S

HILL Richard (a colored man)'s child 12/22/1818 S
HILLARD John 10/16/1811 W
HILLARY L's child 7/28/1808 S
HILLARY Lewis's wife 11/9/1815 W
HILLARY Lewis's wife 8/2/1817 W
HILLARY Miss 2/5/1816 S
HILLARY N D 11/28/1831 S
HILLARY Nicholas for ----- 11/23/1806 W
HILLARY Nicholas's child 9/14/1813 W
HILLEARY John 2/20/1818 M
HILLEARY Lewis (colored man) 10/3/1821 W
HILLEARY Nicholas 11/6/1823 S
HILLEARY Nicholas's child 9/3/1817 W
HILLEARY Tilman's daughter 10/22/1821 W
HILLS Mrs 1/3/1820 W
HILSMER Mrs 3/24/1817 W
HILTEN Thomas's son 5/21/1830 M
HILTON John's child 11/15/1823 W
HILTON Mr's child 9/9/1801 W
HILTON Mr's child 8/27/1817 W
IIILTON Mrs 2/22/1819 S
HILTON Perry's child 7/20/1822 S
HINES Daniel 10/16/1807 W
HINES John 10/8/1816 W
HINES John's child 9/1/1819 W
HINES John's mother-in-law 8/16/1810 S
HINES Mary Ann 5/16/1823 S
HOAGLAND Isaac 11/30/1817 W
HOBLER William C 2/9/1815 W
HODGE Robt (colored man)'s wife's daughter 12/30/1825 W
HODGES Benjamin's daughter 8/14/1815 M
HODGES Thomas C 10/15/1821 M
HODGSON Joseph 5/21/1805 M
HODNET James 5/28/1821 W
HODSON Mrs (colored woman) 10/8/1822 S
HODSON Zarobable 5/3/1829 W
HOLAHAN Andrew 7/21/1830 S
HOLLAND Mr's child 9/25/1815 S
HOLLIDAY William's wife 3/3/1832 W
HOLLINGHEAD John 3/23/1815 M
HOLLY Drady (colored woman) 10/12/1830 S
HOLLY John 2/8/1817 S

HOLLY Reuben (colored man) 4/27/1831 S
HOLLY Ruben (colored man) 9/4/1829 S
HOLLY's mother in law 10/30/1815 S
HOLMAN Mr's black man 3/21/1816 S
HOLMEAD Anthony for ----- 7/5/1806 W
HOLMEAD George of Anthony 1/28/1799 W
HOLMEAD John for ----- 11/1/1802 M
HOLMES Wm 8/29/1825 M
HOLSTON James 11/28/1827 S
HOLT John and Sopha Skagg's child 11/7/1823 W
HOLT John R 1/7/1832 M
HOLT John's child 6/7/1820 M
HOLT Lawrence O 3/23/1818 M
HOLT Mrs 12/20/1819 M
HOLT Mrs 3/15/1820 M
HOLT Ralph 9/9/1827 W
HOLTZMAN Eli 7/10/1828 W
HOLTZMAN George W 10/9/1825 M
HOLTZMAN George's child 3/31/1820 M
HOLTZMAN George's child 10/3/1829 M
HOLTZMAN George's colored girl 12/12/1825 S
HOLTZMAN Harriet 12/15/1824 W
HOLTZMAN Jacob 12/23/1814 M
HOLTZMAN John's child 8/1/1821 W
HOLTZMAN John's child 12/8/1823 W
HOLTZMAN John's child 11/11/1829 W
HOLTZMAN John's child 4/11/1832 W
HOLTZMAN Mrs 7/9/1815 W
HOLTZMAN Mrs George's child 10/12/1827 W
HOLTZMAN Thomas's child 2/27/1832 W
HOMAN Benjamin's child 5/15/1828 M
HOMANS Benjamin 12/11/1823 M
HOMILLER Michael 11/2/1830 W
HOOBLER John 12/26/1827 S
HOOPER Sally 7/17/1830 S
HOOVER Mr 2/15/1810 W
HOOVER Mrs Peter 4/8/1823 S
HOOVER Peter's child 5/22/1817 S
HOOVER Peter's child 9/11/1823 S
HOPE Thos's child 10/22/1818 S
HOPE Tom 1/2/1823 S
HOPE Tom's wife 10/14/1822 S

HOPKINS Edward 3/13/1814 M
HOPKINS Mrs 4/19/1820 W
HOPKINSON Francis 9/30/1823 W
HORROGON John 7/22/1830 S
HOSKINS Jeff 9/29/1824 W
HOSKINS John 1/13/1827 S
HOTT Mr's child 10/3/1813 W
HOWARD John's wife 3/16/1829 S
HOWARD John's wife's mother 3/16/1829 S
HOWARD Mr's child 6/16/1829 S
HOWKE Joseph's child 9/23/1815 W
HOYT E J's child 12/17/1808 S
HUBBARD Dyer's daughter 2/27/1830 S
HUDSON Mr's child 6/6/1830 S
HUDSON Samuel's child 7/13/1832 S
HUFF Mr 10/8/1819 S
HUFF Mrs's child 12/30/1819 S
HUGHES Archy 8/15/1826 S
HUGHES Jacob 12/7/1818 W
HUGHES Jane 4/28/1829 M
HUGHES Miss (at J Laird's) 6/4/1805 M
HUGHES Miss for ----- 10/4/1806 M
HUGHES Miss's negro girl 12/17/1809 S
HUGHES Richard (colored man) 11/14/1827 S
HUGHS J 3/12/1822 W
HULL Jacob 5/12/1820 W
HULL Jacob's child 3/27/1809 W
HULL Mrs's mother 10/21/1822 S
HULL William 9/9/1832 W
HUNT Daniel (colored man) 1/1/1831 S
HUNT Mrs's child 2/15/1818 W
HUNTER Mr 8/15/1819 S
HUNTER Mr's child 11/18/1811 S
HUNTER Mr's child 5/2/1818 S
HURDLE Noble's son 7/24/1832 W
HURDS Mrs (colored woman) 9/9/1832 S
HURDUL John 9/3/1829 S
HURLEY Morris 9/4/1830 S
HURTLE Joseph's child 4/5/1814 M
HUSLER J T 1/6/1829 S
HUSLER Joseph 1/11/1822 W
HUSLER Joseph's child 10/1/1821 W

HUSLER Sarah 8/17/1830 S
HUTCHENS Mr Castar's child 9/9/1821 S
HUTCHENS Mrs 10/26/1820 W
HUTCHENS Susan's child 10/9/1831 W
HUTCHIN Bennet's child 8/26/1831 S
HUTCHIN Mr's child 8/18/1818 S
HUTCHINS F's child 7/12/1831 S
HUTCHINS John's child 11/22/1823 S
HUTCHINS John's child 7/27/1827 S
HUTCHINSON John S 1/7/1827 M
HUTTON Dafny's child 8/31/1820 S
HUTTON James's child 10/21/1823 M
HUTTON Mrs 8/7/1823 M
HYDE James 3/12/1826 W
HYDE Mrs 8/10/1829 W
HYDE Thomas's child 10/26/1807 W
HYDE Thomas's child 6/24/1808 W
HYDE Thomas's colored child 12/24/1803 S
INGEL Thomas 11/24/1828 S
IRWIN William 11/20/1806 M
ISAACS Mr 2/18/1815 W
ISBORN Mrs's child 6/20/1804 W
ISWELL William's child 11/7/1826 M
ITURBIDE Miss 10/2/1828 M
JACKMAN William 3/20/1814 S
JACKSON ------ 12/2/1831 W
JACKSON Ann 5/11/1829 M
JACKSON Benedict (colored man) 4/11/1827 S
JACKSON Jasper 9/6/1820 M
JACKSON John 1/30/1819 M
JACKSON John 4/8/1812 W
JACKSON John's child (colored) 1/6/1829 S
JACKSON Joseph 5/22/1831 W
JACKSON Joseph's child 10/26/1820 W
JACKSON Joseph's child 3/26/1823 W
JACKSON Mr's child 12/18/1830 S
JACKSON Mrs 1/13/1815 W
JACKSON Mrs 3/23/1812 W
JACKSON Mrs 7/4/1823 W
JACKSON Philip's child (colored) 8/14/1826 S
JACKSON Philip's child (colored) 5/25/1828 S
JACKSON Richard 9/16/1823 M

JACKSON Samuel 4/6/1831 S
JACKSON Samuel's child 6/22/1820 S
JACKSON Samuel's child 6/19/1819 S
JACKSON Samuel's child 8/5/1820 S
JACKSON Susan's child (colored) 8/24/1827 S
JACOBS John 5/4/1824 S
JAMES Benjamin 7/13/1818 S
JAMES John's child 3/19/1829 W
JAMES Mrs 10/1/1818 S
JANISELL Mrs's child 3/14/1819 S
JARBOW William 8/1/1821 W
JARVIS John 2/9/1830 S
JARVIS Mrs 10/12/1821 S
JARVIS Mrs 6/27/1819 S
JASON Mrs 12/5/1829 S
JAY Absolom 1/15/1809 W
JAY Julia's child (colored woman) 7/26/1829 S
JEFFERSON William 10/9/1832 S
JENISELL John 2/10/1819 S
JENKINS Dennis 9/3/1832 S
JENKINS Matthew's daughter 11/12/1821 S
JENKINS Mrs 9/9/1823 S
JENKINS Nancy 7/13/1829 S
JENKINS Robert 10/7/1810 W
JENNIFER Mr 8/20/1831 M
JEWELL Wm's child 9/8/1817 W
JEWET Nathaniel's child 6/19/1819 W
JOHN Leonard H's child 2/9/1803 M
JOHN Mrs's colored man 10/24/1832 S
JOHNCHEREZ A L 12/1/1817 M
JOHNCHEREZ A L's child 3/31/1814 W
JOHNS Dennis's child 8/19/1813 M
JOHNS L H (colored man) 7/19/1821 S
JOHNS Leonard H's child 9/8/1815 M
JOHNS Leonard H's child 3/9/1804 M
JOHNS Mr's negro woman's child 9/1/1810 W
JOHNS Mrs 3/28/1815 M
JOHNS Mrs Mary P 12/16/1831 W
JOHNS Richard 4/5/1830 M
JOHNSON (a colored woman)'s child 10/11/1816 S
JOHNSON E 7/31/1816 S
JOHNSON Henry 10/22/1820 S

JOHNSON Isaac 10/13/1826 S
JOHNSON Isaac for ----- 5/25/1807 S
JOHNSON Isaac's colored woman 4/14/1808 S
JOHNSON Isaac's son 2/3/1818 W
JOHNSON John 1/15/1815 S
JOHNSON John's child 9/23/1832 S
JOHNSON Matthew's son 10/21/1831 S
JOHNSON Mrs 10/1/1811 M
JOHNSON Mrs for ----- 10/1/1802 W
JOHNSON Peter (colored man) 5/8/1827 S
JOHNSON Richard 12/14/1831 S
JOHNSON Susan (colored woman)'s child 7/28/1824 S
JONCHEREZ A L's child 8/7/1804 W
JONES C L's child 6/27/1820 S
JONES Dennis's black child 12/21/1820 S
JONES Dennis's child 10/19/1821 M
JONES Edward 9/18/1829 M
JONES Edward for ----- 3/11/1802 M
JONES Edward for ----- 3/3/1802 M
JONES F P's child 8/6/1820 S
JONES F P's child 11/18/1818 S
JONES F P's child 12/31/1821 S
JONES Godfrey 1/9/1829 W
JONES Horatio's colored man 4/18/1827 S
JONES James 1/14/1801 M
JONES James C 2/4/1829 W
JONES John 4/11/1828 W
JONES John 6/9/1817 S
JONES John's child 8/2/1832 W
JONES John's son 8/27/1816 W
JONES Lawrence 5/4/1814 W
JONES Miss 4/22/1822 W
JONES Morris 7/24/1823 S
JONES Mr 4/24/1819 S
JONES Mr T W 10/11/1828 M
JONES Mr's child 9/7/1819 S
JONES Mr's child 9/10/1812 S
JONES Mr's child 5/30/1816 W
JONES Mrs 1/5/1831 S
JONES Mrs 3/20/1822 M
JONES Mrs 4/4/1815 S
JONES Mrs 6/5/1820 W

JONES Mrs's child 9/20/1829 S
JONES Mrs's child 7/4/1828 S
JONES R 9/16/1830 S
JONES R's sister's child 9/18/1819 S
JONES R's sister's child 9/20/1819 S
JONES Richard's child 8/3/1817 S
JONES Richard's child 7/31/1812 S
JONES Richard's mother 12/25/1810 S
JONES Richard's sister 3/14/1819 S
JONES Solomon's child 4/12/1820 S
JONES Susanna 4/11/1812 M
JONES Thomas's child 8/16/1831 S
JONES Thomas's child 1/31/1817 S
JONES Thomas's son 11/27/1815 S
JORDAN Mary's child 9/21/1807 S
KAHOE Patrick 7/20/1830 S
KAVANAUGH Andrew 12/20/1830 S
KEACH Suckey's husband 1/2/1826 S
KEARNES Miss 12/7/1818 W
KEARNS Mr 10/15/1824 S
KEASOM Mrs 7/10/1821 W
KEELER John 2/27/1817 S
KEEN Thomas's child 12/2/1811 S
KEEPHER Henry 3/14/1808 W
KEEPHER Henry for ----- 6/14/1800 S
KEEPHER Henry's child 9/5/1803 S
KEEPHER Henry's child 9/29/1807 M
KEEPHER Henry's child 11/18/1802 M
KEEPHER Mrs 9/24/1815 S
KEEPHER Mrs's daughter 11/27/1812 W
KEHIM Robert 1/4/1823 S
KEILER Mr 2/5/1824 S
KELLENBERGER child 8/6/1812 S
KELLY John 4/22/1823 W
KELLY John's child 9/27/1820 S
KELLY Mr 10/14/1808 S
KELLY Mr's child 10/5/1830 S
KELLY Mrs 8/10/1826 S
KEMP Mr's child 9/4/1829 S
KENDEL Eliza (colored woman)'s child 3/20/1824 S
KENDRICK Benjamin 11/15/1829 S
KENGLA Lewis's child 10/3/1809 W

KENGLEY Lewis 1/11/1829 W
KENNEDY James's child 11/11/1801 W
KENNEDY Matthew's child 8/22/1800 W
KENNEDY Miss 4/26/1816 W
KENNEDY Mr's child 2/5/1814 S
KENNEDY Mrs 10/31/1826 M
KENNY Patrick 10/10/1830 S
KENT Gov.'s wife 8/15/1826 M
KENT Joseph's son 11/11/1826 M
KENT Mrs 11/24/1813 M
KERLY William 11/27/1829 S
KERR Alexander for child 2/17/1808 M
KERR William 1/23/1827 M
KERWAN Richard 8/22/1830 S
KEY F S 's black child 1/15/1812 S
KEY F S' son 7/9/1822 M
KEY F S's black child 11/19/1815 S
KEY Francis's Harry 12/9/1807 S
KEY Mr's black woman 9/24/1819 S
KEY Philip B 7/29/1815 M
KEY Philip B's negro man 7/2/1809 S
KILGORE Mrs 5/23/1822 M
KILRICE Mrs 7/1/1814 W
KINCADE James 6/11/1827 M
KINCADE James's colored child 1/2/1826 S
KINCADE Martha 6/18/1827 M
KING Adam 10/6/1826 W
KING Adam's child 2/11/1804 S
KING Adam's child 1/31/1805 S
KING Adam's child 9/10/1800 W
KING Ambrose's child 9/18/1816 S
KING Andrew's child 10/27/1831 S
KING Andrew's child (colored) 7/23/1826 S
KING Andrew's child 11/5/1827 S
KING Andrew's wife 9/6/1827 S
KING Edward's child 7/25/1822 W
KING Eliza's black child 9/20/1817 S
KING Enoch's mother 5/2/1815 S
KING George 10/11/1821 M
KING George's child 11/2/1800 W
KING George's child 11/20/1811 S
KING George's child 1/18/1809 S

KING George's child 6/23/1821 M
KING George's colored child 4/1/1806 S
KING Henry Senr 8/6/1826 M
KING Ignatious's child 6/19/1820 S
KING Ignatius's child 1/23/1817 S
KING Ignatius's father 3/22/1830 S
KING Ignatius's mother 10/3/1827 S
KING Ignatius's wife at the foundry 11/14/1827 W
KING Isabela 5/10/1816 M [Ed note: Isabela McCullough King was William King's mother. She was b. 21 August 1741 in Ireland.]
KING J H's child 9/29/1827 M
KING James C's child 6/1/1808 W
KING James's child 9/23/1815 S
KING James's child 6/28/1829 S
KING James's mother (at the foundry) 1/11/1824 S
KING John (the labourer)'s wife 2/21/1824 S
KING John 10/24/1821 M
KING John A's colored man 5/20/1831 S
KING Joseph's child 7/14/1813 M
KING Little Hellen 10/18/1814 M [Hellen was the sixth of William King's seven children by his first wife, Mary Fowler. Hellen was b. 7 August 1807 and d. 18 October 1814.]
KING Little Mary 7/10/1814 M [This was William King's youngest child by his first wife, Mary Fowler. "Little Mary" was b. 3 October 1812 and d. 10 July 1814.]
KING Marget 8/27/1806 M [William King's young daughter, b. 25 February 1805, d. 27 August 1806.]
KING Margrat 12/28/1821 M
KING Margrat's son 9/6/1813 M
KING Mary 11/14/1812 M [Mary Fowler King, b. 7 October 1776 in Annapolis, Md., was William King's first wife. They were married 4 November 1798, and she bore him seven children before her death on 14 November 1812 at the age of 36.]
KING Mary 4/6/1815 M
KING Mary Emily (F King's child) 9/21/1832 M [William King's granddaughter, the child of his son Francis.]
KING Melvina 9/14/1818 M [William King's third child by his second wife, Christina Goszler Fowler, and the tenth of his sixteen children. Melvina lived from 12 October 1817 until 14 September 1818.]
KING Miss 1/21/1815 S

KING Miss 10/7/1819 M
KING Mr (Labann)'s child 10/4/1813 S
KING Mr 1/12/1815 S
KING Mr 1/7/1815 S
KING Mrs 12/13/1822 M
KING Mrs Charles 1/14/1832 M
KING Mrs Ignatius 1/6/1829 S
KING Mrs's child 7/18/1822 M
KING Nicholas 5/22/1812 M
KING Nicholas's child 6/27/1801 S
KING Nicholas's child 10/14/1805 M
KING Old Mr 12/22/1813 S
KING William 2/17/1825 S
KING William 7/21/1803 M [This was William King the cabinet'maker's son and second eldest child, b. 11 September 1801, d. 21 July 1803.]
KING William Senior's child 9/27/1796 M
KING William Senior's nurse's child 7/11/1796 S
KING William Sr 10/19/1821 M [This was the uncle of William King; although not father and son, they were referred to as Senior and Junior to avoid confusion in the small village of Georgetown.]
KING William's child 8/3/1821 S
KING William's child 2/17/1825 S
KING William's colored child 6/16/1804 S
KING Zachariah's child 8/26/1819 S
KINSAL Mrs's daughter 9/23/1814 W
KINSEL Mr 11/11/1814 S
KIRBY Charles 10/19/1830 S
KIRBY Michael 7/27/1830 S
KIRBY R's child 7/10/1821 W
KIRBY Robert's child 11/16/1819 W
KIRBY Robert's colored child 9/9/1822 S
KIRBY Robt's colored child 7/9/1825 S
KIRK A M 12/9/1830 S
KIRK A M's child 7/9/1824 M
KIRK Mary 5/8/1826 M
KIRK Mr paid for unknown 7/11/1796 S
KIRK Mrs's colored boy 9/21/1831 S
KIRK Mrs's colored child 6/1/1824 S
KIRK Thomas 11/28/1817 M
KIRKPATRICK Mrs 10/12/1828 S

KIRKWOOD Peter 1/2/1816 S
KITTS Priscilla (colored woman)'s granddaughter 4/23/1825 S
KLEIBER Mrs 7/26/1830 W
KNABS William's child 9/25/1821 W
KNIGHT Mr 4/12/1828 S
KNIGHT Mr's child 6/27/1820 S
KNIGHT Mr's child 4/5/1815 S
KNIGHT Mr's child 2/23/1814 S
KNIGHT Mrs 8/3/1821 W
KNIGHT William 10/6/1821 M
KNOLES Thomas 11/23/1822 M
KNOT Mr's son 6/6/1819 S
KNOTS Daniel's black woman 6/26/1812 S
KNOWLES John 8/4/1823 W
KNOWLES Joseph E's wife 8/11/1800 M
KNOWLES Mr's child 11/5/1800 W
KNOWLES Mrs 4/27/1831 W
KNOWLES Mrs for ----- 9/22/1801 W
KNOWLES Mrs omitted 3/10/1818 M
KNOWLES William's child 11/6/1824 W
KNOX John's child 5/12/1825 S
KNOX John's wife 9/6/1826 S
KNOX Mr 12/26/1829 S
KNOX Mrs 1/19/1822 S
KRAUSE John 9/9/1820 M
KROUSE Everard's child 3/10/1830 W
KROUSE John for ----- 1/25/1805 W
KROUSE John's Harry 3/9/1815 S
KROUSE John's Lewis 9/1/1805 S
KROUSE John's wife 11/11/1803 M
KROUSE Mr 4/5/1799 W
KROUZE Mrs 11/24/1822 W
KUHN Joseph L's child 11/30/1830 M
KUHN Mrs Catherine 12/12/1830 M
KUHNS William 11/10/1823 W
KURTS Daniel's black woman 11/15/1813 S
KURTZ D's child 8/22/1818 W
KURTZ Daniel (colored woman) 1/16/1826 S
KURTZ Daniel's black woman 5/3/1812 S
KURTZ Daniel's black woman 9/4/1820 S
KURTZ David's child 7/19/1823 W
KURTZ David's child 7/21/1828 S

KURTZ Mrs 5/6/1820 M
KURTZ Thomas 5/1/1826 W
KURTZ Thomas for ----- 10/11/1808 M
KURTZ Thomas for Dulen 2/17/1807 S
LACY Benjamin 10/1/1817 W
LACY Benjamin 12/18/1805 W
LACY John's child 9/24/1831 S
LAIDLER Elenor 1/4/1827 M
LAIN Robert 4/13/1814 S
LAINE John 11/22/1814 S
LAINE Mr 10/9/1805 M
LAIRD John for ----- 9/28/1804 M
LAIRD John's black child 10/6/1814 S
LAIRD John's child 1/12/1805 M
LAIRD John's child 8/26/1804 M
LAIRD John's colored child 11/23/1823 S
LAIRD John's housekeeper 10/5/1805 W
LAIRD John's wife 8/31/1804 M
LAIRD Mrs William 6/9/1832 M
LAIRD William's child 3/20/1824 M
LAIRD William's child 4/21/1827 M
LAIRD Wm's child 11/17/1825
LAMAR R 11/6/1820 M
LAMB Mr's child 9/22/1823 W
LAMBERT Edward 12/5/1832 M
LAMBERT Maurice 12/6/1824 M
LAMBERT Morris's child 8/3/1814 W
LAMBERT Mrs 10/26/1826 M
LAMBRIGHT George 8/15/1811 W
LAMBRIGHT George's child 10/4/1806 S
LAMBRIGHT George's child 7/11/1807 S
LANDES Abraham's child 10/27/1817 W
LANDES Mrs Abr's child 7/5/1819 W
LANDIS Abraham's child 7/23/1816 W
LANDIS Abraham's child 7/9/1812 W
LANDSDEL Mr's child 6/4/1814 S
LANDSDEL Mr's child 5/23/1814 S
LANE Mr 2/24/1809 S
LANE Robert's mother 12/16/1811 W
LANEY Charles 3/2/1819 S
LANG John 1/27/1820 M
LANG John for ----- 1/24/1805 W

LANG John's child 4/19/1811 M
LANG Mrs 5/23/1820 S
LANG William's black boy 3/23/1818 S
LANG William's child 8/25/1829 W
LANG William's daughter 12/16/1822 W
LANHAM Aquila 8/28/1829 M
LANHAM Elisha 7/25/1804 S
LANHAM Eliza 8/28/1829 M
LANHAM Marcia's colored woman 5/29/1830 S
LANHAM Mareia 8/29/1829 M
LANHAM Mr's child 7/21/1829 S
LANHAM Mrs A 9/28/1824 M
LANHAM Mrs's child 11/20/1823 W
LANN Mr 11/15/1814 W
LANNIN Elisha 2/2/1822 W
LANNUM Elisha's child 10/7/1820 W
LANNUM Norman 9/16/1818 S
LANNUN Rebecka 11/13/1812 S
LATHROP John 1/30/1820 W
LATHROPE Mr's child 10/19/1818 M
LATIMER Marcus 4/26/1831 W
LATIMORE Stephen 8/22/1818 M
LAUB Jacob 7/27/1820 M
LAW Horace 9/27/1827 S
LAW John 5/30/1831 S
LAW Mr 9/15/1818 S
LAW Mrs 9/17/1811 S
LAY Richard Senr 9/20/1831 M
LAY Richard's child 9/4/1812 W
LAY Richard's child 5/24/1813 W
LAY Richard's child 8/5/1816 M
LAY Richard's son 3/25/1830 W
LAYLAND Mr 3/31/1820 W
LEACH John 12/10/1828 M
LEACH Mrs 12/14/1826 S
LEACH Mrs 5/7/1826 S
LEAR Mr's child 2/21/1796 M
LEAR Mrs 2/21/1796 M
LEAR Tobis 10/14/1816 M
LEAR Walter 11/17/1827 S
LEATHY 3/21/1809 S
LEE Alfred's brother 4/26/1826 S

LEE Caroline 3/24/1823 S
LEE Elinor's child 8/27/1821 W
LEE Jane's child 7/23/1823 S
LEE Miss 9/18/1821 W
LEE Miss Nancy's black child 8/5/1815 S
LEE Mr 4/2/1823 W
LEE Nancy's black man William 2/21/1813 S
LEE Thomas S's wife 1/24/1805 M
LEE William's child 8/31/1812 M
LEEDE Frederick M 10/13/1824 S
LEEK Mr 3/13/1804 S
LEEK Mr's child 12/3/1825 S
LEESH Mr's child 1/30/1825 W
LELAND John 8/7/1827 W
LELAND John's child 1/11/1808 W
LELAND Mr's boy 10/11/1806 S
LEO Mr's black boy 11/3/1813 S
~~LETCHER~~ Care (colored woman)'s mother 3/4/1823 S
LEUCAS Henry 12/29/1825 S
LEUCAS John's wife 4/3/1830 S
LEVERET Mr 8/29/1829 W
LEVETT Samuel 9/9/1819 M
LEVINE Daniel 3/24/1826 S
LEVINE William's wife (colored) 7/21/1827 S
LEVINS Eliza's child (colored) 10/18/1827 S
LEVIS Ed's child 10/12/1825 S
LEVIS Edward's child 7/30/1830 W
LEVIS Mr's child 3/25/1818 W
LEVIS Mr's child 11/27/1822 W
LEWES child 3/10/1821 S
LEWIS Anthony 5/23/1832 S
LEWIS Marcus 4/1/1825 W
LEWIS Mrs 3/28/1819 M
LIBBY (colored woman) 12/8/1828 S
LIBBY Joseph's child 2/11/1824 M
LIBBY William 3/17/1831 W
LIGHTFOOT Mrs 10/7/1830 S
LINAHAN John 10/29/1831 S
LINGAN George 12/9/1827 S
LINGAN James M for Miss P 9/10/1802 M
LINGAN Mrs's black child 10/1/1815 S
LINGAN Nicholas 11/3/1811 M

LINGHAM Mrs Janette 6/29/1832 S
LINKENS Mr's child 7/10/1819 S
LINKIN Mr's child 9/21/1818 S
LINKINS Henry 2/3/1832 W
LINKINS Henry's child 4/5/1830 S
LINKINS Hope 11/8/1832 S
LINKINS James 8/10/1830 W
LINKINS Mrs Henry 1/8/1832 W
LINKINS Sarah (colored woman) 3/19/1832 S
LINTHICUM O M's child 8/5/1824 M
LINTHICUM O M's child 1/30/1832 W
LINTHICUM O M's child 3/16/1827 M
LINTHICUM Otho M's children (two) 12/12/1832 M
LINTHICUM Otho M's child 12/17/1832 M
LIPSCOMB Jesse's child 2/12/1824 W
LIPSCOMB John's child 7/5/1806 W
LIPSCOMB W C's child 11/24/1822 W
LITTLEJOHN A S's child 5/6/1831 W
LITTLEJOHN Alexander's child 3/3/1832 S
LIVELY Mr 10/11/1822 W
LIVERS Anthony's child 7/21/1809 W
LIVERS Ignatious 1/8/1821 W
LIVERS Mr's child 8/2/1802 W
LIVERS Mr's child 6/11/1820 W
LIVERS Mrs J 5/13/1809 M
LIVERY Mrs 1/26/1823 W
LIVINGSTON C 11/6/1822 W
LIVINGSTON Mrs 3/23/1814 M
LODDER Joshua's mother-in-law 9/29/1809 S
LONG James's wife 3/4/1800 W
LONG Madison's wife 2/15/1831 S
LONG Margaret 8/20/1830 S
LONG Samuel 8/17/1809 S
LOUD Mrs 9/17/1831 S
LOUFBOROUGH Nathan's black woman 5/2/1815 S
LOUFBOROUGH: see also LUFBOROUGH
LOUNDS Francis 4/23/1815 M
LOUNDS Mrs 1/5/1815 W
LOUNDS Mrs 7/7/1829 M
LOVE Charles for ----- 5/14/1807 M
LOVE Charles for ----- 8/25/1808 M
LOVE Charles's child 10/14/1806 S

LOVE Mr 2/7/1830 S
LOVE Mrs 8/3/1822 M
LOVE Thomas R's father 7/8/1828 W
LOVEJOY Elizabeth 2/24/1815 W
LOVEJOY John's child 10/7/1804 W
LOVEJOY Samuel 5/23/1807 S
LOVEJOY Zedekiah 9/18/1832 W
LOVEJOY Zedekiah's child 4/5/1824 W
LOVELESS Mr's child 9/23/1818 S
LOVELESS Mrs's child 11/17/1823 S
LOWE Miss 11/15/1820 M
LOWE Miss 11/5/1819 M
LOWE Mr's child 8/22/1809 S
LOWE Mrs 1/27/1818 M
LOWE Walter 3/18/1807 M
LOWERY John's coloured woman 4/27/1815 S
LOWNDES Charles's child 10/21/1797 M
LOWNDES F's Isaac 1/3/1822 S
LOWNDES Francis's colored child 8/25/1832 S
LOWNDS Ann 1/18/1822 M
LOWRIE Cesar 3/8/1807 W
LOWRIE William 9/18/1803 W
LUCAS Bennet's child 8/6/1824 S
LUCAS Bennet's daughter 9/15/1828 S
LUCAS Harrison 9/22/1832 S
LUCAS John's child 8/1/1829 S
LUCAS William's child 9/4/1823 S
LUCKET Mrs 4/12/1812 W
LUCKETT Ig. 9/7/1827 S
LUFBOROUGH Mrs 11/27/1823 M
LUFFBOROUGH Nathan for ----- 7/2/1807 M
LUFFBOROUGH Nathan's child 8/27/1805 M
LUFFBOROUGH Nathan's child 9/10/1809 M
LUFFBOROUGH Nathan's child 8/16/1805 M
LUFFBOROUGH Nathan's colored child 4/4/1807 S
LUFFBOROUGH; see also LOUFBOROUGH
LUPTON Mr's child 9/16/1817 S
LUPTON Mrs 3/13/1828 W
LUTZ John's child 10/5/1813 W
LYLES Jacob 1/31/1815 S
LYLES Lewis 6/17/1828 S
LYLES Mrs 2/4/1815 S

LYLES Mrs 9/6/1832 S
LYLES Semos (colored woman)'s child 11/7/1832 S
LYNCH Michael 8/16/1830 S
LYON John's nephew 11/4/1826 M
LYON Mr's child 6/18/1813 M
LYONS John's black child 7/16/1818 S
LYONS John's black woman 1/18/1818 W
LYONS John's brother-in-law's child 9/13/1819 W
LYONS John's sister 4/3/1828 M
LYONS Miss E 3/7/1823 M
LYONS Mrs (tobacconist's mother) 1/14/1829 W
LYONS Mrs 11/25/1809 S
LYONS Mrs 9/16/1822 M
MACCUBBIN Richard 8/30/1814 M
MacDANIEL G's son 7/27/1821 M
MacDANIEL Mrs 8/24/1821 M
MACKALL B F's child 9/13/1819 M
MACKALL B F's child 9/24/1816 M
MACKALL B's black woman 6/27/1820 S
MACKALL Benjamin's child 3/19/1807 W
MACKALL Benjamin's child 9/15/1818 M
MACKALL Leonard's child 11/23/1801 W
MACKALL Leonard's Dinah 5/30/1826 S
MACKALL Mr's child 10/14/1817 S
MACKALL; see also MAKALL
MACKENALL Mr 12/8/1818 S
MACKEY Alexander 4/22/1816 M
MACKEY Alexander's child 6/16/1804 W
MACKEY Mrs 11/26/1818 M
MACKEY Mrs 4/5/1815 M
MACKEY William 9/10/1825 M
MACKEY William's child 7/2/1816 W
MACKINALL Mr's son 7/24/1818 S
MACOMB 6/5/1831 M
MACOMB Alexander Senr 1/20/1831 M
MACOMB Mrs's child 1/5/1809 W
MADDOX Mr's child 11/12/1823 M
MADERA Mrs's child 8/30/1815 S
MAFFIT Thomas 3/17/1816 M
MAFFITT Samuel 10/26/1813 M
MAFFITT William 11/3/1822 W
MAFFITT William 3/4/1828 M

MAGEE John's child 4/13/1832 S
MAGILL Mrs 9/12/1826 M
MAGRATH Jane's child 2/21/1808 S
MAGRAW Benjamin's child 8/21/1819 W
MAGRAW Mrs 9/17/1818 W
MAGRUDER Alexander 6/27/1812 W
MAGRUDER Dr's black man 8/15/1814 S
MAGRUDER George 8/11/1823 M
MAGRUDER George's wife 1/6/1806 M
MAGRUDER Hellen 8/17/1818 M
MAGRUDER Lewes 11/23/1829 S
MAGRUDER Lycurgus's child 10/14/1821 M
MAGRUDER Mary Ann 9/27/1821 M
MAGRUDER Miss Patty 6/27/1815 W
MAGRUDER Miss Rachal 7/14/1814 M
MAGRUDER Mr 11/27/1821 W
MAGRUDER Mrs 1/31/1815 M
MAGRUDER Mrs 9/27/1819 W
MAGRUDER Mrs D 7/11/1816 M
MAGRUDER Mrs George B 3/16/1827 M
MAGRUDER Mrs S B 7/26/1819 W
MAGRUDER Mrs's child 8/2/1832 S
MAGRUDER Mrs's daughter 8/14/1815 W
MAGRUDER Ninian 3/5/1823 M
MAGRUDER Ninian's black boy 5/5/1807 W
MAGRUDER Patrick for ----- 4/4/1807 M
MAGRUDER Patrick's child 4/6/1816 M
MAGRUDER Robert P 8/11/1822 M
MAGRUDER Samuel (PG Co) 12/25/1825 W
MAGRUDER Samuel B 11/18/1818 W
MAGRUDER Samuel B for ----- 12/26/1806 S
MAGRUDER Thomas 12/9/1817 M
MAGRUDER Thomas 6/6/1832 M
MAGRUDER Thomas 8/15/1830 M
MAGRUDER Wm O 5/5/1819 W
MAGUIRE Hugh 5/8/1828 M
MAHANEY Matthew 7/27/1830 W
MAHONY George's child 10/15/1822 W
MAHORNEY Daniel 9/18/1830 S
MAHORNY Mr 2/18/1815 W
MAKALL Benjamin 12/12/1822 M
MAKALL; see also MACKALL

MALADY Thomas 7/27/1830 S
MALONEY Mrs 11/7/1830 S
MALONY James's wife 7/31/1815 W
MANCHIET Mrs 12/17/1814 W
MANKIN Henry 7/27/1830 S
MANTIGUA Capt. 11/6/1829 S
MANTZ Isaac 8/15/1830 W
MANUAL 10/12/1814 S
MAQUIRE Hugh's wife 9/21/1827 M
MARAND Mr 10/12/1821 S
MARBURY Adam (colored man)'s wife 12/24/1825 S
MARBURY Leonard's child 5/17/1820 M
MARBURY Lucy's child 8/30/1820 S
MARBURY Luke 12/10/1823 S
MARBURY Miss E 1/7/1814 M
MARBURY Mr 10/5/1798 M
MARBURY William's black woman 1/7/1814 S
MARBURY William's child 3/13/1802 M
MARBURY William's child 9/25/1814 S
MARBURY William's colored woman 12/19/1805 S
MARBURY William's colored child 10/24/1821 S
MARBURY William's Maria 7/12/1824 S
MARBURY William's negro woman 9/10/1811 S
MARBURY Wm's black girl 1/23/1818 S
MARCH Hanah's child 8/6/1814 S
MARCH John 6/3/1804 M
MARCH Mrs 8/13/1807 M
MARCHEL Mr (omitted) [12/1812] S
MARCHEL Mr 10/2/1812 W
MARCY Thomas 8/19/1831 W
MARCY Thomas's colored woman 4/20/1831 S
MARKRITIER Stephen 8/12/1823 S
MARKWARD William 11/25/1821 W
MARKWOOD Mrs 7/2/1817 M
MARLBRO John's girl 5/13/1823 S
MARLO Thomas (colored man)'s child 12/21/1824 S
MARON Mrs 8/21/1822 M
MARQUAL Mrs's child 9/11/1815 S
MARQUAN Mr's son 12/10/1809 S
MARQUARD Charles's child 3/1/1822 M
MARRAY Miss 6/17/1796 W
MARSH Sally's child 10/17/1826 S

MARSHAL R H's colored woman 10/6/1823 S
MARTIN Miss's child 11/20/1816 S
MARZINGO Mrs 1/28/1825 M
MASON Ann (colored woman) 1/15/1830 S
MASON Armstead T 2/8/1819 M
MASON Elizabeth 7/18/1819 M
MASON George's child 8/28/1823 M
MASON John Junr's child 8/14/1831 M
MASON John T's child 7/22/1801 M
MASON John T's child 11/7/1801 M
MASON John T's child 6/23/1802 M
MASON John's colored person 6/27/1806 S
MASON John's Tom 1/26/1815 S
MASON Joseph's child (colored) 9/1/1830 S
MASON Mary (colored woman) 10/31/1832 S
MASON Stephen T's child 1/26/1801 S
MASON Thomas 3/12/1813 M
MASSEY Samuel 11/27/1822 W
MASSEY Thomas's child 8/11/1819 S
MASTERS Levi 6/6/1824 S
MATHEWS Mr's child 9/3/1819 S
MATLE Mr 1/26/1798 S
MATTHEWS Allen's child (colored) 7/23/1830 S
MATTHEWS Henry's child 8/27/1828 M
MATTHEWS Henry's child 12/27/1826 S
MATTHEWS Henry's child 8/5/1832 M
MATTHEWS Rezin (colored man)'s child 9/3/1831 S
MATTINGLY Mr 7/16/1825 S
MATTINGLY Mrs 10/29/1821 S
MATTINGLY Mrs 11/2/1824 S
MATTINGLY Susan 9/7/1832 S
MAUGH John 7/17/1822 S
MAUPIN Mrs 11/20/1827 S
MAURY Mrs R B 3/17/1828 M
MAY John 5/22/1827 W
MAY Mr's child 1/18/1823 W
MAY Mrs 8/13/1820 S
MAYER Adam's child 8/12/1820 W
MAYER Henry's child 9/9/1810 S
MAYER Henry's child 8/10/1811 S
MAYFIELD Benjamin 4/23/1826 W
MAYFIELD Benjamin's son 5/30/1821 M

MAYFIELD Henry's child 10/18/1821 S
MAYFIELD Henry's child 8/1/1819 W
MAYFIELD Mrs's child 11/10/1823 S
MAYFIELD William 4/22/1821 W
MAYHUE Jonathan 5/22/1829 S
McCALL Catherine 3/10/1828 M
McCAN Arthur 10/5/1821 S
McCANDLESS's man 1/18/1827 S
McCARTHY Mr's child 6/1/1830 S
McCARTY John 10/22/1830 S
McCARTY John 9/7/1830 S
McCARTY Thomas 4/7/1816 M
McCASHIN Catharine 12/25/1815
McCASLER James 11/26/1809 S
McCAULY William's child 8/18/1820 S
McCHESNEY D's child 10/24/1818 M
McCHESNEY David's child 5/1/1830 M
McCLAIN Duncan's child 10/11/1814 S
McCLANN Robert for ----- 11/14/1809 W
McCLEARY Captain 7/25/1811 M
McCLISH Mrs's child 3/27/1828 M
McCLOSKEY Mr 10/19/1823 S
McCOMB General's child 10/29/1821 M
McCOMB Mrs 9/20/1822 M
McCOY John's child 9/20/1820 S
McCOY Mr's child 8/30/1818 S
McCOY Mr's child 4/12/1820 S
McCOY Mr's child 10/11/1821 S
McCULCHEAR Mrs 11/29/1825 W
McCUTCHEN Thomas 2/3/1815 W
McCUTCHEON James 5/8/1810 S
McCUTCHEON James for ----- 9/17/1809 S
McCUTCHEON James's child 7/21/1803 W
McCUTCHEON James's child 10/15/1803 W
McCUTCHEON John 2/26/1815 W
McCUTCHEON John for Mrs McCoshine 10/8/1808 W
McCUTCHEON Thomas for a girl 10/6/1809 W
McCUTCHEON Thomas for ----- 8/12/1807 S
McCUTCHEON Thomas's child 8/17/1810 W
McDANIEL E 8/29/1820 W
McDANIEL George's child 9/17/1815 W
McDANIEL George's child 9/28/1821 M

McDANIEL John's child 12/16/1813 W
McDANIEL John's child 2/18/1823 W
McDANIEL John's child 8/16/1827 W
McDANIEL Leonard 11/1/1817 S
McDANIEL Mrs's child 8/4/1817 S
McDANIEL T 5/14/1824 S
MCDANIEL Mr's child 7/4/1826 S
McDANIELS Mr's child 6/19/1827 S
McDANIELS Mrs's child 5/1/1827 W
McDONALD Mrs (colored) 2/21/1827 S
McDONALD William (colored man) 4/2/1830 S
McDONNAL L a black man for his mother 6/5/1813 S
McDonald; see also MICDONNAL
McDONOUGH Charles 11/14/1830 S
McDOWELL Mrs 4/1/1829 S
McELAVNAY Thomas 11/21/1829 S
McGENTISS William 4/28/1830 S
McGILL John 1/17/1827 M
McGINNIS Mrs 2/20/1830 S
McILHANEY Mr's child 10/28/1831 W
McILVAINE C's child 7/1/1823 M
McINTIRE ------ 8/31/1832 S
McINTIRE Alexander 9/24/1797 M
McINTIRE Mrs's child 5/15/1832 S
McINTIRE Samuel for ----- 7/15/1808 M
McKEE Mr's child 2/23/1824 S
McKELDEN Andrew 12/5/1816 W
McKELDIN Mrs's child 4/13/1817 W
McKENNAY Samuel's child 8/4/1817 S
McKENNEY T L's Tom 8/7/1821 S
McKENNEY William's black girl 4/15/1814 S
McKENNEY William's black girl 12/2/1813 S
McKENNEY William's child omitted 11/25/1817 M
McKENNEY William's child 10/21/1821 M
McKENNY Samuel's child 11/22/1826 M
McKENNY Samuel's child 12/21/1823 M
McKENNY Thomas L's child 1/27/1811 M
McKENNY William's child 8/24/1819 M
McKENNY William's child 8/20/1819 M
McKEWEN Mr's child 4/26/1824 W
McKIMM John 2/6/1831 S
McLAUGHLIN Charles for ----- 10/5/1802 M

McLAUGHLIN Charles's colored person, 8/28/1800 S
McLAUGLIN Charles's colored person 8/18/1801 S
McMAHON Roger 6/26/1830 S
McMANNERS Ellen's child 10/22/1831 S
McMANNERS Mrs's child 6/18/1819 S
McMULLINS Patrick 7/3/1830 S
McMURRAY Mr's cartman's child 7/27/1805 S
McMURRAY William for ----- 7/27/1811 M
McMURRAY William's child 8/23/1808 M
McMURRY Joseph 9/1/1813 M
McNEAR Daniel's child 9/25/1826 S
McNEAR William's child 11/11/1824 W
McNERHENNY John 10/31/1832 W
McNERHENNY Mrs 8/7/1831 S
McPERSON J H 8/16/1825 M
McPHERSON Daniel 12/27/1831 W
McPHERSON H & J for ----- 12/13/1807 W
McPHERSON Henry's colored child 8/2/1828 S
McPHERSON Henry's colored child 12/31/1826 S
McPHERSON Henry's colored woman 10/19/1832 S
McPHERSON Henry's mother 10/17/1811 W
McPHERSON John 9/16/1823 M
McPHERSON Mrs 1/22/1818 W
McTEVRAN Henry's black man 12/15/1818 S
MEEM George's child 8/20/1821 W
MELLEY Bazil 6/5/1820 S
MELLIGEN Mr 9/30/1799 W
MELVIN Alexander 8/22/1818 M
MELVIN James's child 10/12/1805 M
MELVIN James's child 4/28/1806 M
MELVIN James's child 4/4/1807 M
MELVIN James's negro boy 4/10/1802 S
MELVIN Jas 2/20/1826 W
MELVIN Mrs 8/20/1815 M
MERRY Anthony's Peter 12/3/1805 W
MICDONNAL P 10/6/1822 S
MICHINS Mrs's child 8/16/1808 S
MICKUM William 1/29/1830 S
MIDDLETON Mr's child 8/5/1817 M
MILBURN John 4/21/1828 S
MILES William 9/7/1828 S
MILES William's child 8/21/1823 S

MILLARD Mary's daughter 1/28/1829 S
MILLER Anna Maria 11/7/1828 W
MILLER Captain 9/30/1817 M
MILLER Elizabeth 11/23/1817 W
MILLER George 10/15/1820 W
MILLER Hezekiah's child 2/27/1823 S
MILLER James's child 10/7/1821 W
MILLER James's child 9/18/1820 W
MILLER Mr's child 9/17/1812 W
MILLER Mr's child 2/1/1815 W
MILLER Mrs 9/19/1821 W
MILLER Mrs's daughter 10/19/1821 W
MILLER William 10/23/1826 S
MILLER Wm 3/25/1818 W
MILLIGAN Joseph's child 5/5/1816 M
MILLIGAN Joseph's child 11/4/1822 W
MILLS Mr 5/25/1816 S
MIM Peter 12/3/1813 M
MIM Polly 2/8/1815 W
MIMKIN Mrs's daughter 10/12/1823 S
MINIGHIN Robert 7/23/1829 S
MINN James 7/22/1812 S
MINOR George (Wm Minor's son) 8/18/1831 M
MINOR Mrs 5/1/1811 W
MISCY Mr's child 8/19/1819 M
MITCHEL Hannah's child 4/17/1823 S
MITCHEL J 2/22/1820 S
MITCHELL Doctor 9/30/1804 M
MITCHELL John 7/4/1808 W
MITCHELL John's black child 7/29/1817 S
MITCHELL John's black man 2/20/1815 S
MITCHELL John's child 12/16/1800 W
MITCHELL Judson's brother 12/19/1816 W
MITCHELL Judson's child 5/21/1830 W
MITCHELL Matthew 9/13/1832 W
MITCHELL Miss 3/28/1821 W
MITCHELL Mr 8/10/1827 W
MITCHELL Mr's child 8/5/1803 S
MITCHELL Mrs 1/12/1814 M
MITCHELL Mrs 3/22/1830 W
MIX E's child 2/7/1827 W
MONFORD William's child 12/30/1819 S

MONFORD Wm's child 10/18/1818 S
MONRO Jonathan's child 8/24/1799 S
MONRO Jonathan's wife 8/30/1799 W
MONROE Jonathan's colored child 3/6/1800 S
MONROE Thomas's child 8/13/1810 M
MOODY -------- 8/30/1831 S
MOOR Charles's daughter 11/6/1822 S
MOORE James's child 2/22/1804 W
MOORE John for unknown 4/21/1799 S
MOORE John's child 5/10/1803 W
MOORE Joseph's child 9/17/1818 S
MOORE Nathan for ----- 4/19/1808 S
MORAN Miss 10/1/1818 S
MORAN Mrs 5/25/1827 S
MORDOCK John 6/19/1820 W
MORDOCK John's child 5/21/1820 W
MORDOCK Mrs 11/19/1815 W
MORE Charles's daughter (colored) 10/1/1826 S
MORE Jesse's child 12/22/1823 W
MORE John 12/28/1824 S
MORE John for ----- 4/1/1803 S
MORE John's child 7/11/1822 S
MORE John's child 12/7/1818 S
MORE Joseph's relation (colored woman) 11/2/1822 S
MORE Joseph's wife's sister 2/17/1822 S
MORE Mrs's child 8/30/1816 S
MORE Vincent 11/27/1822 W
MORE William (colored man) 10/21/1826 S
MOREHOUSE Mr 3/24/1824 S
MORGAN Aquila's child 9/28/1826 S
MORGAN Evan's child 4/15/1811 S
MORGAN John's child 8/27/1831 W
MORGAN John's child 8/28/1831 W
MORGAN John's child 8/27/1830 W
MORGAN John's child 10/19/1831 S
MORGAN Mordoca 11/7/1816 W
MORGAN Mr 3/20/1814 S
MORGAN Mr 6/12/1821 S
MORGAN Mr 7/9/1820 S
MORGAN Mrs 11/2/1821 W
MORGAN Mrs 12/8/1822 M
MORGAN William 10/28/1822 W

MORGAN William for ----- 10/20/1806 S
MORGAN William's boy 3/11/1802 W
MORGAN William's child 12/30/1799 W
MORGAN William's grandchild 3/21/1826 W
MORLAND Mrs's child 6/7/1821 S
MORRELL John's child 8/18/1815 W
MORRIS Garret's wife 5/15/1816 S
MORRIS George's child 5/9/1816 W
MORRIS George's sister-in-law 12/18/1811 W
MORRIS Jeret (colored man)'s relation 9/7/1822 S
MORRIS Miss (at Academy) 12/17/1832 M
MORRIS Mr's child 9/24/1813 W
MORRIS Mr's child 6/27/1796 W
MORRIS Mrs 9/20/1829 S
MORRIS Randal for wife 1/14/1811 W
MORRIS Randal's child 7/24/1811 W
MORRIS Randall 7/9/1818 S
MORRIS's child 8/19/1811 W
MORRISON John 12/31/1815 W
MORRISON Miss 9/3/1832 M
MORSELL J S's colored child 3/28/1821 S
MORSELL J S's colored child 2/16/1816 S
MORSELL J S's George 6/23/1822 S
MORSELL James S for ----- 6/24/1802 M
MORSELL Mrs 5/31/1813 M
MORSELL Mrs J S 4/19/1831 M
MORTON Miss Isabella 11/6/1832 W
MORTON William's black child 9/10/1812 S
MORTON William's child 12/23/1823 W
MORTON William's colored child 6/3/1825
MORTON William's negro child 8/6/1810 S
MOUNTS John's child 11/15/1821 M
MOUNTZ Jacob for ----- 2/15/1811 M
MOUNTZ John 10/31/1812 W
MOUNTZ John for ----- 1/24/1807 S
MOUNTZ John for ----- 12/18/1809 M
MOUNTZ John's colored woman 9/23/1831 S
MOUNTZ Mrs (the old lady) 3/5/1832 W
MOXLEY Horatia 11/22/1829 W
MOXLEY Mr's child 12/19/1818 S
MOXLEY Mr's child 12/24/1820 S
MOXLEY Samuel's child 12/3/1827 W

MOXLEY Samuel's child 1/11/1827 S
MOXLEY Samuel's colored man 10/20/1828 S
MOXLEY Samuel's colored man 1/25/1828 S
MOXLEY Samuel's colored child 8/14/1830 S
MOXLEY Samuel's father 5/5/1827 W
MOXLEY's child (colored) 12/5/1826 S
MOYERS Samuel's child 10/17/1814 W
MOYERS Samuel's child 8/13/1808 S
MOYERS Samuel's child 3/15/1823 W
MOYERS Samuel's child 8/26/1819 W
MOYERS Samuel's grandchild 9/22/1822 W
MUD Thomas's child 9/21/1817 M
MUDD Bennett 8/24/1830 S
MUDD Harriet's child 11/22/1823 W
MUDD T J's child 5/8/1819 S
MUDD Thomas J's child 8/30/1819 S
MULLAKIN Mrs 12/20/1824 M
MULLIGAN James 4/1/1816 M
MULLIGAN Mrs 6/15/1815 M
MULLIGAN Thomas 7/23/1830 S
MULLIGEN Mr 1/6/1798 S
MULLIN John's child 4/21/1830 S
MULLIN Mr's child 8/23/1830 S
MUMBY R's child 6/26/1822 W
MUMFORD William (colored man) 2/6/1821 S
MUNFORD Sarah (colored woman)'s child 6/23/1821 S
MUNRO Robt 4/30/1819 M
MURDOCK Addison 1/31/1808 M
MURDOCK Addison's colored women 11/9/1807 S
MURDOCK John 2/17/1830 W
MURDOCK John's child 6/27/1818 S
MURDOCK John's child 11/20/1813 S
MURDOCK Mrs 12/25/1831 W
MURPHY 12/6/1823 S
MURPHY Charles's child 9/3/1830 S
MURPHY Daniel 10/10/1830 S
MURPHY John 12/4/1830 S
MURPHY Martha's child (colored) 6/12/1827 S
MURPHY Mrs 5/11/1827 S
MURRAY Michael 7/21/1830 S
MUSE Lindsay's sister (colored woman) 9/14/1827 W
MUSTIN Thomas's child 11/11/1823 M

MYER Franklin S's child 9/10/1831 M
MYERS John's child 8/16/1812 W
MYERS John's child 1/16/1812 W
MYERS Mr 3/12/1814 W
MYERS Mrs John 6/2/1824 W
NACE Mary's child (colored) 7/10/1826 S
NALLY Mr 2/13/1826 S
NALLY Mr 4/1/1816 S
NAYLOR John H 12/4/1806 S
NEAL James 10/15/1829 S
NEAL John's wife 4/19/1820 S
NEAL Leonard 6/19/1817 M
NEALE John (colored man) 1/12/1829 S
NEALE Leonard 5/28/1826 S
NEALL Charles 11/29/1815 W
NEALL H 6/7/1815 S
NEEDAM George 4/9/1822 W
NEEDAM William A 4/1/1815 W
NELSON Mr 3/1/1806 S
NELSON Mrs William 10/6/1830 W
NELSON Nancy 8/26/1831 S
NELSON Thomas 12/29/1830 W
NEUGENT Eli (colored man)'s child 11/23/1823 S; see also NEWGENT, NUGENT
NEVINS Mr 4/22/1831 W
NEVINS child 8/15/1826 S
NEVIT James 11/3/1813 S
NEVIT John's child 7/20/1822 S
NEVIT Joseph's daughter 2/21/1812 M
NEVIT Mr 1/4/1815 S
NEVIT William's child 10/12/1819 W
NEVITT Mrs 2/5/1826 S
NEVITT Thomas 9/27/1807 S
NEVITT Thomas's child 3/3/1804 S
NEWGENT Eli (colored man)'s child 5/25/1822 S
NEWGENT Eli's mother-in-law 7/25/1822 S; see also NEUGENT, NUGENT
NEWTON Clement's black woman 12/23/1815 S
NEWTON Clement's son 3/25/1817 W
NEWTON James's child 11/22/1823 W
NEWTON John 6/12/1816 W
NEWTON John's child 8/6/1831 S

NEWTON Lewis 9/30/1822 W
NEWTON Miss 7/28/1813 S
NEWTON Mr 9/29/1823 W
NEWTON Mrs W's child 3/10/1827 S
NEWTON Mrs's child 8/13/1832 S
NEWTON Mrs's child 2/21/1813 S
NEWTON Mrs's child 8/2/1831 S
NEWTON Walter 2/14/1826 S
NEWTON Walter's brother 9/29/1814 S
NEWTON Walter's child 8/5/1823 W
NEWTON Walter's child 9/6/1816 W
NEWTON Walter's child 8/25/1813 W
NEWTON Walter's child 8/13/1820 W
NEWTON Walter's child 8/20/1819 W
NICHOLAS (colored man)'s son 2/23/1824 S
NICHOLLS I S's child 9/26/1830 S
NICHOLLS I S's colored child 7/25/1826 S
NICHOLLS Isaiah 5/7/1828 W
NICHOLLS Mrs 4/15/1824 S
NICHOLLS Mrs 9/15/1820 S
NICHOLLS Mrs Sarah 10/14/1827 M
NICHOLLS Mrs's child 8/6/1820 S
NICHOLLS William S's black child 11/26/1812 S
NICHOLLS William S's child 9/19/1816 M
NICHOLLS William S's child 12/11/1813 M
NICHOLLSON Thomas's son 9/19/1826 W
NICHOLS I 2/2/1829 W
NICHOLS Mr 7/1/1820 S
   see also NICOLLS
NICHOLSON George 6/13/1829 S
NICHOLSON James 1/12/1828 W
NICHOLSON Mr 12/22/1818 S
NICHOLSON Mr 3/3/1822 S
NICHOLSON Mr's child 9/9/1819 S
NICHOLSON Mr's father 11/20/1815 S
NICHOLSON Mr's son 8/24/1819 W
NICHOLSON Mrs 10/23/1819 S
NICHOLSON Mrs 2/1/1830 M
NICHOLSON Mrs's child 8/20/1829 W
NICHOLSON Samuel's child 8/25/1829 S
NICHOLSON Thomas 3/14/1829 M
NICHOLSON Thos H 2/25/1818 S

NICOLLS I S's child 3/16/1831 M\
    see also NICHOLLS
NIGHT James's wife 3/16/1804 S
NIXDORFF Mrs 9/16/1830 M
NIXDORFF Tobias's colored child 6/25/1828 S
NOBLE Mrs 4/10/1824 W
NOLAN Thomas's child 9/15/1832 W
NOLAND Mrs 5/13/1829 S
NOLAND Patrick 8/10/1829 S
NORMAN Betsey 7/31/1813 S
NORMAN John's mother (colored man) 6/6/1822 S
NORMAN Patrick's child (colored man) 12/24/1829 S
NORMAN William (colored man) 1/1/1831 S
NORRIS Benjamin 3/18/1815 W
NORRIS Isaac for ----- 12/21/1806 W
NORRIS Isaac's child 3/16/1806 W
NORRIS Isaac's wife 5/3/1804 W
NORRIS James 4/20/1825 S
NORRIS Mr's child 7/2/1817 S
NORRIS Mrs 8/24/1824 S
NORRIS Mrs's child 1/12/1823 S
NORRIS Mrs's child 9/26/1823 S
NORRIS Mrs's child 9/24/1832 S
NORRIS Mrs's child 9/23/1832 S
NORRIS Mrs's son 10/21/1823 S
NORRIS R's sister-in-law 11/3/1826 S
NORRIS Stephen's child 3/20/1818 S
NOURSE Michael's child 10/13/1821 W cherry
NOURSE Mr's child 1/30/1802 W
NOVEL Jane's child (colored) 11/26/1826 S
NOWLAND Thomas's child 6/22/1828 W
NUGENT Eli (colored man)'s child 1/15/1831 S
NUGENT Eli (colored man)'s wife 3/26/1832 W
NUGENT Eli's child 12/28/1818 S
    see also NEUGENT, NEWGENT
O'BRIAN Mrs 4/4/1832 W
O'BRIAN William 6/25/1820 M
O'BRIEN Mrs 11/19/1820 W
O'DONNALL Hugh's mother-in-law 9/30/1829 S
O'DONOGHUE Dennis's child 8/31/1831 W
O'DONOGHUE John 7/17/1830 S
O'DONOGHUE Timothy 6/25/1830 W

O'DONOGHUE Timothy's child 6/2/1830 W
O'FARRELL P 5/11/1801 S
O'NEAL Theodore 9/4/1832 W
O'NEALE Mrs 3/1/1830 W
OAKLY John 5/6/1806 M
OBER Benjamin's child 6/28/1798 W
OBER Gustavus 1/3/1819 m
OBER Robert's child 11/24/1823 M
OBER Robert's child 8/20/1816 M
OBER Robert's child 11/2/1823 M
OBRIAN Joseph 9/26/1816 S
ODEN Benjamin for ----- 2/6/1803 M
ODEN Benjamin's child 11/9/1802 M
OFFIT Mrs 12/3/1819 W
OFFITT Mrs 2/7/1819 W
OFFITT T B 10/2/1820 W
OFFORD Mr for ----- 1/28/1807 W
OFFUT Bazil 5/12/1817 W
OFFUTT Rebecca 3/28/1824 W
OFFUTT William 12/13/1822 W
OGDON Mrs 5/15/1816 M
OGLE Horatio 9/5/1831 S
OGLE Mr's child 9/11/1823 S
OLIGLE Harris's child 10/15/1814 W
OLIVE William 1/23/1812 S
OLIVER Mrs 3/20/1831 W
OLPHIN Mrs 4/3/1824 S
ONEAL John's child 4/21/1817 S
ONEAL John's child 9/3/1816 S
ONEAL Mrs 10/1/1819 W
ORM T's child 9/6/1820 W
ORME Archibald for ----- 4/12/1808 W
ORME Jeremiah's child 12/19/1831 W
ORME Nathaniel 9/12/1804 W
ORMOT Valentine 12/18/1811 S
ORR Mrs 9/29/1830 W
OSBOURN Richard's child 2/27/1830 M
OTT Anne 7/25/1828 M
OTT John 4/9/1818 M
OTT John's child 1/3/1818 M
OTT Mrs 2/4/1815 M
OTTINGER Charles 12/6/1827 S

OULD Robert's child 9/22/1823 W
OULD Robert's colored boy 1/8/1829 S
OULD Robert's son 7/23/1832 S
OVERTON John (colored man) 8/14/1828 S
OVERTON John (colored man)'s child 12/19/1821 S
OVERTON John's child 10/28/1816 S
OVERTON Richard (colored man) 3/28/1832 S
OVERTON Susan (colored woman) 9/5/1832 S
OWEN Colonel 1/30/1812 M
OWENS Elizabeth 3/25/1816 W
OWENS Isaac Jr 9/17/1824 M
OWENS Isaac jr's child 4/1/1824 S
OWENS Isaac's child 8/30/1801 W
OWENS Isaac's child 6/10/1811 W
OWENS Isaac's child 11/19/1810 W
OWENS Isaac's Sam 2/18/1811 S
OWENS Mr 4/30/1802 S
OWENS Mrs Mary 9/7/1832 M
OWENS Singleton 1/29/1817 w
OWING Mrs 7/11/1806 W
PACKHAM Caleb's child 11/10/1815 W
PAGE George 9/21/1830 S
PAGE Mr 10/26/1798; W
PAGET William's child 7/28/1824 S
PAGET William's child 10/1/1829 S
PAIN Mr 12/30/1810 S
PAIN William 1/18/1815 W
PAINE Elizabeth's child 9/15/1818 S
PAINE Jacob's daughter 10/3/1821 W
PAINE Wm's sister 2/16/1818 W
PALMAR Elisha 9/30/1821 W
PALMER Ann 2/21/1826 S
PALMER John 7/3/1826 W
PALMER John's child 9/8/1820 M
PANE William 1/31/1823 W
PARADISE Mr's child 3/13/1818 S
PARDONSON James 5/24/1827 S
PARIE Sarah 9/21/1831 S
PARIS Mrs 4/23/1814 W
PARKE David 9/21/1822 S
PARKER Elonor's black girl 9/6/1818 S
PARKER George Senr 8/14/1826 W

PARKER Mrs 11/9/1818 W
PARKER Thomas's father 6/26/1830 W
PARKER William's child 6/25/1824 W
PARKS John's child 8/27/1816 S
PARROTT Mr (hatter) 11/19/1804 S
PARROTT R's colored man 12/30/1822 S
PARROTT Richard 1/5/1823 M
PARROTT Richard's black boy 1/13/1813 S
PARROTT Richard's black man 5/1/1809 S
PARROTT Richard's child 10/8/1804 M
PARROTT Richard's colored person 1/6/1805 S
PARROTT Richard's colored child 9/26/1821 S
PARROTT Richard's negro woman 11/15/1811 S
PARROTT Richard's negro child 7/7/1809 S
PARSON William's child 5/9/1826 W
PARSON William's father 12/11/1813 W
PARSON William's young man 11/20/1818 S
PARSONS James 2/6/1814 W
PARSONS Mrs 4/14/1821 M
PARSONS William's apprentice (John Reynolds) 5/11/1825 S
PARSONS William's child 6/28/1813 M
PARSONS William's child 2/22/1829 W
PARSONS William's child 4/1/1808 S
PARSONS William's child 11/23/1813 M
PATTEN Mrs 3/15/1826 M
PATTENGER Thomas's child 5/27/1821 M
PATTENGER Thomas's colored woman 5/5/1821 S
PATTERSON Dr's child 9/21/1814 M
PATTERSON Edgar's child 7/2/1816 M
PATTERSON Edgar's child 10/14/1803 M
PATTERSON Edgar's colored child 8/4/1808 W
PATTERSON Edgar's daughter 5/5/1830 M
PATTERSON Edger's colored woman 12/16/1822 S
PATTERSON Edward (colored man) 4/28/1822 S
PATTERSON Miss 11/8/1832 M
PATTERSON Mr's child 5/4/1802 M
PAUL Anthony 9/24/1823 W
PAUL Mrs 2/16/1815 S
PAUL Mrs's child 3/24/1827 S
PAULEY Mrs 4/1/1819 W
PAYN John's father 8/14/1827 S
PAYNE Isaac 3/13/1826 S

PAYNE Jacob 5/22/1827 W
PAYNE Jacob's daughter 10/7/1830 W
PAYNE John 10/4/1831 S
PAYNE Josias 2/9/1826 S
PAYNE Mrs 2/8/1823 S
PAYNE Thomas's child 6/11/1826 W
PEABODY John 2/26/1827 W
PEABODY Miss Adeline 10/10/1817 M
PEABODY Mrs 10/21/1826 W
PEAKE John's child 12/23/1826 S
PEAKE Mr's child 6/16/1832 S
PEALE Charly (colored man) 3/7/1823 S
PEALE Mary 2/4/1818 S
PEARCE Ignatius's child 4/5/1830 S
PEARCE Isaac for ----- 5/1/1804 W
PEARCE Mr's child 9/27/1811 W
PEARCE Mrs's child 8/25/1813 W
PEARCE Mrs's child 9/28/1820 M
PEARCE William 6/8/1822 S
PEARS Aquila 4/12/1829 S
PEAVE Qualia 9/6/1814 S
PECK Joseph 9/15/1809 M
PECK Joseph's wife 9/28/1805 M
PECK M A's black girl 5/16/1813 S
PECKHAM Mrs's son 6/25/1823 W
PECKHAM William 1/20/1823 W
PELTON Asahel 8/27/1825 S
PENDELL Mrs's child 9/8/1830 S
PENDRED Mrs 1/28/1815 W
PERLEY Mr 5/14/1829 S
PERLEY Mr's child 11/2/1823 S
PERLEY Mrs's child 7/26/1826 S
PERRY Benjamin's child 10/25/1830 S
PERRY Mr 1/15/1815 W
PERRY Mrs 8/31/1823 W
PERRY Mrs's child 3/27/1830 S
PETER Alexander 10/26/1807 M
PETER Columbia 12/4/1820 M
PETER David 12/2/1812 M
PETER David's child 4/17/1803 M
PETER David's chld 7/22/1808 M
PETER Elizabeth 11/4/1821 M

PETER George's black man 10/24/1813 S
PETER George's child 5/28/1814 M
PETER George's child 3/31/1814 M
PETER George's child 3/25/1824 M
PETER George's colored woman's child 7/28/1825 S
PETER George's colored woman's child 7/31/1825 S
PETER John (colored man) 4/8/1822 S
PETER John 10/21/1804 M
PETER John's brother 7/22/1811 M
PETER John's child 9/11/1823 M
PETER John's child 8/27/1810 M
PETER John's colored child 10/1/1803 S
PETER John's negro woman 2/9/1804 S
PETER John's sister 3/30/1810 M
PETER Mr's child 9/4/1820 M
PETER Mrs 8/21/1813 M
PETER Mrs Ann 2/9/1814 M
PETER Mrs Elinor 2/7/1812 M
PETER Mrs George 5/14/1824 M
PETER Robert 11/16/1806 M
PETER Robert Junior 11/11/1809 M
PETER Sarah 10/8/1823 M
PETER Thomas's child 10/3/1807 M
PETER Thomas's child 4/29/1809 M
PETER Thomas's child 9/1/1800 M
PETERS Harriet (colored woman) 9/12/1826 S
PETTENGILL Mr's child 9/19/1821 W
PETTET Mrs 2/6/1822 W
PETTINGALE Mr's child 9/20/1823 W
PETTINGILL Mr's child 8/25/1822 W
PETTIT William 11/21/1823 W
PHELAN Stephen's child 8/9/1831 S
PHILIPS Mr 2/17/1815 S
PHILIPS Mrs 2/14/1828 S
PHILIPS's child 8/31/1815 S
PHILISTIN Mrs 2/6/1824 W
PICKERELL Benjamin's child 10/17/1818 S
PICKERELL Benjamin's child 9/16/1818 S
PICKFORD John B 6/20/1818 W
PICKRELL B's woman 5/8/1818 S
PICKRELL John's child 4/22/1816 W
PIERCE Ignatius 9/22/1831 S

PIERS Aquila's wife 1/28/1827 S
PIFER Henry's child 8/12/1817 M
PIFER Mr 6/13/1820 S
PIFER Mr's child 6/13/1820 S
PILES Mrs 6/10/1819 W
PINDELL Mr 7/23/1828 S
PITT George 5/25/1816 M
PLANT Eliza's child (colored woman) 2/9/1822 S
PLANT Eliza's child 8/28/1826 S
PLANTS Eliza's child 10/5/1831 S
PLATER Mr's woman 9/14/1824 S
PLATER Patsey Miss 9/14/1824 M
PLATER Thomas 5/3/1830 M
PLATER Thomas for a boy 11/22/1803 M
PLATOR (colored man) 1/12/1831 S
PLATOR Mrs 7/14/1814 M
PLATOR Thomas (black man) 2/15/1815 S
PLATOR Thomas's child 6/28/1800 W
POINTER Ann's child 8/24/1818 S
POLK Charles P for ----- 11/25/1810 M
POLK David's child 12/31/1823 M
POLKINHORN Henry 10/15/1813 W
POLKINHORN Henry's child 10/2/1808 S
POOL Ann 10/14/1821 S
POOL Lewis's child 3/13/1816 W
POOL Mrs 11/17/1817 W
POOL Mrs 12/18/1820 S
POOL Nancy's child 8/13/1815 S
POOLEY Mrs 12/24/1826 S
PORTER Dorey 11/18/1830 S
PORTER William's sister 9/15/1831 S
PORTER's child 6/10/1813 S
POST Peter L 6/17/1831 S
POTTS Samuel J's child 6/26/1824 M
POTTS Samuel's child 12/16/1822 M
POTTS Samuel's colored man 1/19/1823 S
POTTS Samuel's colored child 2/23/1824 S
POWEL Ann (colored woman)'s child 12/17/1823 S
POWELL Mary 11/5/1811 S
POWELL Mrs 2/25/1830 S
POWER Frederick's child 9/3/1829 S
POWERS Alexander 8/7/1832 S

POWERS Edward 2/26/1830 S
POWERS Frederick's child 7/30/1831 W
POWERS Mrs 9/2/1814 S
POWERS R's child 1/15/1822 S
PRATER Mrs 2/22/1831 S
PRATHER Mr 8/7/1825 S
PRATT John W's child 7/17/1805 M
PRATT Mrs's black child 7/31/1818 S
PRESSEY Mrs 10/7/1819 S
PRICE Mr 11/22/1815 W
PRICE Mr's child 9/6/1802 M
PRICE Samuel for ----- 10/18/1806 S
PRICE Samuel's child 3/5/1808 S
PRICE Thomas 4/14/1815 W
PRINGLE John's uncle 6/28/1798 W
PRIOR George (colored man) 4/16/1827 S
PRITCHARD Benjamin's child 6/10/1814 W
PRITCHARD Benjamin's child 11/20/1805 W
PRITCHARD Benjamin's child 12/20/1807 W
PRITCHARD Mr 4/8/1815 W
PRITCHARD Mr's child 11/5/1821 S
PRITCHARD Mrs Benjamin 1/28/1810 W
PRITCHARD Mrs's child 10/17/1821 S
PROCTOR Benedict (colored man) 9/21/1821 S
PROCTOR Polly (colored woman) 7/25/1830 S
PUMFREY Lloyd's woman 5/18/1819 S
PUMPHREY Lloyd's child 8/2/1828 W
PUMPHREY Lloyd's child 1/7/1830 S
PUMPHREY Lloyd's child 8/27/1823 M
PUMPHREY Lloyd's child 10/12/1832 W
PUMPHREY Lloyd's child 8/27/1829 W
PUMPHREY Lloyd's father 8/14/1827 S
PURDY Mr 6/9/1812 S
PURPOX John (colored man) 6/15/1826 S
PUTMAN Mr's child 7/27/1816 W
PYE Mrs for ----- 12/31/1803 M
PYFER Henry's child 2/9/1821 M
PYFER Henry's child 1/26/1826 M
PYFER Henry's child 10/11/1822 M
PYFER Henry's child 11/29/1832 M
QUADE Mrs 3/3/1812 S
QUADE Walter for ----- 7/21/1806 S

QUADE Walter for ----- 4/27/1806 S
QUADE Walter's father 3/1/1810 S
QUANDER Sally (colored woman) 3/17/1826 S
QUEEN Anthony (colored man) 9/3/1822 S
QUEEN Austin 8/4/1819 S
QUEEN Mr Richard's child 8/7/1823 W
QUEEN Mrs 2/21/1817 W
QUEEN Samuel 1/18/1831 W
RABBIT Mr's child 3/24/1821 S
RABBIT Thomas's child 12/13/1830 W
RADCLIFFE Mrs 2/16/1825 M
RAGAN Bazil's son 2/12/1820 W
RAGAN Ed 5/16/1831 S
RAGAN John 5/5/1816 W
RAGON Basil's child 8/7/1812 S
RAGON Basil's grandchild 8/16/1826 W
RAGON Bazil 10/28/1829 W
RAGON Bazil's child 11/14/1811 S
RAGON Daniel 2/23/1824 S
RAGON Daniel's child 9/16/1800 W
RAGON Daniel's child 10/10/1806 W
RAGON Daniel's child 11/2/1802 W
RAGON Mary 8/23/1821 W
RAGON Richard 9/23/1832 W
RAGON Richard's wife's mother 10/11/1829 S
RAIN Lawrence 8/23/1831 S
RAMSEY Andrew's child 9/10/1814 M
RANDOLPH Mr's man 3/14/1818 S
RANKIN Mr's child 7/25/1804 M
RANNALS Jessee (colored man)'s child 12/10/1832 S
RATCLIF Mrs 9/21/1812 W
RATCLIFF Joseph's child 10/17/1819 M
RATCLIFFE George's child 10/28/1832 W
RATCLIFFE Joseph's child 10/9/1826 M
RATCLIFFE Joseph's child 7/29/1828 M
RATCLIFFE Mary 11/4/1828 M
RATCLIFFE Mr a colored man's child 12/21/1818 S
RATHIN R 3/6/1821 S
RATRIE William Senr 9/23/1827 W
RAWLINGS Samuel 9/13/1825 W
RAY Mr, a boatman 3/17/1829 W
RAY Mr's child 8/16/1818 W

REACH William's child at the foundry 10/28/1829 S
READ child 2/9/1820 W
READEN Henry 5/12/1812 S
READEN Mrs 10/5/1812 S
REAVER Mr's child 10/29/1822 S
REDEN Henry 7/5/1812 S
REDHEFFER Mr 2/20/1821 M
REDMAN Catherine 11/30/1828 M
REDMAN James 11/23/1823 M
REED James 8/14/1829 W
REED Jane 5/1/1816 W
REED Mr 3/13/1815 W
REED Mr's child 8/15/1818 W
REED Mrs 3/14/1821 M
REED Mrs 8/13/1817 S
REED Mrs's child 4/20/1817 S
REED William (colored man) 2/9/1831 S
REEDER John 3/6/1821 W
REEDER Mr's child 10/13/1822 W
REEDER Mrs's child 10/25/1821 W
REEDER Thomas 9/15/1832 S
REEDER Thomas's child 6/21/1820 M
REES Major 2/28/1806 W
REEVES Mrs 3/3/1825 S
REGEN Henry's child 7/21/1829 W
REINTZEL Anthony 9/14/1817 M
REINTZEL D's black woman 11/20/1820 S
REINTZEL Daniel 11/19/1828 W
REINTZEL Maria 11/18/1814 W
REINTZEL Samuel's child 10/30/1823 W
REINTZEL Samuel's child 7/18/1830 W
REINTZEL's Charles 6/17/1827 S
REINTZLE Anthony 5/21/1806 W
REINTZLE Daniel for a lad 1/31/1807 W
REINTZLE Daniel's child 12/20/1810 M
REINTZLE George 9/29/1800 W
REINTZLE John 3/13/1811 M
REINTZLE John's wife 1/16/1806 M
REINTZLE Mrs Daniel 9/20/1832 M
REINTZLE Samuel's child 7/27/1832 W
REINTZLE Valentine's wife 3/19/1804 M
REMICK M D 1/22/1827 S

REMINGTON Mr's daughter 1/9/1816 S
REMMINGTON J A 2/22/1831 W
RENALDS John's child 8/8/1815 M
RENNELLS Mrs's child 7/17/1831 S
RENNER Christian's child 8/6/1830 S
RENNER Daniel 1/30/1830 M
RENNER Daniel's child 7/17/1817 M
RENNER Daniel's child 9/27/1820 S
RENNER Daniel's child 8/30/1819 M
RENNER Daniel's Gilbert 6/28/1828 S
RENNER John's child 7/4/1831 S
RENNER John's negro man 4/8/1811 S
RENNER Mrs Helen 2/23/1802 M
RENSHAR Mr 2/12/1820 W
RENSHAW Mrs for ----- 10/8/1801 W
RENTZEL Andrew 5/12/1816 W
RENTZEL Valentine's black man 10/15/1816 S
RETCLEF Joseph's black woman 4/1/1816 S
RETCLIF Joseph's child 3/11/1816 W
RETEN Jacob's child 11/9/1808
REVEL James 5/12/1830 S
REYNOLDS Mrs's child 10/3/1821 W
RHEY Mr's child 10/30/1823 S
RHODES George's child 9/21/1807 W
RHODES William 2/13/1828 M
RICE George 12/8/1823 S
RICH Mr 7/22/1820 W
RICHARDS Caleb 12/15/1822 W
RICHARDS Mrs 2/22/1823 S
RICHARDS Mrs 3/26/1821 S
RICHARDSON J's child 10/7/1823 S
RICHARDSON Jessee (colored man) 1/5/1832 S
RICHARDSON Mrs 1/7/1812 W
RICHARDSON Thomas 11/13/1812 W
RICHARDSON Thomas's child 7/23/1812 W
RICHEY Mrs's daughter 11/23/1832 W
RICHEY Mrs's son 11/24/1832 W
RICHMOND Mr 4/8/1796 M
RICHMOND Mr's child 10/7/1813 S
RICHMOND Mrs 10/7/1813 S
RIDGELY Wm G's child 9/14/1818 M
RIDGEWAY Eden's child 9/30/1818 S

RIDGEWAY John 9/3/1832 W
RIDGEWAY Mr's child 7/11/1825 S
RIDGEWAY Mr's child 9/12/1818 S
RIDGEWAY Mr's child 9/8/1824 S
RIDGEWAY Mrs 1/27/1825 S
RIDGEWAY Mrs 11/26/1826 S
RIDGEWAY Mrs's child 9/8/1832 S
RIDGEWAY Mrs's child 9/26/1832 W
RIDGLEY William G's child 5/28/1816 M
RIDGLEY William G's child 10/20/1812 S
RIDGLEY William G's child 4/15/1816 M
RIDGWAY James 3/24/1815 S
RIDGWAY John F's child 9/18/1831 W
RIDGWAY Leven 1/30/1816 S
RIDGWAY Leven's child 9/7/1815 S
RIDGWAY Levin 5/21/1824 S
RIDGWAY Mr 3/14/1815 S
RIDGWAY Mr's child 8/21/1815 S
RIDGWAY Mrs 11/21/1821 W
RIDGWAY Mrs 3/30/1815 S
RIESE Mr's child 7/20/1830 S
RIFFLE G 2/7/1832 S
RIFFLE Joseph 9/22/1827 S
RIFFLE Mr's sister's child 8/27/1818 S
RIGDEN Mrs 8/26/1826 W
RIGDEN T for Mr Mitchell 11/9/1808 S
RIGDEN Thomas's child 3/4/1812 W
RIGDEN William's child 4/23/1811 S
RIGGS Mrs 4/18/1817 M
RIGGS Romulus's child 11/13/1821 M
RILEY Joseph 9/11/1830 S
RIND Mrs 4/25/1822 W
RIND Mrs Samuel 11/9/1830 M
RIND W A Jr's child 7/22/1822 W
RIND William A's child 8/3/1808 M
RIND William A's child 7/24/1803 M
RIND William's child 6/15/1820 W
RIND Wm A's child 7/14/1816 S
RINGGOLD Mary 6/11/1826 M
RINGGOLD Miss Sophia 5/15/1832 M
RINGGOLD Mrs 11/29/1813 M
RINGGOLD Tench's colored man 3/9/1815 S

RISZNER Mrs 5/3/1812 W
RITCHIE Abner 9/27/1819 M
RITCHIE John 6/27/1831 M
RITCHIE Mrs 10/1/1829 W
RITCHIE William 9/15/1832 W
RITTENHOUSE John B 6/5/1814 M
RITTENHOUSE John B's child 10/23/1810 M
RITTENHOUSE John B's negro woman 10/11/1810 S
RITTENHOUSE Mrs 5/10/1829 M
RITTENHOUSE Mrs's black child 12/6/1819 S
RITTENHOUSE Thomas's black girl 2/2/1812 S
RITTER Jacob 10/1/1813 W
RITTER Jacob's child 7/25/1812 W
RITTER Mrs 3/3/1816 W
RITTER Peter's brother 1/15/1816 W
RITTER Peter's child 8/19/1812 M
RITTER Peter's child 7/6/1812 M
RITTER Peter's colored child 10/1/1831 S
RITTER Peter's colored child 12/4/1829 S
RIYE Mrs' child 4/14/1816 S
ROACH James 7/21/1830 S
ROADS William 10/24/1816 S
ROBB John 2/16/1824 W
ROBERDEAU Isaac 1/17/1829 M
ROBERT a colored man 5/25/1816 S
ROBERTS Henry 11/7/1830 W
ROBERTS Mr's child 1/17/1817 M
ROBERTS Mrs 1/8/1817 M
ROBERTS Wm's black child 8/30/1818 S
ROBERTSON Ann's child 9/30/1831 W
ROBERTSON Charles (colored man) 9/20/1832 W
ROBERTSON George 10/23/1831 W
ROBERTSON H B's colored child 2/11/1824 S
ROBERTSON H B's child 6/18/1830 W
ROBERTSON H B's child 11/8/1814 S
ROBERTSON Henry 9/17/1831 M
ROBERTSON Henry B's child 9/26/1832 W
ROBERTSON Henry B's child 8/29/1831 W
ROBERTSON J P 2/18/1827 W
ROBERTSON John's child 7/31/1820 W
ROBERTSON John's child 12/22/1818 W
ROBERTSON John's child 10/2/1823 S

ROBERTSON John's daughter 7/2/1830 W
ROBERTSON Joseph 10/6/1814 S
ROBERTSON Kitty (colored woman)'s sister 7/10/1831 S
ROBERTSON Lamkin's child 9/20/1829 S
ROBERTSON Mary 1/17/1831 W
ROBERTSON Mr (laborer)'s child 3/20/1822 S
ROBERTSON Mr 2/19/1823 W
ROBERTSON Mr's child 5/20/1813 S
ROBERTSON Mr's child at Curtis 8/13/1821 W
ROBERTSON Mrs 1/26/1816 W
ROBERTSON Mrs 11/15/1822 S
ROBERTSON Mrs 3/8/1815 W
ROBERTSON Mrs 4/24/1819 W
ROBERTSON Mrs 9/13/1815 S
ROBERTSON Mrs Eliza 5/20/1825 M
ROBERTSON Mrs's child 9/8/1818 S
ROBERTSON Mrs's colored man 7/3/1823 S
ROBERTSON Mrs's mother (pauper) 2/2/1824 S
ROBERTSON Peggy (colored woman) 3/21/1832 S
ROBERTSON Thomas' colored boy 4/13/1815 S
ROBERTSON Thomas's brother 11/6/1811 M
ROBERTSON Thomas's son 10/2/1813 W
ROBERTSON William 11/16/1820 S
ROBERTSON William 4/9/1800 W
ROBERTSON William B 9/5/1831 W
ROBERTSON Wm 6/13/1819 S
ROBINSON James 11/11/1830 S
ROBINSON John's child 12/20/1823 W
ROBINSON John's child 7/24/1824 W
ROBINSON Mr 7/21/1830 S
ROBINSON Mrs 9/29/1821 W
ROBY Leonard 1/4/1816 S
ROBY Mr 10/5/1822 W
ROCH Mrs 2/4/1815 S
ROCK Mr 12/7/1806 S
RODES Mrs's child 4/11/1814 S
RODGERS Major 9/5/1810 M
RODGERS Mrs 2/13/1818 M
RODGERS Thomas's child 8/21/1808 M
RODIER Peter's child 10/12/1825 S
RODS Mrs 4/20/1814 S
ROLLING William's daughter 8/15/1826 S

ROLLINGS Thomas (colored man) 8/28/1832 S
ROLLINGS William's child 8/13/1829 S
ROSATER Thomas's wife 11/27/1832 S
ROSE Mrs 4/2/1829 W
ROSS Andrew 1/13/1822 M
ROSS Andrew for wife 9/17/1808 M
ROSS Charlotty 7/3/1816 S
ROSS Charlotty's child 6/29/1816 S
ROSS Lamkin 5/8/1820 S
ROSS Mr 6/6/1821 M
ROSS Mrs 11/8/1819 M
ROSS Richard 9/27/1831 M
ROSS Richard seaman 2/18/1826 S
ROSS Richard's nephew 8/16/1830 M
ROSS William's child 11/20/1820 S
ROSS William's wife 11/14/1832 S
ROUNDS Ezeikel (colored) (don't know him) 5/19/1828 S
ROUNDS Ezekiel 3/20/1824 S
ROUNDS Lettie (colored woman)'s child 9/13/1823 S
ROUNDS Martin 7/8/1827 S
ROUNDS Zekel's child 12/31/1814 S
ROWE James 7/19/1819 S
ROWLES Joseph E 9/10/1811 M
ROWLES Joseph E's child 7/23/1809 M
ROWLES Joseph E's child 10/29/1803 M
ROWLUND George 12/10/1814 S
ROWS Mr 10/14/1803 W
RUFFINS Robert 9/6/1814 S
RUMNEY John's child 6/17/1806 W
RUNNALDS Mr 10/19/1829 S
RUNNELS Margrat 11/15/1813 S
RUSH Paty 4/25/1822 S
RUSH Samuel 5/24/1817 S
RUSHER Richard's child 6/19/1812 M
RUSSEL John 11/16/1811 S
RUSSELL Basil 3/6/1817 S
RUSSELL Bill's child 9/13/1829 S
RUSSELL F A's child 6/9/1817 M
RUSSELL F A's child 7/11/1818 M
RUSSELL Judson's brother 1/18/1830 S
RUSSELL Mr 12/22/1818 S
RUSSELL Mrs 9/25/1813 W

RUSSIE Mrs 9/23/1817 W
RUTH Henry 3/6/1815 W
RUTHFORD Mrs 4/12/1821 W
RUTRIE William 8/2/1827 W
RYAN Patrick 8/31/1829 S
RYAN Patrick's child 6/5/1830 S
RYAN Richard's child 7/21/1830 S
RYE Mr's child 7/3/1827 S
RYE Mr's child 11/7/1823 S
RYE Mr's child 8/29/1832 S
RYE Mr's child 10/21/1832 S
SALMON Mrs 2/24/1815 S
SALTER Ann 11/5/1818 S
SAMON John 10/11/1831 S
SAMSON James 8/21/1829 S
SAYERS James's wife 11/13/1832 W
SAYERS John 1/8/1809 M
SAYERS Mr's child 10/21/1808 M
SAYERS Mr's child 8/31/1805 M
SCHELL Seth 9/1/1832 W
SCHLEY Mrs 4/12/1826 W
SCHULTZ Henry 7/7/1820 M
SCOTT Alexander's Sam 8/3/1820 M
SCOTT Alexander's son 10/11/1820 M
SCOTT Allen's colored woman 11/20/1822 S
SCOTT Allen's colored child 3/27/1831 S
SCOTT Gustavus 12/29/1800 M
SCOTT James (Washington) 5/10/1829 S
SCOTT James's son (Washington) 4/10/1829 S
SCOTT James's son (colored man) 11/13/1827 S
SCOTT Jessee 7/23/1830 M
SCOTT Jessie's colored child 7/21/1827 S
SCOTT John's child 7/19/1803 M
SCOTT Margaret for ----- 4/5/1806 M
SCOTT Miss Margarett 1/16/1800 M
SCOTT Mr William A's wife 8/20/1830 W
SCOTT Mr's child 10/27/1821 S
SCOTT Mrs 10/23/1821 M
SCOTT Mrs 9/12/1823 S
SCOTT Mrs A (Montgomery County) 10/7/1825 W
SCOTT Mrs Horatio 10/2/1827 M
SCOTT Mrs J's colored child 3/26/1831 S

SCOTT Mrs William (Montgomery County) 6/20/1832 W
SCOTT Mrs's child 7/21/1830 S
SCOTT Mrs's colored child 2/9/1831 S
SCOTT S C's child 3/24/1829 M
SCOTT Sabrett 10/11/1824 W
SCOTT Sabrett E's child 4/20/1831 M
SCOTT Thomas 9/24/1820 W
SCREVENER Mr 4/25/1815 S
SEDGWICK H's child at Paget's 2/28/1829 S
SEDGWICK Harriet 10/4/1828 S
SEMMES Cravan 1/31/1815 W
SEMMES James 8/26/1829 W
SEMMES James's child 11/18/1818 W
SEMMES Joseph 3/29/1832 W
SEMMES Joseph's George's wife 4/12/1805 S
SEMMES Joseph's wife 10/29/1803 M
SEMMES Mary 1/12/1813 M
SEMMES Mrs 8/15/1819 W
SEMMES Raphel's child 9/23/1820 M
SEMMES's George's child 6/4/1809 S
SEMMY R T's child 8/29/1819 W
SEWALL Clement 1/8/1829 W
SEWALL Lewis's child 8/27/1824 S
SEWALL Mrs (Virginia) 10/21/1830 W
SEWALL Mrs 9/10/1827 W
SEWELL Joseph's son 3/25/1820 W
SHAAF Mrs's colored child 9/8/1824 S
SHAAFF Arthur 5/17/1817 M
SHAAFF J 5/1/1819 M
SHAAFF Mrs's colored boy 9/17/1821 S
SHAAFF Mrs's colored child 5/9/1830 S
SHAAFF Mrs's colored child 7/6/1831 S
SHAAFF Mrs's son 8/12/1820 M
SHAAFFER George 9/11/1832 S
SHAHAN Mr 7/23/1830 S
SHANAHAN Timothy 12/13/1830 S
SHANKS Wm 3/22/1819 S
SHANLEY Patrick 8/17/1830 S
SHARP Mrs 6/30/1815 W
SHARP Mrs 9/24/1818 S
SHARP Mrs' child 8/20/1818 S
SHAW & BIRTH for ----- 10/12/1804 S

SHAW Catherine 2/22/1824 M
SHAW Charles T 12/26/1830 W
SHAW James 12/27/1814 W
SHAW John 6/22/1815 W
SHAW John's child 11/18/1832 S
SHAW L's daughter 11/19/1826 M
SHAW Lemuel's colored child 1/30/1827 S
SHAW Lemuel's colored child 8/17/1829 S
SHAW Mrs 8/17/1826 W
SHAY John 10/26/1830 S
SHAY Mr's child 9/28/1818 S
SHEAKMAN Mr's child 4/13/1830 S
SHEAPARD L's child 7/19/1821 W
SHEAPARD Mr's child 9/27/1812 W
SHEAPERD L's child 4/11/1821 W
SHECKELL Levi's child 8/8/1828 S
SHECKELL R's child 9/13/1817 W
SHECKELL Richd's child 6/8/1825 W
SHECKELLS Mrs 11/6/1831 S
SHECKELLS Thomas 10/3/1831 W
SHECKELS Richard's child 8/9/1824 W
SHEID Miss Ann J 8/31/1821 M
SHELBY Mrs 2/9/1814 S
SHELTON Captain 1/9/1809 M
SHEPPARD Walter for ----- 10/18/1802 S
SHERLEY Mr 9/10/1812 S
SHERLOCK John's child 9/21/1814 S
SHERMAN Peter 11/5/1823 W
SHERRIFF Mrs of Bladensburg 4/14/1827 W
SHIELD Mr's child 8/18/1818 S
SHIELDS Patty 1/3/1828 S
SHIPLEY Mrs's daughter 7/22/1830 S
SHIVELY Mrs 10/16/1827 S
SHIVENER John 2/14/1821 M
SHLEY John D 12/28/1819 W
SHOEMAKER Charles 4/5/1807 S
SHOEMAKER David Jr 4/4/1828 W
SHOEMAKER George's child 10/5/1830 W
~~SHOEMAKER Mrs 2/9/1822~~
SHORTER A (colored man) 10/25/1826 S
SHORTER Abraham's mother 12/26/1811 S
SHORTER Abram's brother 5/18/1810 S

SHORTER C (colored man)'s mother 8/30/1821 S
SHORTER Clem 2/27/1826 S
SHORTER Jessee (colored man)'s wife 3/6/1832 S
SHORTER Ned's child 10/17/1816 S
SHORTER Philip's child 3/14/1830 S
SHREVE Benjamin of Virginia 1/27/1827 W
SHREVE Mr's child 8/18/1815 S
SHREVES Mr 4/18/1815 W
SHREVES Samuel 7/5/1828 W
SHRYBROCK Mr's child 1/12/1826 S
SIFFORD Isaac 6/12/1824 S
SIFFORD Miss 4/14/1832 S
SIFFORD Mrs 11/28/1817 W
SIFFORD Mrs's child 6/22/1826 S
SIFFORD Mrs's child 7/29/1824 S
SILPS Thomas's child a colored man 11/25/1816 S
SIM Doctor Thomas 9/16/1832 M
SIM Doctor's black boy 6/4/1827 S
SIM Mrs 9/4/1815 M
SIM Mrs Thomas 7/13/1831 M
SIM Thomas for colored woman 9/6/1823 S
SIM Thomas's black man 10/30/1819 S
SIM Thomas's black girl 12/4/1819 S
SIMMES Ignatious' child 10/5/1816 M
SIMMES Paul a colored man 3/4/1814 W
SIMMON William's wife 11/20/1808 M
SIMMONDS William's child 9/13/1803 M
SIMMONS Elizabeth 9/14/1831 S
SIMMONS Miss 2/28/1814 M
SIMMONS Mrs 12/11/1825 S
SIMMONS Mrs 3/14/1815 W
SIMMONS Mrs 7/16/1818 M
SIMMONS Mrs's grandchild 5/1/1830 S
SIMMONS Robert 2/17/1831 S
SIMMONS Samsen 6/3/1822 W
SIMMONS William for a girl 9/3/1811 M
SIMMONS William's child 4/19/1809 M
SIMMONS William's child 4/12/1809 M
SIMMONS William's child 2/17/1808 M
SIMMS Joseph M's child 10/5/1805 W
SIMONDS Nelly's grandchild 10/13/1826 S
SIMPSON Captain 1/27/1819 S

SIMPSON James 5/25/1806 S
SIMPSON John's child 1/6/1809 W
SIMPSON Mrs 9/5/1831 W
SIMPSON Mrs's daughter 7/1/1811 S
SIMPSON Sam (colored man) 8/4/1830 S
SIMSON Kitty 5/1/1814 S
SIP Mr's child 11/2/1813 S
SIPS Mr's child 7/20/1811 S
SKEGS William 3/26/1821 S
SKIDMORE George 7/27/1830 S
SKIDMORE Jared's wife 7/28/1831 S
SKIDMORE Mr's child 9/18/1823 W
SKIDMORE Samuel 11/21/1814 S
SKINNER Mr's child 10/1/1820 W
SLATOR Davis 10/31/1815 M
SLATOR Mr 11/11/1807 S
SLATOR Thomas for ----- 8/7/1803 S
SLATOR William 10/24/1813 S
SLYE Mrs (Robert's wife) 2/6/1823 M
SLYE Mrs Thomas G 9/18/1832 S
SLYE Robert A 10/2/1832 M
SLYE Robt's child 3/8/1824 M
SLYE Thomas G's child 6/21/1809 W
SMALLWOOD Daniel's wife 1/30/1827 S
SMALLWOOD Horatio's child 9/7/1819 W
SMALLWOOD Lewis (colored man) 3/27/1830 S
SMALLWOOD Mr 9/10/1810 S
SMALLWOOD Mrs's boy 9/7/1823 S
SMART John's child 8/14/1828 W
SMART Mrs's child 12/7/1823 W
SMITH Abner (colored man)'s child 10/6/1823 W
SMITH Ann's child 3/20/1822 S
SMITH Athony's child 11/3/1818 W
SMITH Captain Thomas 2/15/1818 S
SMITH Captain's child 11/26/1811 S
SMITH Caroline 1/24/1824 M
SMITH Clement's black child 5/30/1815 S
SMITH Clement's black man 11/2/1818 S
SMITH Clement's boy 7/12/1826 S
SMITH Clement's child 1/11/1819 M
SMITH Clement's child 7/14/1814 M
SMITH Clement's child 4/8/1822 M

SMITH Clement's child 1/19/1812 M
SMITH Clement's colored woman 10/9/1832 S
SMITH Clement's colored woman 11/24/1832 S
SMITH Clement's colored child 12/30/1823 S
SMITH Clement's overseer 8/2/1828 S
SMITH Clement's two children 7/3/1818 M
SMITH David 1/29/1830 S
SMITH Doctor 8/28/1796 W
SMITH Doctor Clement 12/12/1831 M
SMITH Edward L for ----- 6/26/1809 M
SMITH Edward L's child 6/24/1808 M
SMITH Henry (colored man)'s child 5/12/1821 S
SMITH J K for G McCandless 2/26/1809 S
SMITH J K's colored child 3/17/1819 S
SMITH John K for ----- 1/7/1805 M
SMITH John K 7/24/1818 M
SMITH John K's black child 9/23/1817 S
SMITH John K's colored child 11/3/1804 S
SMITH John K's child 8/15/1825 M
SMITH John's child 10/19/1823 W
SMITH Josias (colored man)'s child 9/12/1821 S
SMITH Josias's sister's child 4/2/1831 S
SMITH Josias's sister's child (colored woman) 9/6/1829 S
SMITH Lewis's child 7/21/1826 S
SMITH Lewis's son 9/22/1826 W
SMITH Major 12/27/1805 W
SMITH Mr (colored man) 7/12/1821 S
SMITH Mr 10/14/1817 W
SMITH Mr's child 8/21/1819 W
SMITH Mr's child 9/20/1819 M
SMITH Mr's child omitted [9/1817] S
SMITH Mr's child 7/14/1814 W
SMITH Mrs 12/25/1831 S
SMITH Mrs 2/8/1823 W
SMITH Mrs 3/23/1814 M
SMITH Mrs 6/9/1819 S
SMITH Mrs 9/28/1819 W
SMITH Mrs 9/2/1815 M
SMITH Mrs M's daughter 11/3/1811 W
SMITH Mrs's child 12/21/1831 S
SMITH Mrs's child 9/22/1812 M
SMITH Robert 12/30/1830 M

SMITH Thomas (colored man)'s child 8/8/1825 S
SMITH Thomas 1/11/1831 S
SMITH Thomas's child (colored) 1/7/1829 S
SMITH Thomas's child 4/15/1822 S
SMITH Thomas's child (colored) 8/27/1827 S
SMITH Thomas's son 2/10/1815 S
SMITH Walter for ----- 9/17/1809 M
SMITH William (colored man) 8/18/1832 S
SMITH William 5/22/1809 W
SMITH William's daughter 12/16/1808 W
SMITH Wm 4/25/1818 W
SMOOT Charles 7/2/1811 S
SMOOT Mrs's child 5/5/1821 M
SMOOT Mrs's Milly 6/10/1832 S
SMOOT Samuel's child 5/25/1825 S
SMOOT Samuel's child 4/26/1823 S
SMOOT Samuel's child 12/20/1811 S
SMOOT Walter's colored woman 10/2/1832 S
SNIDER Mr's grandchild 8/12/1829 S
SNOWDEN Mrs 10/6/1830 W
SNOWDEN Richard 9/4/1823 M
SNYDER Mr's daughter 9/25/1829 S
SOMMER Nathan's mother 5/28/1816 S
SOMMERS John 9/27/1828 M
SONN Doctor 2/17/1814 S
SOUTHALL Daniel 10/16/1830 M
SOUTHERLAND Thos Y 5/8/1825 M
SOUTHERON Susannah's woman 3/3/1830 S
SOUTHNER Mrs 11/3/1821 W
SPALDING Enoch 2/2/1828 S
SPALDING Mr 5/24/1829 S
SPALDING Mr for ----- 12/16/1809 M
SPALDING Mrs 11/7/1818 S
SPALDING Mrs 4/30/1821 W
SPALDING Richard 1/18/1826 S
SPARROW John 6/25/1816 S
SPARROW John 8/31/1830 W
SPARROW Mr 11/27/1823 S
SPARROW Mr's child 8/28/1821 W
SPARROW Mr's child 8/21/1827 S
SPARROW Mr's child 4/2/1817 S
SPARROW Mrs 5/2/1826 S

SPEAK Mrs's negro child 3/14/1808 S
SPEAK Mrs's Negro child 1/3/1804 S
SPEAKE Captain's child 6/7/1803 M
SPEAKE Mrs 3/20/1810 M
SPEAKE Mrs's child 11/18/1803 S
SPEAKMAN Mr's child 3/8/1829 S
SPEAR Mrs's child 12/8/1821 S
SPENCER, Doctor's son that died at Holbrook's 4/8/1829 W
SPOWROW Mr's child 10/28/1816 S
SPRIGG Mrs 2/7/1812 M
SPRIGG Orsburn 5/8/1815 m
SPRIGG Richard 12/12/1829 S
SPRIGG Samuel's child 2/16/1816 M
SQUAW William 1/16/1817 S
STAHL Jacob's child 8/12/1832 S
STANFORD Richard 4/10/1816 M
STANLY Mr for ----- 3/29/1802 S
STARNES Mrs's child 10/8/1819 W
STAUNTON Richard's child Alexander 7/1/1831 M
StCLAIR John 10/15/1811 M
STEEL Matthew for a girl 11/1/1805 W
STEEL Mr's child 10/22/1820 W
STEEL Mr's child 8/18/1820 W
STEEL Mrs 10/15/1820 S
STEELE Charles's child 11/13/1823 S
STEELE Mr 9/21/1810 W
STEELE Mrs 10/25/1824 W
STEELE Mrs's child 7/20/1812 S
STEELE Samuel's daughter 10/15/1827 W
STEMBLE Henry's colored child 11/6/1822 S
STEMPLE Mr's child 8/23/1812 W
STEPHENS James for ----- 7/16/1806 M
STEPHENS Miss 12/31/1814 W
STEPTOE Caroline's child 7/31/1807 S
STEPTOE Henrietta's child 12/20/1805 S
STEVENSON Betsey (colored woman)'s child 5/4/1824 S
STEVENSON Mrs 12/17/1831 W
STEVENSON Mrs' daughter 10/21/1830 S
STEWART David 3/9/1815 M
STEWART Doctor for ----- 9/30/1811 M
STEWART Henry 8/31/1823 W
STEWART Hugh 1/26/1820 M

STEWART Mary 7/14/1829 S
STEWART Miss 12/8/1823 W
STEWART Miss Margaret 1/22/1823 M
STEWART Mrs's child 11/30/1819 S
STEWART William's child 7/20/1820 M
STEWART William's child 12/18/1821 M
STEWART William's child 10/15/1811 M
STEWART William's child 5/1/1813 M
STILES Mr 4/5/1825 W
STILES Mrs's mother 4/8/1817 S
STILLING Mrs 6/20/1815 S
STILLS Mr's daughter 2/19/1821 W
STINCHCOMB A S's child 10/3/1824 S
STINCHCOMB A S's child 6/27/1823 S
STODDART Benjamin for ----- 2/13/1802 M
STODDART Mr 2/7/1827 W
STODDART Mr's child 12/29/1824 S
STODDERT Benjamin 12/19/1813 M
STONE Edward's child 5/14/1813 W
STONE Edward's child 8/26/1819 W
STONE John B 9/1/1818 S
STONE John for ----- 7/31/1798 M
STONE Mrs 2/12/1815 M
STOOPS William's wife 3/10/1800 W
STORM James's child 9/4/1813 M
STORY Mr 12/8/1806 S
STOUT Mr 3/22/1825 W
STRECH Mrs 2/20/1816 M
STRICH Mr 7/22/1822 M
STROMAN Mr's child 7/23/1825 S
STROMAN Mr's child 9/16/1826 S
STROMAN Mrs's child 5/26/1829 S
STULL Captain's child 4/15/1813 M
STULL J J's colored woman 10/9/1829 S
STULL J J's colored child 11/22/1829 S
STULL John J's child 6/20/1830 M
STULL John J's colored woman 8/26/1832 S
STULL John J's child 12/7/1823 M
STULL John's colored child 10/12/1828 S
STULL Mrs 8/17/1826 M
STURTEVANT Seth's colored man 10/27/1832 S
SULLIVAN John 3/15/1830 S

SULLIVAN Mrs's child 8/8/1824 S
SUPPLE Pat 7/29/1830 S
SUTER A's colored child 11/10/1824 S
SUTER Alexander's black child 9/27/1812 S
SUTER Alexander's brother Robert 5/20/1810 M
SUTER Alexander's colored woman 4/15/1809 S
SUTER Alexander's daughter 1/3/1832 W
SUTER Alexander's negro child 7/19/1810 S
SUTER Ann 9/24/1831 M
SUTER Mrs 7/4/1812 M
SUTER Richard's grandchild 3/30/1827 S
SWAIN William 11/19/1823 S
SWAN J 10/9/1820 S
SWAN Major's child 7/17/1807 M
SWAN Mr's child 10/26/1814 S
SWAN Mr's child 4/17/1817 S
SWAN Nancy (colored woman) 10/30/1822 S
SWANN Caleb 11/30/1809 M
SWANN Nathan's child 8/1/1828 W
SWEENEY George's child 6/20/1830 S
SWETT Samuel Junr 3/14/1818 M
SWIFT Lieut.'s child 10/3/1827 M
SWINK W 1/27/1822 W
SYLVESTER Mr's child 8/8/1827 W
SYLVESTER Mr's child 10/16/1828 W
SYMINGTON James's child 10/2/1822 W
SYMINGTON Peter's child 4/12/1829 S
TABLER John's child 8/6/1829 W
TAILOR Benjamin's child 7/1/1813 S
TAILOR Captain's child 9/16/1812 S
TAILOR Miss at Nelson 8/30/1821 S
TALMIE Mr 9/13/1805 W
TANEY A J 10/23/1823 M
TANNAR Mr 8/8/1815 W
TANNER Mr 9/11/1825 S
TANNER Paul 9/15/1826 S
TANNEY Francis L 9/20/1802 S
TATEHAM Colonel's boy 7/21/1816 S
TAVANCE John for ----- 8/24/1809 M
TAVANCE John's child 9/3/1808 W
TAYLO John's child 5/6/1820 S
TAYLOE Charlotte's mother 6/27/1819 S

TAYLOE John 3/1/1828 S
TAYLOE John's child 9/24/1822 M
TAYLOE Mrs's colored boy 10/16/1828 S
TAYLOR Daniel 12/16/1822 S
TAYLOR Mr's child 11/4/1815 S
TAYLOR Mr's child 8/13/1808 S
TAYLOR Mrs 4/15/1832 W
TAYLOR Mrs's child 5/20/1825 S
TAYLOR Nellie's grandchild (colored) 8/13/1827 S
TAYLOR Nelly's child (colored woman) 4/27/1829 S
TAYLOR Sally 11/22/1826 S
TAYLOR Winder's child 8/26/1832 W
TENNESON I's colored man 10/16/1830 S
TENNEY Isaac 3/15/1817 M
TENNISON Joshua 8/24/1832 M
TENNY Isaac for ----- 1/22/1803 M
TERRY Andrew's child (colored) 4/25/1828 S
TERRY Andrew's daughter (colored woman) 8/15/1828 S
THACKER James's child 7/23/1830 W
THAW Benjamin 5/2/1832 M
THAW Joseph's child 5/4/1821 M
THAW Joseph's child 5/12/1821 M
THAW Joseph's wife 1/3/1805 M
THAW William 4/4/1832 M
THECKER Mr's child 11/20/1806 S
THECKER Mrs 6/16/1811 W
THERLY Mr 7/31/1820 S
THOMAS Anthony's father (colored) 2/8/1828 S
THOMAS Captain's wife's child 9/11/1821 S
THOMAS Henry's child 12/11/1831 S
THOMAS Henry's wife 6/21/1809 S
THOMAS Jared (colored man)'s child 4/11/1824 S
THOMAS Jennet's child 8/28/1820 S
THOMAS John 3rd black child 11/11/1809 S
THOMAS Lewis (colored man)'s grandchild 12/13/1831 S
THOMAS Lewis (colored man)'s child 8/10/1831 S
THOMAS Miss 8/18/1819 W
THOMAS Mr 7/13/1818 S
THOMAS Mrs 11/29/1829 W
THOMAS Mrs 12/23/1819 S
THOMAS Richard's wife 9/21/1830 S
THOMPSON Benjamin 1/3/1823 S

THOMPSON Captain John 10/1/1831 M
THOMPSON James (colored man) 9/25/1832 S
THOMPSON James for ----- 3/7/1805 M
THOMPSON James's child 6/21/1805 M
THOMPSON James's child 9/4/1806 M
THOMPSON James's colored girl 4/16/1831 S
THOMPSON Juliana 6/2/1826 S
THOMPSON Mr's child 10/1/1817 S
THOMPSON Mrs 10/16/1823 S
THOMPSON Mrs's colored man 10/28/1832 S
THOMPSON Mrs's colored girl (Seth) 10/14/1826 S
THOMPSON Susanah 7/1/1826 S
THOMPSON William 8/9/1830 M
THOMPSON William Jr's child 4/16/1823 M
THOMPSON William Senr 11/23/1823 M
THOMSON Charles 9/2/1815 S
THOMSON George 6/23/1810 M
THOMSON John 3/12/1813 S
THOMSON John 5/11/1805 S
THOMSON John 9/14/1832 M
THOMSON John C's child 9/20/1812 W
THOMSON John C's child 10/5/1815 W
THOMSON John for ----- 4/27/1809 M
THOMSON Miss Isabella 9/17/1832 M
THOMSON Mr 10/10/1813 M
THOMSON Mr for a boy 12/24/1811 M
THOMSON Mr's child 9/25/1815 S
THOMSON Mrs 2/11/1814 S
THOMSON Mrs 8/25/1821 W
THOMSON Mrs's mother 11/6/1810 W
THOMSON Nancy 12/23/1816 S
THOMSON Rachel 12/29/1829 W
THOMSON William (colored)'s child 11/21/1821 S
THOMSON William's colored woman 8/28/1822 S
THORNTON Sarah 7/24/1828 S
THORP Thomas's child 10/27/1813 S
THRELKELD John 8/31/1830 M
THRELKELD John for mother 9/10/1801 M
THRELKELD John's Grace 11/30/1816 S
THRELKELD Miss E 8/28/1826 M
THRELKELD Mrs E 8/20/1826 M
THUMBERT William's boy 11/23/1813 S

THUMBERT William's child 8/27/1817 M
THUMBERT William's child 6/24/1822 M
THUNBLERT William's child 12/8/1820 M
TIERNAN Mr 9/8/1825 S
TIFFIN Edward's child 7/16/1813 M
TILLEY Charles's child 12/30/1823 W
TILLEY Charles's child 10/22/1825 W
TILLEY Henry W's child 2/19/1830 M
TILLEY Henry's colored woman 9/20/1832 S
TILLY James 9/4/1821 W cherry
TIMS Mr 12/11/1828 W
TIVINE Mrs 11/17/1820 S
TOLBERT Mr (of Alexandria)'s son 8/25/1820 S
TOLIVER James for a soldier 9/18/1814 S
TOLIVER James for 2 soldiers 9/2/1814 S (2 coffins, both S)
TOLMEY James 10/8/1822 W
TOLMIE Mrs's grandchild 10/9/1821 W
TOLSTON Sarah's child colored 9/14/1813 S
TOODY Michael 12/27/1830 S
TOOLEY Thomas 1/9/1830 S
TOPHOUSE Samuel's child 10/6/1803 W
TOPPAN Mrs 4/15/1796 S
TOULSON Nancy (colored woman) 1/28/1826 S
TOWNLEY James's child 4/19/1830 M
TOWNLY Charles 8/3/1826 S
TOWNLY Mrs's child 7/24/1818 M
TOWNSEND Henry for ----- 1/25/1804 S
TOWSON Colonel N's child 7/15/1823 M
TRACY Mr's child 12/8/1832 S
TRAIL Mr 3/25/1818 S
TRAVERS Chas 1/31/1826 S
TRAVERS George 3/11/1819 M
TRAVERS John 11/5/1821 M
TRAVERS John's black boy 9/8/1817 S
TRAVERS John's black child 7/15/1820 S
TRAVERS Mr 6/30/1823 W
TRAVERS Mrs 3/21/1820 W
TRAVERS Nicholas for ----- 10/1/1809 M
TRAVERS Nicholas's apprentice Walter 9/11/1809 S
TRAVERS Nicholas's child 4/22/1825 W
TRAVERS Nicholas's child 4/18/1830 W
TRAVERS Sarah's colored child 6/5/1830 S

TRUNNEL Henry's child 7/24/1820 W
TRUNNEL Horatio's child 9/23/1803 S
TRUNNEL Horatio's child 10/29/1815 S
TRUNNEL Horatio's son 3/11/1818 W
TRUNNEL Mr's mother-in-law 11/19/1820 W
TRYON Mrs 9/25/1823 W
TUBBERVIL Richard 9/15/1814 M
TUCKER Benjamin 4/26/1815 S
TUCKER Enoch's child 8/6/1818 M
TUCKER Enoch's child 9/7/1823 M
TUCKER Enoch's child 2/19/1830 M
TUCKER Mr 3/11/1805 W
TUCKER Samuel's child 10/9/1822 S
TUCKER Samuel's child 10/14/1825 W
TUEL Mrs 3/26/1824 S
TUEL Richard's father 10/27/1810 W
TUEL Ross's child 6/27/1824 S
TURBY John 10/6/1826 S
TURNAR Jane 4/23/1824 S
TURNBUL Mrs's child 11/12/1806 S
TURNER Betsey's child 8/9/1814 S
TURNER Billy (colored man)'s wife 12/1/1831 S
TURNER Dennis 11/30/1830 S
TURNER James 4/15/1822 S
TURNER Mary 9/1/1819 M
TURNER Mrs 12/15/1817 M
TURNER Nathan (colored man) 4/29/1830
TURNER Samuel 2/3/1824 M
TURNER Samuel for Mr Grimes 8/5/1809 M
TURNER Samuel's child 5/21/1817 M
TURNER Samuel's child 3/28/1796 M
TURNER Sara 1/12/1817 S
TURNER Thomas 3/16/1816 M
TURNER Thomas for ----- 5/21/1811 M
TURNER Thomas's child 12/3/1804 M
TURNER Thomas's child 5/7/1811 M
TURNER Thomas's child 10/29/1808 M
TURNER Thomas's child 12/10/1825 S
TURNER Thomas's child 4/1/1830 M
TURNER Thomas's colored child 4/5/1830 S
TURNER Thomas's colored child 1/25/1828 S
TURNER Thomas's colored woman 9/2/1822 S

TURNER Thomas's John 2/19/1828 S
TURNER Thomas's negro child 8/29/1810 S
TURNER William's child 8/14/1825 S
TURVEY William 11/2/1830 S
TUTTLE Mrs 3/10/1813 S
TWINE William (colored man) 9/11/1832 S
TWYFORD Smith's child 1/4/1828
TYLER John 7/11/1829 S
TYLER Minty 9/1/1831 S
TYLER Mr 5/23/1818 M
TYLER Mrs 3/13/1822 W
UPPERMAN George's child 5/8/1813 W
UPPERMAN Henry's child 11/26/1811 W
UPPERMAN Henry's child 9/20/1822 M
UPPERMAN Henry's colored man 9/26/1832 S
UPPERMAN Jacob 9/29/1821 W
UPPERMAN Mr 12/14/1822 W
UPPERMAN Mrs 7/25/1822 W
VALLARD R H L's child 7/27/1820 W
VALLY Mr 7/22/1830 W
VANDERHOOF Daniel 8/10/1829 W
VANESSEN Peter's colored child 8/2/1827 S
VANESSON Peter's child 8/29/1821 W
VANHORN Mrs 4/10/1826 S
VANNESIN Peter's child 9/6/1822 M
VANNESSEN Mrs Peter 11/13/1832 M
VARDEN Mrs 8/3/1815 S
VILLARD Mrs Sophia 6/22/1825 M
VINSON John 7/17/1813 S
WADE Mr's child 8/27/1820 W
WADE Mrs for ----- 8/2/1800 S
WAGNER Jacob's black child 4/6/1813 S
WAIN Mr for ----- 2/13/1808 W
WALES Mrs's child 6/27/1813 M
WALKER Ann 1/16/1829 S
WALKER David's child 5/15/1826 M
WALKER Edward's child 3/3/1830 S
WALKER Elijah 8/17/1811 M
WALKER Elizabeth (colored woman)'s child 6/11/1825 S
WALKER Elizabeth 7/16/1819 W
WALKER James for ----- 12/17/1805 W
WALKER Mr's child 4/18/1817 M

WALKER Mrs 3/28/1826 S
WALKER S S's child 8/28/1827 M
WALL John 7/13/1818 S
WALLACE Margarett 2/28/1831 M
WALLAN Mr 10/20/1832 W
WALLAND Mr's child 9/20/1812 S
WALLER William's child 7/18/1831 S
WALLICE Mrs 12/13/1821 W
WALTERS T's black child 1/25/1814 S
WALTON James's (colored man) child 9/11/1810 S
WARD Elizabeth's child 9/1/1812 S
WARD George 6/20/1830 W
WARD John's child 7/9/1832 S
WARD Mr's child 8/9/1826 S
WARD Mrs Eliz 10/1/1824 S
WARD Ulysses's nephew 10/2/1820 W
WARDELL S's sister's child 9/28/1830 S
WARFIELD Doctor's Mordecai 2/27/1831 S
WARING Henry's colored man 9/13/1832 S
WARING Miss Nelly 7/5/1822 M
WARING Miss Susan 12/19/1832 M
WARNER Mrs 4/10/1828 S
WARNER Nicholas's daughter (colored) 1/22/1827 S
WARREN Benjamin 10/2/1830 S
WARREN William 10/29/1830 S
WARRING Mrs 11/23/1823 M
WARRING Mrs's boy 2/16/1815 S
WARTON James's child 12/15/1817 W
WARTON James's son 1/12/1817 S
WASHBURN Daniel 12/6/1829 W
WASHINGTON George's child 9/17/1815 M
WASHINGTON George's child 12/6/1817 M
WASHINGTON George's child 2/2/1809 M
WASHINGTON George's child 2/12/1812 M
WASHINGTON George's son 6/11/1820 M
WASHINGTON Lund's child 9/17/1822 M
WASHINGTON Lund's grandchild 4/26/1825 S
WASHINGTON Mrs 7/2/1820 M
WASHINGTON William A 10/4/1810 M
WATERS Jno 12/25/1825 W
WATERS John's child 6/26/1822 W
WATERS John's child 9/22/1820 W

WATERS John's child 1/13/1827 W
WATERS Mr 9/21/1818 M
WATERS Mr T G 11/1/1825 M
WATERS Mr's child 10/3/1809 W
WATERS T G's mother 12/20/1824 M
WATERS T G's colored child 1/21/1823 S
WATERS T G's child 12/25/1819 M
WATERS Thomas G's colored man 9/14/1832 S
WATERS Thomas G's colored man 7/19/1832 S
WATERS Thomas's black woman 8/13/1817 S
WATERS Thomas's black child 8/13/1817 S
WATERS Thomas's child 10/18/1818 M
WATERS William (Virginia) 3/29/1827 W
WATERS William's wife 1/26/1808 W
WATHEN Mrs 2/19/1818 S
WATKINS Mr's child 7/27/1821 S
WATKINS Mrs 10/17/1815 M
WATKINS Mrs's black child 9/8/1818 S
WATKINS Stephen 12/25/1828 S
WATKINS W W's child 6/30/1831 W
WATSON James 10/13/1822 M
WATSON Mrs Jane 11/9/1831 W
WATSON Thomas's child 8/13/1806 S
WATTERS T's black man 3/6/1820 S
WATTS Mary's child (colored) 1/30/1827 S
WATTSON Mr 1/20/1828 M
WAUGH Mr's child 2/17/1826 W
WAYMAN Charles 9/27/1805 M
WEASNER Mr 2/27/1817 S
WEAVER Michael's child 9/8/1831 S
WEAVER Mr 6/10/1821 S
WEAVER Mr's child 9/27/1813 S
WEBB John 2/2/1822 S
WEBB Mr 9/3/1817 W
WEBSTER E 12/8/1818 W
WEBSTER Miss 11/15/1818 W
WEBSTER Mrs's grandchild 7/4/1824 S
WEBSTER Samuel P's colored child 5/15/1832 S
WEDLOCK Sam's child, colored 7/27/1830 S
WEDLOCK Samuel's child (colored) 2/10/1829 S
WEEDEN Mrs's son 2/27/1815 S
WEEDEN William 12/27/1820 S

WEEMS Doctor John 11/11/1808 M
WEEMS Elisha's black woman 10/11/1820 S
WEEMS John's child 7/28/1806 M
WEEMS Mrs's black girl 12/27/1813 S
WEIGHTMAN Mr's child 7/28/1826 S
WEIGHTMAN Mr's child 12/10/1817 W
WEIGHTMAN Mr's child 7/31/1826 S
WEISNER Mr 4/6/1818 W
WEISNER Mrs 2/6/1828 S
WEISNER Thomas 1/31/1825 S
WELCH David 9/16/1830 S
WELCH Methew 4/28/1814 W
WELCH Michael 10/2/1830 S
WELCH Miss 2/12/1820 S
WELCH Mrs 10/2/1811 S
WELLS Mrs 1/19/1822 S
WELLS Richard's child 5/9/1823 M
WELLS Richard's child 7/5/1820 M
WELLS Richard's child 8/20/1816 M
WELLS Richard's child 12/19/1830 S
WELLS Richard's child 6/30/1832 M
WELSH Hugh 4/17/1831 S
WELSH Mr 11/13/1811 S
WENTWORTH Matthias 6/1/1826 S
WEST John's child 7/23/1812 M
WEST Mr 1/8/1815 S
WEST Mrs 4/24/1815 M
WETNEY Mr's child 9/15/1821 W
WETZEL F 10/31/1820 W
WETZEL John 8/16/1824 W
WHALEN Bridget 9/16/1825 S
WHALEN Michael 10/5/1826 S
WHALEN Mrs 1/29/1815 S
WHALEN Nicholas's child 8/14/1817 S
WHALEN Nicholas's child 12/16/1814 S
WHALIN Mary 10/31/1814 S
WHANN David 5/24/1813 M
WHANN Mrs 5/12/1820 M
WHANN William's black child 3/31/1814 S
WHANN William's black boy 3/10/1814 S
WHANN Wm's black woman 4/11/1818 S
WHARTON James 8/10/1830 W

WHARTON Mrs 3/1/1818 M
WHEATLEY Mr's child 2/19/1824 W
WHEATLEY Mrs 10/16/1821 W cherry
WHEELER Clement 8/11/1822 M
WHEELER Ignatius colored man 10/7/1823 W
WHELAN Mr's mother-in-law 7/12/1831 S
WHELAN Mrs 7/2/1820 S
WHELAN Mrs Rebecca 9/11/1832 W
WHELAN Thomas's father 9/23/1832 W
WHELAN William 12/11/1830 S
WHITE Benjamin 4/7/1802 W
WHITE C C 's child 8/10/1819 W
WHITE C C's (colored) child 8/2/1821 S
WHITE C C's child 12/2/1821 W
WHITE Charles C's child 12/24/1815 M
WHITE Charles C's child 7/16/1820 W
WHITE Charles C's child 7/5/1814 W
WHITE Eliza's child 2/28/1825 S
WHITE James 10/25/1801 S
WHITE James's child 9/2/1799 S
WHITE John's child 8/25/1826 W
WHITE John's child 4/24/1831 W
WHITE John's child 5/1/1831 W
WHITE Josabed 2/2/1829 W
WHITE Josabed's wife 10/7/1827 W
WHITE Joseph for a girl 7/31/1811 W
WHITE Mr 11/22/1821 S
WHITE Mr's child 4/16/1809 W
WHITE Mr's child 4/16/1813 S
WHITE Mr's mother 4/15/1822 S
WHITE Mrs 10/18/1822 S
WHITE Mrs 9/9/1812 M
WHITE Richard's child 8/11/1826 W
WHITE Robert's child 8/7/1819 W
WHITE Robt's child 5/19/1825 W
WHITE Thomas C 3/24/1824 W
WHITEWOOD Mrs Elizabeth 7/29/1809 M
WHITLAW John's child (colored man) 11/2/1829 S
WHITLOW J B (colored man)'s child 12/13/1826 S
WHITMORE Benjamin for ----- 4/17/1805 S
WHITMORE Benjamin's child 11/9/1805 S
WHITNEY --------'s child 8/16/1831 S

WHITNEY Jared's child 2/1/1824 W
WHITNEY Mr's 2 children 8/5/1819 S
WHITNEY William's father 1/8/1828 W
WHITNEY William's mother 9/14/1831 W
WIDDOWS Isaac 1/9/1831 S
WILBERTON Hiram 3/13/1830 S
WILEY John 3/21/1819 M
WILEY John's black boy 10/3/1818 S
WILEY John's child 4/22/1818 M
WILEY Mary 1/21/1817 W
WILEY Mrs 5/16/1818 W
WILHOUN George's colored child 8/3/1821 S
WILKINS Mr 8/19/1830 S
WILLIAM James's child 11/13/1821 S
WILLIAM Jeremiah's black child 9/16/1820 S
WILLIAM Lieut.'s child 8/10/1829 M
WILLIAMS Benjamin's mother 5/8/1815 S
WILLIAMS Brooke's colored woman 3/20/1826 S
WILLIAMS Captain's negro boy 3/22/1804 S
WILLIAMS Charles (colored man)'s child 7/7/1831 S
WILLIAMS Daniel 9/12/1820 S
WILLIAMS Eli 12/30/1822 M
WILLIAMS Eli's colored woman 9/19/1816 S
WILLIAMS Elisha O 12/15/1805 M
WILLIAMS George (colored man) 8/5/1832 S
WILLIAMS George 10/4/1831 S
WILLIAMS James (a black man)'s child 6/12/1813 S
WILLIAMS James (colored man)'s son 12/30/1831 S
WILLIAMS James 9/18/1828 W
WILLIAMS James's child 2/23/1824 S
WILLIAMS Jeremiah's black woman 1/9/1812 S
WILLIAMS Jeremiah's black child 1/9/1812 S
WILLIAMS Jeremiah's boy 4/23/1824 S
WILLIAMS Jeremiah's child 1/2/1808 M
WILLIAMS Jeremiah's colored boy 11/8/1828 S
WILLIAMS John 6/21/1823 S
WILLIAMS John a black man 5/15/1813 S
WILLIAMS John S's child 3/3/1816 S
WILLIAMS Joseph's wife 5/2/1826 S
WILLIAMS Major 10/26/1818 M
WILLIAMS Mr (stage driver) for ----- 11/13/1802 S
WILLIAMS Mr 3/6/1814 M

WILLIAMS Mr 4/20/1824 S
WILLIAMS Mr's boy 5/4/1822 S
WILLIAMS Mr's child at the foundry 3/25/1824 W
WILLIAMS Mr's child 1/16/1830 S
WILLIAMS Mr's child 7/22/1809 S
WILLIAMS Mrs 1/23/1814 W
WILLIAMS Mrs 10/31/1816 M
WILLIAMS Mrs 9/29/1823 S
WILLIAMS Mrs 9/3/1815 W
WILLIAMS Mrs 9/28/1816 M
WILLIAMS Mrs 9/11/1826 W
WILLIAMS Mrs Philip 9/14/1831 M
WILLIAMS Mrs's child 11/24/1824 S
WILLIAMS Mrs's child 11/25/1830 W
WILLIAMS Mrs's child 4/24/1831 S
WILLIAMS Nace (colored man)'s child 7/30/1831 S
WILLIAMS Rosanna (colored woman)'s child 8/29/1831 S
WILLIAMS Samuel 9/22/1802 S
WILLIAMS Thomas 3/12/1810 M
WILLIAMS William 9/6/1819 M
WILLIAMS William's child 8/5/1815 W
WILLIAMS William's child 9/8/1816 W
WILLIE John 9/10/1826 S
WILLS Mr's child 8/23/1812 S
WILLSON James C's child 8/1/1827 M
WILLSON Jeffry (colored man) 8/12/1832 S
WILLSON John 9/25/1827 S
WILLSON John A's colored child 8/19/1827 S
WILLSON Mrs E 11/8/1830 S
WILLSON Mrs Isaac 2/19/1827 W
WILLSON Mrs's colored woman 9/26/1827 S
WILLSON Sarah for Miss Dashiell 10/1/1808 M
WILLSON Z 11/18/1826 W
WILLY Jarvander 4/16/1816 W
WILSON Grace's child 7/14/1820 M
WILSON H G's brother 5/5/1826 W
WILSON Henry G's child 3/26/1832 W
WILSON Isaac's child 4/29/1824 M
WILSON Isaac's child 9/4/1813 M
WILSON James R 8/18/1819 M
WILSON James's child 10/21/1818 M
WILSON John 4/7/1829 W

WILSON John A (George) 1/18/1815 S
WILSON John A's black child 5/30/1818 S
WILSON John for ----- 12/12/1807 S
WILSON John's child 3/31/1813 S
WILSON John's child 10/1/1811 M
WILSON John's child 9/27/1806 M
WILSON John's child 10/4/1813 M
WILSON Lawrence 2/6/1823 S
WILSON Levi 8/2/1819 W
WILSON Mr 2/21/1815 W
WILSON Mrs 7/5/1816 W
WILSON Mrs's child 5/18/1814 S
WILSON Richard 3/13/1815 M
WILSON Thomas 10/30/1814 W
WILSON Thomas 6/28/1824 M
WILSON William 3/12/1817 M
WILSON Zadock's wife 4/7/1802 W
WIMEN Mrs's child 12/19/1818 S
WIMSETT John 5/30/1828 S
WIMSETT Mrs 4/28/1826 S
WINDBURY Mrs 2/12/1815 W
WINDOM Charles's child 8/10/1814 W
WINEBURGER J's relation 9/25/1822 W
WINEBURGER Jacob's child 6/14/1812 W
WINEMILLER Mrs 7/12/1830 W
WINFRED Mrs 9/22/1810 S
WINGARD A's child 4/9/1819 M
WINGARD Abraham 1/11/1820 M
WINGARD Abraham's son 7/3/1817 M
WINTER Mary C 12/30/1831 M
WIPOR Ruben's child 7/18/1816 W
WIPPLE Oliver 3/16/1813 M
WIRT John 3/25/1818 M
WIRT John's child 4/7/1817 M
WIRT John's child 1/23/1814 M
WIRT John's child 5/16/1815 M
WIRT Philip 9/18/1818 W
WIRT Philip's child 2/1/1816 M
WIRT Sarah's daughter 3/20/1826 W
WISE Charles 10/7/1820 W
WISE Helen 2/3/1819 S
WISE Mr (Alexandria) 11/3/1807 W

WISE Mr 11/27/1819 W
WISE Mr's child 9/13/1816 S
WISE Mrs 7/31/1812 S
WITHERS E D's colored man 7/10/1831 S
WITHERS E D's colored woman 4/25/1830 S
WITHERS E D's child 10/21/1830 S
WITING Colonel 9/4/1810 M
WOLTZ Henry 8/23/1831 W
WOLTZ Mrs 4/30/1827 W
WOOD Ann 9/6/1818 M
WOOD Basil's mother 12/24/1830 S
WOOD Doctor for ----- 6/13/1811 M
WOOD E's daughter 11/4/1820 S
WOOD John 3/10/1818 S
WOOD Mr 2/19/1813 W
WOOD Mrs Ann 11/1/1824 W
WOODLAND Jane's husband 12/31/1814 S
WOODMAN Mr 4/17/1822 S
WOODS Charles's wife 10/3/1830 W
WOODS Joseph's child 10/10/1831 S
WOODS Joseph's wife 9/13/1832 W
WOODS Mr's child 9/8/1830 S
WOODSIDE John's negro girl 2/1/1806 S
WOODSIDES Mr for ----- 8/28/1807 S
WOODWARD Mr's child 2/29/1812 S
WOODWARD Sedley's child 5/10/1831 W
WOODWARD Sedley's son 9/3/1831 W
WOODWARD Sylvester 9/9/1832 S
WOODWARD Thomas's child 3/26/1830 M
WOODWARD Thomas's child 4/5/1830 M
WOOLHAM Mr 7/7/1822 S
WOOLLAND Mrs 1/24/1832 S
WOOLLARD Samuel 12/13/1820 S
WOOLLARD Samuel's child 1/11/1819 S
WORTHINGTON Dr's wife 1/21/1798 M
WREN John 9/3/1821 M
WRIGHT John 7/13/1828 W
WRIGHT Thomas C's child 9/1/1806 W
WROTH Mrs 11/2/1820 S
YATES John 1/2/1823 M
YATES Mrs 2/16/1817 W
YATS Mrs's daughter 3/12/1817 S

YEATS Lieutenant 9/10/1814 S
YOUNG Adam's wife 12/3/1826 W
YOUNG Benjamin's child 8/7/1831 M
YOUNG Charles 2/23/1814 M
YOUNG Jacob 8/6/1823 W
YOUNG Martha 5/25/1815 M
YOUNG Mr 9/18/1812 M
YOUNG Mrs 3/14/1832 S
YOUNG Thomas 10/12/1832 W
YOUSH Mr's child 10/21/1801 W

ABOUT THE AUTHORS

JANE DONOVAN has written extensively on Washington, D.C., and United Methodist history. Her books include *Historical Dictionary of Washington*, *Many Witnesses*, *Lafayette Life*, and *Records of Dumbarton United Methodist Church*. She is a candidate for the MTS in the history of Christianity from Wesley Theological Seminary.

CARLTON FLETCHER is the history columnist for *The Glover Park Gazette*. He received a citation from the Daughters of the American Revolution for identifying and locating the only Revolutionary War veteran grave in Georgetown.

www.ingramcontent.com/pod-product-compliance
Lightning Source LLC
Chambersburg PA
CBHW050139170426
43197CB00011B/1891